Plato's Socrates on Socrates

Plato's Socrates on Socrates

Socratic Self-Disclosure and the Public Practice of Philosophy

Anne-Marie Schultz

LEXINGTON BOOKS
Lanham • Boulder • New York • London

Published by Lexington Books
An imprint of The Rowman & Littlefield Publishing Group, Inc.
4501 Forbes Boulevard, Suite 200, Lanham, Maryland 20706
www.rowman.com

6 Tinworth Street, London SE11 5AL

Copyright © 2020 by The Rowman & Littlefield Publishing Group, Inc.

All rights reserved. No part of this book may be reproduced in any form or by any electronic or mechanical means, including information storage and retrieval systems, without written permission from the publisher, except by a reviewer who may quote passages in a review.

British Library Cataloguing in Publication Information Available

Library of Congress Control Number: 2020933373

Library of Congress Cataloging-in-Publication Data Is Available

ISBN 978-1-4985-9964-1 (cloth)
ISBN 978-1-4985-9966-5 (pbk.)
ISBN 978-1-4985-9965-8 (electronic)

Contents

Acknowledgments		vii
Overview		1
1	Recovering Socrates the Narrator in Plato's *Theaetetus*	11
2	Socratic Self-Disclosure in Plato's *Symposium*	25
3	Three Imitations of Socratic Narration	41
4	Socratic Self-Disclosure in Plato's *Apology*	61
5	Socratic Self-Disclosure in Plato's *Phaedo*	73
6	Listening to Socratic Voices	101
Postscript: Becoming a Public Philosopher		117
References		121
Index		133
About the Author		141

Acknowledgments

In a book about the Socratic practice of self-disclosure, it seems fitting to tell a bit of my own story. My interest in Plato's use of narrative began over thirty years ago. I was an English major who wandered into a philosophy classroom because of a general education requirement. I liked philosophy enough to take another course. I loved Greek mythology as a child. The History of Ancient Greek Philosophy struck me as ideal. Midway through that semester, we read Plato's *Symposium*. I was captivated by Diotima's vision of love. Almost simultaneously, the intricate narrative structure of the dialogue sparked a flame of desire in my English major mind. Many unanswered questions buzzed about in my head: Who were these crazy people who told us this story? Why did they love Socrates so much? Why did Plato include them in the tale? How did this bizarre opening shape our understanding of the beautiful itself? I was transfixed. Simply put, I fell in love with a dialogue about love. I fell in love with the philosophical content and the literary form of this special dialogue. These dual loves carried me to graduate school at The Pennsylvania State University where I wrote a dissertation on the narrative structure of the *Symposium* under the late Stanley Rosen.[1]

As I began my teaching career, I imitated a rather standard conception of Socratic pedagogy. Much like Aristodemus imitated Socrates by going around barefoot, I embraced "the Socratic method." The rigorous process of elenchus, of refutative questioning and answering, aims at drawing out the correct answers from the souls of the willing and unwilling participants in the process.[2] However, the elenchus often left me feeling detached from my students. I wondered what my role as educator was *beyond* facilitating their understanding of ideas. I wondered where to situate myself in the story of philosophy that I was inviting the student to love. In my own way, I began to ask Hesiod's query in the *Theogony*: "But what is all this to me, the story of the oak and the boulder?" (1968, 35). Reading bell hooks' *Teaching to Transgress* when it was first published in 1994 started the revolution in my thinking about the kind of teacher I aspired to be. I was in the second year of my teaching career. I knew I wanted to be a teacher who educated for "the practice of freedom" (hooks 1994, 4). I began to examine my own practice. Why was I always positioning myself as the questioner? Why did I simply imitate Socrates? Why didn't I speak from my own experience and love of philosophy? I went back to the source: the Platonic dialogues. I started to look more carefully at everything Plato's Socrates did when he attempted to engage his interlocutors. In addition to argumentative refutation, he cites Homer regularly. He makes countless jokes. He tells myths of the ascent of the soul to the place beyond being and the journey of the soul in the afterlife. I reflected again and again on his query in the *Phaedrus* where he wonders what kind of creature he is. He explains his interest in self-inquiry to Phaedrus, asking, "Am I a beast more complicated and savage than Typhon, or am I a tamer, simpler animal with a share in a divine and gentle nature?" (*Phdr.*, 230a). After a while, I noticed that he told a lot of stories about himself, his philosophical practices, and what he learns from his teachers. His pedagogical methods involve autobiography and strategic self-disclosure as much as they depend on the elenchus, perhaps more so. As I explored these Socratic stories, I also started to share some of my own stories with my students. As a few semesters passed, the classroom dynamic shifted. My teaching became more conversational and egalitarian. I hope that, after reading this book, you will see Socrates in a new light and that you, like Socrates, will share your stories of philosophy with students and with the broader public as well. I also hope that we will all become better able to listen and learn from each other in the public sphere.

As always, I have a number of people to thank for their sustained support of my work. I enjoyed one semester of research leave at the start of writing of this book. I thank Dean Nordt and The College of Arts and Sciences at Baylor University for this generous support. The Baylor Philosophy Department and The Baylor Interdisciplinary Core, in addition to being filled with wonderful colleagues, also provided abundant travel support to conferences to present portions of this work. The Boston Area Colloquium in Ancient Philosophy, The Ancient Philosophy Society, The History of Philosophy Society, and The Southwestern Seminar in Continental Philosophy have all provided hospitable spaces and valuable interlocutors for early formulations of this project. Emma Bianchi, Sara Brill, Jessica Decker, Ryan Drake, Jill Gordon, Danielle Lane, Marina McCoy, Kris Mclain, Shannon Mussett, Mike Shaw, and Kristi Sweet have been particularly supportive over a long period of time. I am grateful to have so many philosophical friends! I am thankful for the current members of my writing group: Lenore Wright, Paul Carron, Mike Whitenton, and Jacque Mougouè for their ongoing willingness to read and critique my work. Thank you for providing so much occasion for genuine laughter along with the serious play of exchanging ideas with each other. The undergraduate and graduate students in my ancient survey courses, Plato seminars, and reading groups at Baylor have been ready interlocutors as well. You are all why I do what I do. A special thanks goes to Sabrina Little. She is the best research assistant I have had the pleasure of working with in my twenty-five years at Baylor. Thanks again to Leslie Ballard for his excellent copyediting work. All of you played an important in role in bringing this book about Socratic storytelling to light.

My own story began, of course, with my parents, Andrea and Michael Frosolono. My sister, Christina Frosolono Sell, arrived in the world shortly after I did. It is difficult to imagine the story of my life without her love and support in it. My family now extends well beyond this nuclear beginning. My brother in law, Kelly Sell, along with Christina, deserves enormous thanks for providing a new home for my parents during a difficult chapter in their lives. As you will learn in chapter 5, my mother passed away when I was writing this book. We all miss her greatly. I would also like to thank my in-laws (Jon, Suzette, Marc, Kris, Madison, Caleb, and now Gracie) for welcoming me into the Schultz family. My husband, Jeff, Milo the golden retriever, and Dante the Rhodesian ridgeback infuse each day with love and joyful play. Dante was particularly helpful in keeping my writing space squirrel-free. Again, I dedicate this book to Jeffrey Randall Schultz. Thank you for being such a wonderful part of the story of my life.

Permissions:

Like most long-term projects, portions of this work have appeared in print previously.

- An early version of the *Theaetetus* chapter appeared as "Listening to Socrates' Voice in the *Theaetetus*: Recovering a Lost Narrator." In *Second Sailing: Alternative Perspectives on Plato*. Eds. Debra Nails and Harold Tarrant, Helsinki: *Societas Scientiarum Fennica* 13 (2015): 248–265.
- The initial formulation of the overall project appeared as "Socrates on Socrates: Looking Backward to Bring Philosophy Forward." *Proceedings of the Boston Area Colloquium in Ancient Philosophy* 30 (2015): 123–141.
- Some of the Ta-Neishi Coates and Cornel West material in chapter 6 appears in "Stirring up America's Sleeping Horses: Cornel West, Ta-Nehisi Coates, and Socratic Parrhesia and Platonic Writing in the Public Sphere." *Southwest Philosophical Review* 34 (2018): 1–16.

- Part of the *Apology* chapter appears as "Socrates as Public Philosopher: A Model of Informed Democratic Engagement," *The European Legacy* 24, no. 7–8 (2019), DOI: 10.1080/10848770.2019.1641312.

I thank all the publishers for permission to reprint.

I used the translations of Plato found in *Complete Works* edited by John Cooper (Hackett 1997). The copyrights for these translations appear below.

Plato, Paul Woodruff and Alexander Nehamas, trans., *Symposium*. (Hackett 1989).
Plato, M. J. Levett. trans., rev. Myles Burnyeat, *The Theaetetus of Plato*. (Hackett 1990).
Plato, GMA Grube, trans., rev. John M Cooper, "Apology" and "Phaedo" from Five Dialogues (Second Edition) (Hackett 2002).

Quotes are reprinted by permission of Hackett Publishing Company, Inc. All rights reserved.

NOTES

1. See Frosolono (1993).
2. For an excellent reassessment of the Socratic method, see Scott (2004).

Overview

In *Plato's Socrates on Socrates: Socratic Self-Disclosure and the Public Practice of Philosophy*, I turn to an overlooked dimension of the Platonic dialogues to help us engage with the pressing social and political problems. I explore Plato's presentation of Socrates as a philosopher who tells personal narratives about his educational experience in a variety of public contexts. I hope that an increased awareness of, and appreciation for, this Socratic practice of self-disclosure will encourage more academic philosophers to engage in the public sphere more actively and contribute to the conversation about what it means to be an engaged citizen of the world today. I also hope that recognizing the pedagogical and political importance of self-disclosive speech will encourage everyday citizens to tell their own stories and listen to the stories of others.

With this larger contemporary context in mind, I analyze the philosophical and political implications of Plato's presentation of Socrates' self-disclosive speech in four dialogues: *Theaetetus, Symposium, Apology,* and *Phaedo*. These moments of Socratic self-disclosure are important for several reasons. First, they show that Plato's presentation of "Socrates the narrator" is much more pervasive than the secondary literature typically acknowledges.[1] Despite the pervasive appearance of a Socrates who describes his own experience throughout the dialogues, Socratic autobiographical self-disclosure has received surprisingly little scholarly attention. Plato's use of narrative, particularly his trope of "Socrates the narrator," is often subsumed into discussions of the dramatic nature of the dialogues more generally rather than studied in its own right. Thanks to the work of numerous scholars over the past several decades, there is now a general acceptance of the importance of the dramatic aspects of Plato's dialogues. Gerald Press notes, "the question was no longer whether to take textual, contextual, literary, and dramatic aspects of the dialogues into consideration, but how" (2018, 10). However, even within this new landscape, the narrative dimensions of Socrates' practice within the dialogues are not typically regarded as central to understanding how his philosophy functions in the public sphere.[2] This lack of attention is unfortunate because these carefully crafted narrative remarks add to the richness and profundity of the Platonic texts on many levels. I examine these embedded Socratic narratives to illustrate how they contribute to the portrait of Socrates as a public philosopher in Plato's dialogues.[3]

Let me say, at the outset, that I am not arguing that we should regard these stories as true accounts of what actually happened to the historical Socrates. The question of whether or not these narratives reliably report events that happened to the historical Socrates is not my primary concern.[4] I am, however, keenly interested in a different set of questions. Why does Plato portray his character Socrates as someone who tells stories about himself and particularly stories about his educational experience? What does this rhetorical decision on Plato's part tell us about his understanding of philosophical practice? What might we, as contemporary educators, learn from listening to these Socratic stories of self-discovery? How might these Socratic stories shape the philosophical stories we tell our students and our larger communities? As we consider these questions, keep in mind that I am not advocating that we tell untruthful stories, but that we shape our stories in such a way that they have whether there is a productive pedagogical and political function. In *Hillbilly Elegy*, J. D. Vance describes his own truth-telling process, "Though I sometimes change the names of people to protect their privacy, this story is, to the best of my recollection, a fully accurate portrait of the world I've witnessed . . . I am sure this story is as fallible as any human memory" (2016, 9). He mentions that his sister remembers events in a different order, but keeps his order "because I think there is something to learn in how I've organized the events in my own mind" (2016, 9). Though self-disclosive speech has certain limitations, it is still a valuable mode of public discourse.

An interest in the pedagogical value of self-disclosive speech motivates my exploration of Plato's use of narrative more broadly. Simply put, I am interested in how and why Plato depicts Socrates as a character who tells stories about himself, not just in the dialogues he narrates but throughout the Platonic corpus. These moments of Socratic self-disclosure enhance our understanding of the political dimensions of the practice of philosophy.[5] They show Socrates emphasizing the value of his philosophical education in politically charged settings in which the other characters, either implicitly or explicitly, reject the importance of living the examined life. As a result, the capacity that these characters have for functioning as productive citizens in their community diminishes greatly. Socrates shares his own stories as a means of drawing others into the ongoing practice of living the examined life as well. I am aware that some might find my use of the word "autobiographical" to describe Socrates' self-disclosive practices problematic. Some might regard my claim that Plato consistently presents Socrates as autobiographer with skepticism and charges of anachronism. Isn't autobiography a modern notion? Can there really be autobiography without a modern notion of self? Is there truly autobiography if there's no written account of a life? I would like to bracket these larger questions about the nature of autobiography. I am using "autobiography" in a rather broad sense, to mean the public recounting of aspects of one's life and inner experiences to others.

Second, taking these Socratic narratives into account helps solve ongoing interpretive problems of each individual dialogue. For example, consider the *Theaetetus*. Many scholars of the dialogue regard the opening discussion between Euclides and Terpsion where Euclides admits to erasing all references to Socrates' narrative voice (*Tht.*, 143c) as signaling Plato's own decision to abandon the narrative framing techniques he uses in many other dialogues.[6] However, it is possible to retrieve elements of Socrates' narrative practice throughout the dialogue. The narrative composition of the *Theaetetus*, taken as a whole, offers us clues about how the dialogues fulfill a Socratic philosophical and political legacy of self-care and communal practice. In the *Symposium*, Socrates' narrative presentation of his encounters with Diotima illustrates the deeply pedagogical nature of the dialogue. Furthermore, the three imitations of Socratic narration offered by Alcibiades, Apollodorus, and Aristodemus offer the possibility of seeing these characters in a more favorable light than is generally acknowledged in the secondary literature. They also demonstrate the importance of bringing philosophical pedagogy into the political sphere and the dangers that arise when philosophers cede a place in political discourse. The four autobiographical moments in the *Apology* show how Socrates' philosophical practice is informed by his care for his fellow citizens. The narrative dimensions of the *Phaedo*, both Socrates' self-disclosive speech and Phaedo's account of Socrates' final day, offer a different way of understanding immortality of the soul. This concept of narrative immortality is untethered from a traditional Homeric view of personal glory commemorated in poetic narrative. The narrative dimensions of the *Phaedo* also call us to develop philosophical communities of care where we can support one another.

Third, as I mentioned above, these self-disclosive narratives present a model that we would do well to embrace in our contemporary politically divisive times. The model is of Socrates as a public philosopher. I regard Socrates as a model public philosopher for several reasons. First, he practices his philosophical way of life in the public spaces of Athens. Second, he asks questions of vital importance to average Athenian citizens, questions about education, citizenship, religious practice, and the teachability of virtue. Third, he engages the "popular" Greek traditions, not just philosophical ones. He attends festivals; he mixes with sophists and other important thinkers. He reassesses culturally influential poetry such as the Homeric epics, Hesiod's cosmogony. He attends tragic and comedic performances much like we might watch a movie or a Netflix series today. Fourth, he tells stories about himself and his engagement with these cultural touchstones. These tales serve to both make him more relatable and allow him to model philosophical engagement for a broad public audience. I suggest we follow Socrates into the agora and share the stories of our philosophical lives both inside and outside of the classroom. Insofar as we value Socrates as a model philosopher, we should consider the philosophical value of self-disclosure for ourselves and our communal spheres of influence.

PUBLIC PHILOSOPHY

Before going much further, let me step back a moment and address, in good Socratic fashion, the larger question. What is public philosophy? While I do not think there is any single answer to this question, public philosophy involves a willingness to engage in philosophical conversation in the public sphere.[7] For example, several philosophers are writing blogs that bring issues of academic discourse into direct conversation with everyday life concerns.[8] There are also professional and lay philosophers engaging the public through podcasts like *Sacred and Profane Love* and *The Partially Examined Life*.[9] There are also online forums like The Electronic Agora (https://theelectricagora.com/) and The Humanities Commons (https://hcommons.org/) where scholars can share ideas in a public venue. Many academic philosophers are active on Twitter and Facebook. Some philosophers on Twitter include Leigh Johnson (@DrLeighMJohnson), Chris Long (@cplong), Robin James (@doctaj), Adriel Trott (@AdrielTrott), Kate Manne (@kate_manne), Jennifer Frey (@jennfrey), Francis Beckwith (@fbeckwith), Christian Miller (@charactergap), Mary Townsend (@chezaristote), Nigel Warburton (@philosophybites), and Peter Adamson (@HistPhilosophy). This list is, by no means, exhaustive. It provides a representative sample of philosophers from a broad range of philosophical perspectives who use Twitter in philosophically productive ways that bring philosophy into the public sphere. Public intellectual bell hooks describes one of the results of her decision to leave academia to teach in diverse public settings outside the traditional academic context. She writes, "the most exciting aspect of teaching outside conventional structures and/or college classrooms has been sharing the theory we write in academia with nonacademic audiences, and most importantly, seeing their hunger to learn new ways of knowing, their desire to use this knowledge in meaningful ways to enrich their daily lives" (hooks 2003, xi). hooks' extensive body of work is saturated with autobiographical self-disclosure and provides one model of how philosophers and other academics might integrate self-disclosure and autobiography into their professional written work as well.

It is not just that the public will benefit from more academics engaging in public political discourse. It is a two-way street. Academics and the Academy itself will benefit from this public engagement. Long explains, "From one direction, the prevailing winds of public sentiment bring an abiding wariness of academics in general, and of philosophers in particular. From the other, hot air rises from the academy, carrying its discourse high above the public upon which the academy too often looks down in disdain" (2018, 1). Sustained public engagement may also decrease the negative perception that many people have about the academy. Plato's portrait of Socrates as autobiographer has two important dimensions that make it particularly applicable to our current social and political realities, both inside and outside the academy. First, Socratic self-disclosure is engaging. This aspect of his philosophical practice provides an accessible model by which virtually anyone can imitate and begin to practice philosophy.[10] Everyone has an important story to tell. Second, by sharing his philosophical narratives to a wide range of audiences, Plato's Socrates provides a model for philosophers to enter into the diverse discourse in the public sphere and enhance our impoverished political dialogue about the public good. By recognizing the political and philosophical value of Socrates' autobiographical narratives, we can also recognize a broad range of writers engaging in what Socrates calls the "true democratic art" (*Grg.*, 521a).

SOCRATES' NARRATIVE PRACTICE OF PHILOSOPHY

Before presenting a chapter-by-chapter summary of this book, I offer a brief overview of Socrates' narrative practice of philosophy as Plato depicts it in the dialogues where Socrates serves as primary narrator. As a narrator, Socrates focuses on his thought process, his emotional states, the emotional states of others, and the social dynamics of the situation in which he finds himself. Taken together, these aspects of Socrates' narrative commentary suggest that the emotions play an important role in bringing people to the philosophical life and in the ongoing practice of the self-reflective philosophical life itself. Viewed in this way, Socrates' use of personal narrative liberates the emotions from the confines of centuries of negative judgment about their place in philosophical reflection. Socrates uses the emotional dimensions of his narrative remarks to engage the auditor in the details of his report. More importantly, they stimulate a process of philosophical thinking by drawing the auditors' attention to important moments in the argument and the dramatic action. Since I have presented elsewhere a detailed analysis of how this narrative process works (Schultz 2013), I will limit myself to mentioning six basic aspects of Socrates' narrative style.

First, Socrates' narrative commentary often discloses Socrates' inner states of mind. They reveal that Socrates' emotions are an important feature of his inner life. He is not unemotional. He often interweaves emotional experience into his philosophical thought process. Second, they illustrate a profound sensitivity to the emotions of his auditors and a corresponding ability to use this awareness to facilitate a process of critical reflection in the auditor. Third, Socrates uses the social context in which he narrates, which is often emotionally fraught, to emphasize the value of the practice of philosophy as a therapeutic mode of self-care, a mode of philosophical inoculation against potentially harmful influences such as various forms of sophistic teaching. Fourth, Socrates appears to narrate stories about himself to people he is on friendly terms with. Although we know little about the exact identity of Socrates' auditors, with the exception of Crito in the *Euthydemus*, the narrative setting generally suggests some level of friendship between Socrates and his auditors. In this way, it sets the stage for recognizing the importance of communal responsibility in the practice of philosophy. Fifth, often Socrates' narrative commentary diminishes as the dialogue progresses. There seems to be some implicit expectation on Socrates' part that the auditor will begin to engage in philosophical reflection about the story that Socrates has just told him. If the auditor finds the inner resources to meet Socrates' expectations, the auditor himself becomes more philosophical in the process. Finally, though this is obvious, it is worth stating explicitly. In the act of narrating his philosophical experience, Socrates tells stories about himself. Viewed in this way, the narrative dialogue itself becomes an autobiographical act. Through this narrative presentation of himself, Socrates conveys a strong sense of accountability for his words and deeds. His self-disclosing narratives also illustrate the responsibility he feels to bring others into philosophical community with him.

CHAPTER-BY-CHAPTER SUMMARY

Chapter 1 begins with the *Theaetetus*. In many ways, the *Theaetetus* is a bridge dialogue, at least in terms of its narrative structure, between the Socratically narrated dialogues that I examine in *Plato's Socrates as Narrator: A Philosophical Muse* and the non-Socratically narrated dialogues that are the subject of my in-progress book, *Telling Tales of Socrates: Becoming Philosophers of the Future*. The dialogue as we currently have it is presented by a character, Euclides, who heard the account from Socrates himself while Socrates was in prison awaiting his death (*Tht.*, 143a–b). Euclides tells Terpsion how he created his own version of the conversation between Socrates,

Theodorus, and Theaetetus. Euclides makes clear that he deliberately removed Socrates' narrative voice from his version of the story (*Tht.*, 143c).[11] In doing so, Euclides ignores an important part of the story he received from Socrates. He discounts Socrates' own voice. Nonetheless, I argue that we can recover remnants of Socrates' narrative voice in a dialogue that claims to obscure it at the outset. The *Theaetetus* begins with Euclides telling Terpsion that he heard about the philosophical conversation between Socrates and Theaetetus from Socrates himself. While Socrates was in prison, awaiting execution, Euclides would visit him. After each visit, Euclides would go home and write down what he remembered of Socrates' narrative. At some point, Euclides decides to write his own version of the story. He tells Terpsion he "removed those bothersome bits of Socratic narration" (*Tht.*, 143c). Despite this textual obscuring, the *Theaetetus* also testifies to the original Socratic narrative source just ten lines earlier (*Tht.*, 143b). I draw on the work of Harold Tarrant (2010) and Holger Thesleff (1982) to support my recovery of these trace elements of Socratic narration. Their work suggests that the way Plato uses Greek in the *Theaetetus* strongly resembles the way he uses Greek in other Socratically narrated dialogues. Furthermore, passages like Socrates' description of himself as midwife are evocative of the self-descriptive comments he makes in the narrated dialogues. This process of narrative recovery shows that Plato's rhetorical use of Socrates as a narrator is much more pervasive than previously recognized. In addition, the *Theaetetus* contains several examples of Socrates disclosing aspects of his life as he does when he is a character in the dialogues that are narrated by characters other than Socrates like the *Symposium* and the *Phaedo*.[12]

In chapter 2, I turn to the *Symposium*. Socrates tells the story of Diotima at a dinner party at Agathon's house in 416 BCE. The *Symposium* does not begin with this narrated account. Rather, we hear Socrates' narrative voice through a series of nested autobiographical narratives that frame the dialogue. The *Symposium* opens with Apollodorus' boastful claim: "I am not unprepared to tell the account you ask of" (*Symp.*, 172a). Apollodorus, the narrator of the entire dialogue, offers us an imitation of Socratic storytelling. Apollodorus tells about his preparation as storyteller, as keeper of the Socratic legacy. His story depends on another autobiographical account, namely, Aristodemus' version of the story Socrates told at the party. Apollodorus makes clear that he checked the story with Socrates. Apollodorus preserves the autobiographical aspect of the transmission by telling his friend that he would rather tell the story "just as Aristodemus told the story to him" (*Symp.*, 174a). Through this layered narrative filter, we learn how Phaedrus, Pausanias, Eryximachus, Aristophanes, and Agathon each define love. We also hear how Socrates questions Agathon (*Symp.*, 199d–201c). Agathon admits, perhaps a bit too readily, that "he really didn't know what he was talking about in his speech" (*Symp.*, 201c). After Agathon admits aporia, Socrates reports his encounters with Diotima: "I shall try to go through for you the speech about Love I once heard from a woman of Mantinea, Diotima—a woman who was wise about many things besides this: once she even put off the plague for ten years by telling the Athenians what sacrifices to make" (*Symp.*, 201d). Socrates explains how he will narrate the account: "I think it will be easiest for me to proceed the way Diotima did and tell you how she questioned me" (*Symp.*, 201e). Socrates emphasizes his affinity with Agathon: "I had told her almost the same things Agathon told me just now; that Love is a great god and that he belongs to beautiful things" (*Symp.*, 210e). Just as he tells the Myth of Er to benefit Glaucon, he tells the story of himself and Diotima to benefit Agathon. Socrates articulates Agathon's views as if they were his own past beliefs. His subsequent autobiographical narrative conveys how Diotima changed his philosophical perspective.

Chapter 3 unfolds in the following manner. First, I briefly reconsider the overall dramatic structure of the *Symposium* to emphasize that Socrates presents his autobiographical account of his lessons with Diotima as a means of philosophical provocation. This philosophical provocation offers us the opportunity to assess three other autobiographical accounts that frame the dialogue as a whole, namely, Alcibiades' praise of Socrates, and the dual narrative frames provided by Apollodorus that preserve Aristodemus' version of the story. Second, I turn to Alcibiades' speech, which shares many elements of Socrates' own autobiographical account of his lessons on love. Third, I consider Apollodorus and Aristodemus' accounts of the events surrounding Socrates' speech. I explore these three imitations of Socratic autobiography to illustrate the pervasiveness of autobiographical narratives in the *Symposium*. Each of these characters practice the art of Socratic narrative autobiography to varying degrees of philosophical success. These aspects of the *Symposium* make it possible to regard them in a more favorable light than is often the case in the secondary literature.

Chapter 4 considers the numerous autobiographical elements in the *Apology*. Plato's *Apology* offers us a rich set of Socratic autobiographical reflections. There are four autobiographical accounts that Socrates offers as part of his defense in the *Apology*. The first autobiography, and the one most often commented on in the secondary literature, is Socrates' lengthy report of how he tests the Delphic oracle (*Ap.*, 21a–23a). Working in the order that they appear in the text, the next autobiographical moment occurs when Socrates describes his conflict with the Athenian Council concerning their attempt to try ten generals for war crimes *en masse* (*Ap.*, 32a–c). The third autobiographical moment occurs almost immediately following. Socrates refers to his protest of the actions of the Thirty regarding the recall of Leon from Salamis (*Ap.*, 32c–33d). The fourth autobiographical moment involves Socrates' account of the daimon appearing to him since childhood (*Ap.*, 32d–e). I explore each of these narratives and suggest that Socrates consistently appropriates moments of his life story to illustrate his ongoing commitment to exhorting his fellow citizens to care about the good and the grounding role it should play in their lives.

In chapter 5, I turn to the *Phaedo*. The *Phaedo* recounts the death of Socrates in 399 BCE. The narrator, Phaedo, describes Socrates' final hours to a group of Pythagoreans in Phlius sometime after Socrates' death occurs.[13] As I do in the exploration of the *Symposium* in chapter 2, I will focus on how the character Socrates uses self-disclosive speech and autobiographical narrative within the reported events of this dialogue. This chapter unfolds in the following manner. First, I focus on three important moments of Socratic self-disclosure: his reinterpretation of his ongoing dreams that have commanded him to make and practice music, the result of which is that he sets Aesop and the Homeric hymns to verse (*Phd.*, 60b–61b); his reference to being like Apollo's swans (*Phd.*, 84d–85b); and his admission that he is in danger of not having a philosophical attitude in the face of death (*Phd.*, 91a–c). Second, I turn to the famous "second sailing" passage where Socrates tells his intellectual autobiography about his encounters with Anaxagoras' writings, his subsequent disillusionment with them, and his turn away from natural philosophy to the development of his own linguistic mode of inquiry into the fundamental nature of reality (*Phd.*, 96a–100a). Third, I suggest that Socrates may be offering a different understanding of immortality through this autobiographical self-disclosure that is aimed not at personal glory, but at communal obligation. His self-disclosive speech and autobiographical narrative help create a new communal space for future philosophical dialogue. Fourth, I examine Phaedo's narrative retelling of the events of Socrates' last day to illustrate how autobiographical narrative can help create philosophical communities of care. I conclude this chapter by offering an autobiographical reflection about how philosophy shaped my experience of my mother's passing.

In the final chapter, I summarize the overall effect of Socrates' self-disclosive practices. I then examine three contemporary writers who employ autobiographical discourse in what I regard as a Socratic manner: bell hooks, Kathy Khang, and Ta-Neishi Coates. Hopefully, as we begin to share our own stories and expand the circles of our intellectual work, we will come to recognize that a broad range of voices express a Socratic commitment to awaken fellow citizens from unreflective complacency and privilege. I then offer a postscript containing three short self-disclosive stories that illustrate my journey toward becoming a public philosopher.

NOTES

1. My treatment of these autobiographical accounts grows out of the narrative methodology I established in Schultz (2013). However, this book does not depend on the reader having read the first book.

2. Exceptions include Finkelberg (2018), Schultz (2013), and Collins (2015). See also Morgan (2004). Careful treatments of the narrative frames and commentary appear in extended studies of the dialogues I am considering. I make note of them in the chapters on the individual dialogues.

3. Catherine Zuckert recognizes the importance of these three autobiographical accounts and considers them in terms of how Plato presents Socrates' development as a philosopher. She writes, "But in three later dialogues Plato does present three retrospective statements by Socrates describing parts of his development. Plato leaves it to his readers to put these parts together" (Zuckert 2009, 180).

4. For an excellent treatment of the current state of scholarship on "The Socratic Problem," see Dorion (2018).

5. I use the term "self-disclosive speech" to refer to remarks that Socrates makes about himself. I use "autobiographical reflection" to refer to more sustained narratives that Socrates tells about some event from his past. I see autobiography as a particular mode of self-disclosive speech.

6. On the abandonment of the narrative frame in Plato's "later" works, see Nails (1995), Tarrant (1996), Benardete (1997), Thesleff (2002), and Blondell (2002).

7. For an excellent discussion of the various forms that public philosophy can take and for very helpful guidelines for practicing and supporting it, see Nguyen (2019).

8. Some examples include Jennifer Frey, n.d., *The Virtue Blog* (blog), accessed September 18, 2018, thevirtueblog.com ; Sabrina Little, n.d., *I Run Far* (blog), accessed September 18, 2018, iRunFar.com ; Adriel Trott, n.d., *The Trott Line* (blog), accessed October 20, 2018, https://adrieltrott.com ; Leigh Johnson, n.d., *ReadMoreWriteMoreThinkMoreBeMore* (blog), accessed September 18, 2018, ReadMoreWriteMoreThinkMoreBeMore.com ; Chris Long, n.d., *The Long Road* (blog), accessed September 1, 2018, http://www.personal.psu.edu/cpl2/blogs/TheLongRoad/blog ; and my own website, n.d., *Thoughts on Teaching Philosophy and Yoga* (blog), accessed September 1, 2018, http://www.teachingphilosophyandyoga.blogspot.com . Academics in other disciplines are also engaging in this work. See Lynn Murphy, n.d., *Separated by a Common Language* (blog), accessed September 1, 2018, http://separatedbyacommonlanguage.blogspot.com ; Paul Larson, n.d., *The Spanish Medievalist* (blog), accessed September 1, 2018, http://spanishmedievalist.blogspot.com ; and Mark Osler, n.d., *Osler's Razor* (blog), accessed September 1, 2018, http://oslersrazor.blogspot.com .

9. Jennifer Frey is the primary organizer of this podcast. She describes its public impact here: n.d., APAOnline (website), accessed September 20, 2018, https://blog.apaonline.org/2019/04/03/sacred-and-profane-love-podcast-philosophy-outside-academia/. *The Partially Examined Life* has four primary contributors: Mark Linsenmayer, Seth Paskin, Wes Alwan, Dylan Casey. This podcast is extremely popular. It has been downloaded 25 million times. See Mark Linsenmayer, Partially Examined Life, n.d., October 20, 2018, https://blog.apaonline.org/2018/08/28/the-partially-examined-life-podcast-philosophy-outside-academia/ .

10. There is an abundance of cognitive narratological work that suggests the very act of reading or hearing a narrative automatically prompts audience members either toward or against emulation. See Bergen (2012), Bortolussi and Dixon (2003), Cupchik (1997), Tan (1995), Carsetti (2010), Iacoboni (2009a, 2009b), Keysers (2011), and Williams et al. (2001).

11. Scholars frequently point to the second-century *Anonymous Commentary* on the *Theaetetus* as evidence that there was an earlier version of the *Theaetetus*. The *AC* offers little in the way of support of whether that earlier version had a Socratic narrator. But it is clear that there was some earlier version of the dialogue. See Tarrant (2010) and Thesleff (1982).

12. For an early formulation of this chapter, see Schultz (2015a). In that work, I focus primarily on the recovery of Socrates' narrative voice and not so much on Socrates' self-disclosive practices.

13. See Bowery (2003).

Chapter One

Recovering Socrates the Narrator in Plato's *Theaetetus*

I begin this chapter by describing two common assumptions about the *Theaetetus*. First, scholars who are concerned with determining the chronology of Plato's written work typically regard the *Theaetetus* as a dialogue that Plato wrote late in his life.[1] On a surface reading, so-called late dialogues like the *Theaetetus*, *Sophist*, and *Statesman* appear to contain fewer dramatic elements than dialogues written in the early elenchic and middle highly dramatic periods of his authorship.[2] Scholars typically regard this "late" form as resulting from Plato's decision to move away from the narrative aspects of the dialogues as he develops his own mature philosophical positions.[3] In fact, they often point to Euclides' decision to take out the bothersome "bits of narrative in between the speeches" (*Tht.*, 143b) as an indication of Plato's own views about the overall value of the narrative dialogue as a philosophically beneficial mode of writing.[4] Second, the *Theaetetus* is often grouped with the three other dialogues that have non-Socratic narrators: *Parmenides*, *Symposium*, and *Phaedo*. These stylistic classifications of the *Theaetetus* have some value in that they point us to important thematic aspects of the dialogue and uncover its relationship to other works in the Platonic corpus. Unfortunately, these classifications of the *Theaetetus* obscure how Plato's character Socrates practices the narrative art of autobiography in the dialogue. His self-disclosing discourse shares many similarities with Socrates' autobiographical practices in the five dialogues where he serves as narrator.[5]

In this chapter, I explore how the Socratic autobiographical dimensions of the *Theaetetus* help us better understand the dialogue's pedagogical, philosophical, and political implications. The chapter unfolds in the following manner. First, I draw upon the work done by Holger Thesleff (1982) and Harold Tarrant (2010) to establish that there was an earlier version of the

Theaetetus in which Socrates served as primary narrator of the dialogue. I argue that it is possible to recover remnants of Socrates' narrative voice in the version of text that has been transmitted to us as contemporary readers. Second, I explore the dialogic exchange between Euclides and Terpsion in light of its references to an earlier version of the story that Socrates narrated to Euclides.[6] Third, I consider other passages throughout the *Theaetetus* with an eye toward uncovering any remnants of Socrates' narrative voice from the original version.[7] Even within Euclides' revised reported account that takes out the bothersome "bits of narrative" (*Tht.*, 143c), Euclides' version of the character Socrates does tell stories about himself and makes important self-disclosive remarks throughout the text. Fourth, I offer one possible explanation for Plato's revision of the dialogue to the form we currently have it—the possibility that Socrates' narrative perspective might reinforce a kind of Protagorean relativism.[8] Even though Plato may have "abandoned" Socrates the narrator in this dialogue, I argue that there is much to gain from exploring the ways that Plato portrays Socrates as an autobiographer of his own pedagogical experiences. Socratic storytelling provides a powerful model that we can employ as we come to understand ourselves and others with greater depth and nuance.

STYLOMETRIC ANALYSIS OF THE *THEAETETUS*

Holger Thesleff on the *Theaetetus*

In his discussion of the *Theaetetus*, Holger Thesleff asserts, "It can be regarded as fairly certain that the dialogue was subjected to revision" (1982, 153) by Plato. Thesleff describes how he envisions the early Theaetetus. He suggests that it was "a reported dialogue in the style of the *Charmides*, yet probably with a frame dialogue in the manner of *Euthydemus*, presenting Socrates in conversation with Eukleides" (Thesleff 1982, 153). Thesleff allows that "separating two layers and dating them is no easy task" (1982, 153). Thesleff hears the voice of the Socratic original report in "The easy-going style of the first scene with Theaitetos, 144b–146c (but not the more formal opening exchange of speeches between Socrates and Theodorus), [in] Socrates' presentation of *maieutics* 150b–151d, and [in] the conclusion 201b–d" (1982, 153). Thesleff also suggests that "the extant version of this frame was most probably written for the revised version of the dialogue, and thus it is important to note its easy-going style and the somewhat broad setting presented here" (1982, 182). Some years later, Thesleff elaborates on how Plato revised the dialogue: "Having begun the dialogue as a *Charmides*-like piece in the mid-370s, Plato some years later I believe, remodeled it for internal use in the Academy and included up-to-date reference to his theory of knowledge and polemics against various recent trends of criticism" (1989,

18–19). In this way, Thesleff's work supports the view of other scholars who regard the *Theaetetus* as being written later in Plato's philosophical career.

When assessing these remarks about the *Theaetetus*, it is important to consider Thesleff's overall view of Platonic literary production. He argues that there is a movement away from Socratically narrated dialogues to dramatic dialogues in Plato's trajectory as a writer. Thesleff explains, "So we are again facing the possibility that Plato began his literary career by writing speeches and reported dialogues, and that the dramatic form was introduced later" (1982, 64). Thesleff continues to hold this view throughout his long and distinguished career. Thesleff emphasizes, "There is a trend in Plato's literary production away from the narrated dialogue form to the direct dramatic form" (2002, 292). However, even in a dialogue that claims to explicitly move away from reported narrative form, we will see that traces of Socrates the narrator, an autobiographer of his thoughts, emotions, words, and deeds, remains.

Plato probably did not invent the reported dialogue form. Indeed, most of the early *Socratikoi logoi* probably had Socrates as narrator. Thesleff notes that "a reported dialogue is better suited for publication in written form and for reading unprepared by a single person . . . the narrative of the report gives the necessary hints" (1982, 63). Gary Alan Scott calls them "narrative precautions" (2000, 193n6). Thomas Szelzák calls them a "hermeneutic key" (1999, 28–29) that helps unlock the philosophical meaning of the dialogue.[9] Thesleff explains further, "Once the Academy had been established, and the writing of dramatic dialogues had become an institutionalized practice there, the frame narrative with its inserenda . . . could be easily dropped. The opening of the *Theaetetus* tells us in so many words how this could be done" (2002, 293). Thesleff asserts that the content of the *Theaetetus* did not have broad appeal, unlike the *Gorgias*. For example, he writes, "The text was read at the Academy as an exercise. Like *Lysis* and *Charmides*, Plato found the problems it raised sufficiently interesting to be worth reconsidering, and he began to rewrite it at a later occasion" (2002, 153–54). Thesleff also believes that this "final" revision was extensive because there are traces of the older and the newer layers throughout the expanded and revised dialogue that is our *Theaetetus*. Although our current version of the *Theaetetus* does not have a Socratic narrator, Thesleff's work creates the possibility of uncovering the Socratic narrative traces that remain within it.

Harold Tarrant on the *Theaetetus*

The weight of the stylometric analysis that Harold Tarrant brings to the linguistic evolution of the *Theaetetus* is impressive. Tarrant suggests two possible hypotheses that would explain the similarities that the *Theaetetus* has with other Socratically narrated dialogues: "Either (1) the *Theaetetus* was a dramatic dialogue written over the same period as the narrative dialogues, so as to show similar linguistic trends or (2) the *Theaetetus* is a revised version of a dialogue that was originally written in narrative mode" (2010, 12). Tarrant's additional analysis reveals that "it continued to show strong affinities with the narrative dialogues (when supplemented by *Protagoras* and *Republic* V)" (2010, 12). Based on these considerations, Tarrant maintains "that the *Theaetetus* has much in common with the narrative dialogues, and perhaps especially with *Republic* V, is not in doubt" (2010, 13). He suggests further that, "In the case of the *Theaetetus* one might infer from the prologue not only that there was such an original, but also that it was Socrates himself who was originally performing the narration" (2010, 14). Tarrant ultimately concludes, "What statistical analysis has shown is that the whole *Theaetetus* is stylistically closer to the works that employ the mediating voice of Socrates to narrate a conversation than to the shorter dramatic form" (2010, 16).

How should we read the *Theaetetus* if it has much in common with *Republic V* and the other Socratically narrated dialogues? Tarrant begins to answer this question by turning to the critique of narrative enactment in the *Republic*. Tarrant takes up Plato's concerns about the dangers of dramatic engagement for the guardian class in the *Republic* and suggests that the Socratic narrator somehow safeguards dramatic engagement with ideas.[10] In terms of Socrates' narrative style itself, Tarrant says relatively little other than the reference to word choices that he analyzes and his observation that there are no characters "unworthy of a philosopher to imitate" and that Socrates is "apt to be particularly self-critical" (2010, 16). These word choices exist in Socratic narration more globally, but these linguistic aspects of Socrates' narrative style do not capture the full range of Socratic narrative activity as portrayed in the five Socratically narrated dialogues. To his credit, despite his expert use of stylometric analysis, Tarrant argues that "stylometry can only inform one's thinking" about this matter and that it must be supplemented by "subtle examination" (2010, 16) of the prologue. In the following section, I build on Tarrant's provocative research by bringing a more fully developed account of Socrates as a narrator into a reading of the *Theaetetus*. I know that people might be skeptical about this endeavor. Can we really recover the erased Socrates? Not entirely, to be sure. However, the linguistic similarities with the Greek of the narrated dialogues like the *Republic* suggest the possibility of uncovering some aspects of Socrates' narrative voice. Let us see what we might learn about the *Theaetetus* by bringing these Socratic narrative traces into the light of our philosophical considerations about the role of the philosopher in the polis.

REFERENCES TO A SOCRATIC ORIGINAL IN THE PROLOGUE

The prologue of the *Theaetetus* contains several references to a version of this story that Socrates himself narrated to Euclides. The first two references occur when Euclides reflects on Socrates' observations about Theaetetus' character. He tells Terpsion,

> As I was coming back, I thought of Socrates and what a remarkably good prophet he was—as usual—about Theaetetus. It was not long before his death, if I remember rightly, that he came across Theaetetus, who was a boy at the time. Socrates met him and had a talk with him, and was very much struck with his natural ability; and when I went to Athens, he repeated to me the discussion they had had, which was well worth listening to. And he said to me then that we should inevitably hear more of Theaetetus, if he lived to grow up. (*Tht.*, 142d)

In this passage, Euclides names Socrates as the original source of his account; Socrates "repeated" or, more accurately, "narrated" the discussion he had with Theaetetus. Euclides emphasizes the fact that Socrates told it to him when he affirms it "was well worth listening to" (*Tht.*, 142d). Euclides' evaluation of the merits of the narrative underscores its Socratic source. Euclides reinforces his Socratic source again, saying, "[H]e said to me then [i.e., at the time of Socrates telling Euclides the narrative], that we would hear more of Theaetetus" (*Tht.*, 142d). Euclides does not make any reference to Socrates mentioning Theodorus' part in the conversation. No one else is mentioned as being present when Socrates tells Euclides the story.

The third reference Euclides makes to Socrates is the narrative source that occurs in his response to Terpsion's question. Terpsion asks him; "But what was the discussion? Could you tell it to me?" (*Tht.*, 143a). Euclides' response distinguishes his version from the Socratic original:

> Good Lord, no. Not from memory anyway. I made some notes of it at the time, as soon as I got home; then afterwards I recalled it at my leisure and wrote it out, and whenever I went to Athens, I used to ask Socrates about the points I couldn't remember, and correct my version when I got home. The result is that I have got pretty well the whole discussion in writing. (*Tht.*, 143a)

In this brief passage, Euclides emphasizes how the written text before them is *his* account. He makes notes when he gets home. He recalls it at leisure. He writes it out. He checks his memory with Socrates and corrects his version. Euclides leaves no room for doubt. This is Euclides' account of events, not Socrates' own. Capturing the essential elements of discussion by distilling out the Socratic narrative commentary is Euclides' unique artistic rendering, albeit one that seems to remove the received artistry of Socrates.

Euclides seems interested in the discussion itself, not Socrates' way of reporting it. In this way, he resembles Glaucon and the unnamed friend in the opening of the *Symposium* (173a and 173e) in their eagerness to hear the speeches on love from Apollodorus. Actually, it is not just Socrates' "extraneous" words he tries to remove. He removes Socrates' insights into the thoughts and behaviors of his interlocutors. Benardete notes that in Socratically narrated dialogues we also hear "Socrates' understanding of what his interlocutors had in mind in saying what they did and what his own intentions were. All of this vanishes in Euclides' representation" (1984, 86). Benardete writes, "Euclides' manner of writing does not preclude the possibility that within its limitations ways could be found to express both bodily movements and silent intentions, but it would surely require that Euclides be as skilled as Plato" (1984, 87). Benardete continues, "Rather than to attribute to Euclides so large a talent, we could suppose that either Socrates said nothing about anyone's expressions or intentions and refrained from all interpretation, or Socrates himself, knowing the pedantry of Euclides (Socrates chose him, after all, as the most suitable recorder of this dialogue), smuggled into the speeches all that he suspected Euclides would have otherwise omitted" (1984, 87). The next two references to a Socratic narrative original occur when Euclides describes what they are about to hear the slave read.[11] Sedley notes, "The transcript that Euclides' slave is now asked to read out, and which will constitute the main body of the dialogue, purports within the dramatic fiction to take us straight back to a vividly historical Socrates, frozen in time by a verbatim record of his words, at the moment in his life when he was about to hand on the torch to his successors" (2004, 17).

> This is the book, Terpsion. You see, I have written it out like this: I have not made Socrates relate the conversation as he related it to me, but I represent him as speaking directly to the person with whom he said he had this conversation. These were, he told me, Theodorus the geometer and Theaetetus. I wanted, in the written version, to avoid the bother of having the bits of narrative in between the speeches—I mean when Socrates, whenever he mentions his own part in the discussion, says, "And I maintained" or "I said," or, of the person answering, "He agreed" or "he would not admit this." That is why I have made him talk directly to them and have left out these formulae. (*Tht.*, 143c)

When Euclides says that he wants to avoid the bother of transcribing Socrates' own part, the Greek word he uses is *"pragmata"* (*Tht.*, 143c10). Howland rightly notes, *"pragmata* are more literally 'deeds'—items that Euclides finds troubling philosophically" (1998, 43). Quite literally, then, Euclides admits that he has obscured the deeds of Socrates just as he has obscured the words. The Anonymous Commentator dismisses the reason stated in the text for the revision, at least from the Platonic perspective. He writes, "For it was not for the reason he gives—that the dialogue would be impeded by inserting 'and I said,' and 'I spoke,' and, for the interlocutor, 'he agreed' and 'he didn't agree.' For he has used this style in other dialogues and it is not annoying in them" (1995, IV).[12] Perhaps this stated reason is true for Euclides, but not for Plato. In fact, Benardete (1984, 86) suggests that the dialogue has two authors, Plato and Euclides. However, even in Euclides' own narrator-less creation, remnants of a narrating Socrates are present. We find them in the autobiographical aspects of Socrates' words that Euclides chooses to keep in his story about Socrates and Theaetetus.

LOCATING THE REMAINS OF SOCRATES' NARRATIVE VOICE IN THE *THEAETETUS*

As I mentioned in the introduction to this chapter, Socrates' narrative commentary has many recognizable stylistic features. He often interweaves emotional experience into his philosophical thought process. He exhibits a profound sensitivity to the emotions of his auditors and an awareness of the social context in which he narrates. His narrations vary based on the context of social friendship with the auditor. As it turns out, many of these aspects of Socrates' narrative commentary appear in Socrates' words and deeds as recorded by Euclides. I will focus on three aspects of Socrates' characterization of his internal thought processes: his focus on his emotional states, his description of his mental activities, and his practice of telling a story about himself.

First, consider how Socrates' opening greeting to Theodorus focuses on his emotional state.

> If Cyrene were first in my affections, Theodorus, I should be asking how things are there, and whether any of your young people are taking up geometry or any other brand of philosophy. But, as it is, I love Athens better than Cyrene, and so I'm more anxious to know which of our young men show signs of turning out well. That, of course, is what I am always trying to find out myself, as best I can, and I keep asking other people too—anyone round whom I see the young men are inclined to gather. (*Tht.*, 143d)

In this passage, Socrates mentions his preference and affection for Athens over Cyrene twice. Socrates' love of his city leads him to have concern for its youth as they will mature and become citizens themselves. He ties his philosophical interest in the youth to his emotional concern for them. Socrates mentions his affective state again when he tells Theaetetus he is "anxious to learn" (*Tht.*, 145d). Socrates explains that he is anxious to learn "from Theodorus or from anyone who seems to me to know about these things. But although I get on with them pretty well in most ways, I have a small difficulty, which I think ought to be investigated, with your help and that of the rest of the company" (*Tht.*, 145d). A little later, he shares his hope that "my love of argument is not making me forget my manners—just because I'm so anxious to start discussion and get us all friendly and talkative together" (*Tht.*, 146a).

Second, Socrates describes the mental activity associated with his philosophical process. Socrates says to Theodorus that he desires to talk with Theaetetus: "I wish you would ask him to come and sit with us over here" (*Tht.*, 144d). Then he explains to Theaetetus, "I want to see for myself what sort of face I have. Theodorus says I am like you. But look, if you and I had each a lyre, and Theodorus had told us that they were both similarly tuned, should we have taken his word for it straight away?" (*Tht.*, 144e). Socrates also mentions his aporetic state of mind: "I have a small difficulty, which I think ought to be investigated, with your help and that of the rest of the company" (*Tht.*, 145d) and emphasizes it again: "Now this is just where my difficulty comes in. I can't get a proper grasp of what on earth knowledge really is" (*Tht.*, 146a). Socrates also emphasizes the aporetic dimensions of his activity as midwife, "I myself am barren of wisdom" (*Tht.*, 150c).

Third, Socrates' willingness to tell Theaetetus a story about himself, namely, how he became a midwife, offers one other discernable remnant of his own narrative voice. Socrates begins this autobiographical moment of self-disclosure by asking Theaetetus, "Then do you mean to say you've never heard about my being the son of a good hefty midwife Phaenarete?" (*Tht.*, 149a). He presses Theaetetus further: "and haven't you ever been told that I practice the same art myself?" (*Tht.*, 149a). Socrates then presents this account in direct contrast to the other narratives being told about him, "You see, my friend, it is a secret that I have this art. That is not one of the things you hear people saying about me, because they don't know; but they do say that I am a very odd sort of person, always causing people to get into difficulties. You must have heard that surely" (*Tht.*, 149a). Socrates describes his activity as divinely sanctioned. He proclaims, "God compels me to attend to the travail of others, but has forbidden me to procreate. So that I am not in any sense a wise man; I cannot claim as the child of my own soul any discovery worth the name of wisdom" (*Tht.*, 150d). He emphasizes the divine nature of his practice again: "At times, Theaetetus, I come across people who do not seem to me somehow to be pregnant. Then I realize that they have no need of me, and with the best will in the world I understand the business of match-making; and I think I am good enough—God willing—at guessing with whom they might profitably keep company" (*Tht.*, 151b).

Socrates also describes how this art affects others: "Sometimes they come back, wanting my company again, and ready to move heaven and leave earth to get it. When that happens, in some cases the divine sign that visits me forbids me to associate with them; in others it permits me, and then they begin again to make progress" (*Tht.*, 151a). He emphasizes the torment of the process: "They suffer the pains of labor, and are filled day and night with distress; indeed they suffer far more than women. And this pain my art is able to bring on, and also to allay" (*Tht.*, 151b). Socrates ends his account by describing it as a narrative, "Well, my dear lad, this has been a long yarn; but the reason is that I have a suspicion that you (as you think yourself) are pregnant and in labor. So I want you to come to me as to one who is both the son of a midwife and himself skilled in the art" (*Tht.*, 151c). It is striking that the passage on midwifery is one of the places that Thesleff sees the earlier layer of the dialogue because it links this moment of Socratic autobiographical self-disclosure with his narrative practices in the dialogues that he does narrate.

Now consider the conclusion of the dialogue (*Tht.*, 210b–d), where Thesleff (1982, 153) suggests that the earlier layer exists, to see if it bears any similarity to Socrates' narrative style. Socrates summarizes the aporetic state they have reached: "And so, Theaetetus, knowledge is neither perception nor true judgement, nor an account added to true judgement" (*Tht.*, 210b). Theaetetus agrees, and Socrates brings up his art of midwifery again. In this way, he links the conversation back to his previous description of his maieutic art (*Tht.*, 151a–c) where there were some similarities with Socrates' overall narrative style. Socrates brings Theaetetus himself into this practice by asking him, not just if he is still pregnant, but if we are: "Well, now, dear lad, are we still pregnant, still in labor with any thoughts about knowledge? Or have we been delivered of them all?" (*Tht.*, 210b). Socrates' language suggests that Theaetetus has become a midwife along with Socrates. Theaetetus himself continues to separate himself from Socrates, continuing to make him the object of Socrates' practice. Theaetetus remarks, "As far as I'm concerned Socrates, you've made me say far more than ever was in me" (*Tht.*, 210b). However, Socrates, for his part, continues to see it as a joint endeavor, "When then, our art of midwifery tells us that all of these offspring are wind-eggs and not worth bringing" (*Tht.*, 210b).

As the dialogue ends, it is almost like Socrates is addressing Theaetetus as if he were an auditor listening to an account of the events that he reports (*Tht.*, 209c–210b). Theaetetus seems to be a more engaged auditor than most of Socrates' auditors. He answers Socrates' direct questions about the events that transpired and offers his own opinions about the outcome. Nonetheless, he seems not to recognize Socrates' implicit invitation to become a midwife for himself. This treating of Theaetetus as if he were an auditor continues into Socrates' final remarks. First, he tells Theaetetus not to worry because if he does conceive of any new theories they will likely be better on account of what they have gone through, and even if he does "remain barren, your companions will find you gentler and less tiresome; you will be modest and not think you know what you don't know" (*Tht.*, 210c). In other words, the effect of this encounter with Socrates, much like the effect of listening to a Socratic narrative, results in philosophical advancement.[13]

At this point, Socrates' tone shifts and becomes even more like the final summation of a story he is reporting,

> This is all my art can achieve—nothing more. I do not know any of the things that other men know-the great and inspired men of today and yesterday. But this art of midwifery my mother and I had allotted to us by God: she to deliver women, I to deliver men that are young and generous of spirit, all that have any beauty. And now I must go to the King's Porch to meet the indictment that Meletus has brought against me; but let us meet here again in the morning, Theodorus. (*Tht.*, 210d)

As Euclides' constructed report of Socrates' conversation ends, it contains more and more of Socrates' own voice.[14] Benardete remarks, "He is less faithful to what he had heard than either the *Symposium's* Apollodorus or the *Parmenides'* Cephalus, both of whom usually keep themselves distinct from the several voices of their informants. Euclides, in contrast, in eliminating Socrates, also eliminates himself" (1984, 186). The dialogue does not return to the constructed outer frame conversation between Euclides and Terpsion. Rather, Euclides' account brings us back to the narrative traces that he tried so hard to obliterate. Euclides' written account brings us back to Socrates' own voice. We end with Socrates' summary of his activity. Much like he ends the account in the *Protagoras*, he alludes to a pending appointment and then tells the auditor "our conversation was over so we left" (*Prt.*, 362a). Here, he alludes to his meeting to receive his indictment. Then, Socrates explicitly invites those listening to him to engage in additional philosophical conversation tomorrow. This reference to an anticipated future conversation that will give birth to new knowledge is quite different from how Socrates usually ends his narratives. Generally speaking, in the narrated dialogues, the invitation to take up the philosophical life is more implicit as Socrates' narrative voice tends to fade away as his narratives unfold. Typically, we do not see how the auditor responds to Socrates' philosophical provocation any more than we see Euthyphro's final response to Socrates' philosophical provocation on the porch of the king Archon. The ending of the *Euthydemus* is a striking exception. There, Socrates tells Crito, "Then don't do what you ought not to, Crito, but pay no attention to the practitioners of philosophy, whether good or bad. Rather give serious consideration to the thing itself; if it seems to you negligible, then turn everyone from it, not just your sons. But if it seems to you to be what I think it is, then take heart, pursue it, practice it, both you and yours, as the proverb says" (*Euthyd.*, 307c).

THE THREAT OF PROTAGOREAN RELATIVISM: DID PLATO ABANDON SOCRATES THE NARRATOR?

These "narrative" qualities of Socrates' speech offer additional indications that there may have been a Socratically narrated *Theaetetus*. If so, one of course cannot help but ask, along with countless commentators of the ages, why the change? Why this Platonic revision of Socrates' narrative voice? Is it simply bothersome, as Euclides suggests? Is it an indication of the abandonment of narrative in the "late dialogues" more generally? Does it signify some deeper philosophic divide between Socrates and his character? Questions and answers to this problem pervade the secondary literature. I would like to leave extra-dialogic speculations aside and consider one aspect of the dialogue itself that may have motivated Plato's rhetorical choice: the refutation of Protagorean perspectivism. This worldview has three main components: 1. Human perception is the measure of all things; 2. There is no objective standpoint for truth other than the individual perspective; 3. What an individual perceives is true not for that person only, but true *as such* because that is the only kind of truth that there is.[15]

According to this anti-Pythagorean interpretation, the *Theaetetus* aims to refute the view that knowledge is "merely" perception. If Socrates' narrative voice consistently revealed his own perceptive process, the auditor's (or reader's) attention would perceive Socrates as the perceiver of truth. Moving attention away from a compelling human perspective and toward another understanding of truth *not* grounded in human perception is more difficult to accomplish when a compelling human perspective is precisely the means whereby we are receiving the information and forming our own perceptions about what we hear. On this point, Kathryn Morgan urges us to "consider the significance of Protagorean relativism for our understanding of Platonic (or any other fiction). Protagoras maintains that what is present to our senses is true for us" (2003, 107). She describes how we get "carried away" by listening to a narrative, and "we enter it, if briefly, as a type of reality" (Morgan 2003, 107). It is reasonable to ask if Socrates' narrative voice functions in this way. Does his narrative voice convey only *his* perspective? A brief look at the *Protagoras*, a dialogue Socrates narrates, suggests that the answer might be yes.[16] In the *Protagoras*, Socrates' narrative commentary is filled with references to his own perceptive process. As the narrative unfolds, Socrates describes his own actions and inner experiences. Some observations may seem mundane. For example, he tells the auditor that he recognizes Hippocrates' voice (*Prt.*, 310b) and that he sees Hippocrates blush (*Prt.*, 312a). By noting his visual and aural perceptions, Socrates emphasizes that he presents the story as it appeared to him. When he reports his initial encounter with Hippocrates, Socrates refers to his own perceptive process four times (*Prt.*, 309b, 310b, 311b, 312a). He continues to underscore his perceptive process as he relates the events at Callias' house. For example, he finds the group surrounding Protagoras particularly pleasing. He observes "how beautifully they took care never to get in Protagoras' way" (*Prt.*, 315b); he "perceived Hippias of Elis" (*Prt.*, 315c), and "saw" Prodicus (*Prt.*, 315d), and he tells the auditor that he and Hippocrates "went inside and spent a little more time looking at everything" (*Prt.*, 316b). Socrates does not embellish his perceptive ability, but he consistently calls attention to his perceptive process as a means of conveying his state of mind to the auditor.[17] It is true that the auditor cannot, or at least does not, escape the Socratic narrative filter that conveys the information to him. Socrates' perceptive stance serves as the auditor's own. Furthermore, at least in the *Protagoras*, the auditor never questions the mechanism by which he receives this information.[18] Socrates' narrative voice, as a result, becomes not just what Socrates knows and perceives about the events he relates to the auditor but what the auditor knows and perceives about the events as well. Through Socrates, the auditor learns of Hippocrates' entrance into Socrates' bedroom, their walk around the courtyard, and Hippocrates' blush in admission that he wants to study with a sophist. Socrates' narrative vision controls the auditor's perception of the sophists and their entourages (*Prt.*, 315a–b). It intervenes at crucial points in the dialogue. For example, Socrates' narrative voice controls how the auditor hears about the vanquishing of Protagoras (*Prt.*, 335b) and Socrates' desire to leave the gathering early (*Prt.*, 335d); the narrative voice also conveys Alcibiades' crucial role in the unfolding of events (*Prt.*, 348c). Socrates emphasizes his narrative control at the end of the dialogue, saying, "our conversation was over so we left" (*Prt.*, 362a). When Socrates stops narrating his experience, the auditor's experience ends as well.

When talking about Socrates' narrative perspective in the *Charmides*, Benardete notes, "Narration is the retrospective equivalent of what in the present would be universal tyranny" (1986, 15). Under this view, the control that Socrates maintains over the retelling of the events can become the philosophical equivalent of tyranny. Socrates' perspective becomes the perspective of truth, which is precisely the Protagorean perspective that much of the *Theaetetus* seeks to undermine. One could argue that this is true of writing in general, not just narrative—the writer controls what the reader hears and envisions. Socratic narrative is more insidious as we are explicitly directed to look at these restrictions, namely, Socrates' limitations as observer.

The narrative framework makes explicit the limitations of the speaker by making the speaker obvious to us when, in reality, we should always be thinking in these terms and ask about authorship when we read anything. I believe that a Socratic narrative perspective does not necessitate such a perspective. In fact, many aspects of Socrates' narrative style work directly against this tendency in narrative. For example, Socratic narrative perspective is not wholly *perspectival*, but beckons the auditors to pay attention to aspects of the conversation and interlocutors that they wouldn't otherwise see. Socratic narrative actually allows for a wider variety of interpretations than a traditional authored text while, at the same time, pointing the audience to come to their own conclusions about the information they are receiving. As we will see in the following chapters, Socrates' autobiographical self-disclosure does not function as a totalizing narrative perspective which conveys only his view about the world. In fact, his autobiographies about his intellectual journeys in the *Symposium, Apology,* and *Phaedo* do just the opposite. They bring the listener into the experience of philosophical reflection by portraying the learning process as perspective changing, as life changing. However, the apparent movement away from Socrates' narrative perspective in the *Theaetetus* does raise the question about which philosophical narratives are appropriate for philosophers to tell. Indeed, some might find my call for public autobiographical reflection at odds with Socrates' plea to Theaetetus to keep his art a secret (*Tht.*, 149a).[19] I would say in response that Socrates shares a great deal about his art. A more global look at Socrates' philosophical practices in the dialogues will reveal a Socrates who self-discloses and practices sharing stories of his philosophical encounters. This practice suggests that sharing stories about philosophical transformation can be an important mode of public philosophical engagement. Nonetheless, his plea to Theaetetus raises the question about what kinds of stories are appropriate for philosophers to share in public. I do not think there is one answer to this question that will fit every philosopher. Some might well choose to say nothing at all outside the confines of academia. However, I believe sharing our stories that illustrate the value of education, the joys and challenges of teaching, and the joys and challenges of being a student will enhance our individual and collective lives as we seek to find solutions to the challenges of living together in troubled times.

NOTES

1. On Plato's developmentalism, see Vlastos (1973), Chappell (2005), Kahn (2013), and Gill (2012). An array of scholars argue against the developmental view. See, for example, Press (2000). For compelling discussions of the limitations of stylometric analysis as a basis for determining Plato's "developmentalism," see Nails (1993) and Howland (1991). Sara Ahbel-Rappe (2018) also argues against a stream of developmentalism in her excellent *Socratic Ignorance and Platonic Knowledge in the Dialogues of Plato*. Other scholars have developed alternate ways to organize the dialogues. For example, Catherine Zuckert (2009), in *Plato's Philosophers*, organizes them by their dramatic date. William Altman proposes a nuanced reading order for the dialogues. See Altman (2012, 2016a, 2016b, 2018a).

2. Several important works have successfully argued that this view of the so-called later dialogues is deeply flawed. See Hyland (2015), Rosen (1999) and Sallis (2004). Also, see Altman (2016a, 2016b).

3. See Chappell (2005, 12–24) for a concise summary of several basic interpretive positions, including this one.

4. On the abandonment of the narrative frame in Plato's "later" works, see Nails (1995), Tarrant (1996), Benardete (1997), Thesleff (2002), and Blondell (2002).

5. See Schultz (2013).

6. Sedley (2004, 6–8). Benardete's (1997) article nicely articulates the many levels of retelling and rewriting that stand between us as readers and the actual conversation.

7. Thesleff (1982, 153) suggests three passages were the earlier layer: 144b–146c, 150b–151d, and 210b–d.

8. On this point, see Morgan (2003a).

9. (1982, 63), Scott (2000, 193n6), and Szelzák (1999, 28–9).

10. I am not entirely in agreement about that aspect of his argument in that I think Plato and his character, Socrates, both saw the importance of robust artistic education for the guardian class. However, I do take the conclusions of the stylometric analysis of the *Theaetetus* seriously.

11. See Sedley (2004, 17).

12. See Bastianini and Sedley (1995a, vol. 4).

13. On the *Theaetetus* as a genuinely aporetic work, see Bostock (1988, 13–14), Gulley (1962).

14. See Benardete (1997, 25–53).

15. On Protagoras' philosophy, see Lee and Taylor (2016).

16. Seth Benardete (1984, 1–85) notes, "The structure of the *Theaetetus* most resembles that of the *Protagoras*." In both dialogues, Socrates is the narrator. In the *Protagoras*, he reports almost directly to us; in the *Theaetetus*, he reported to Euclides, who then took the trouble to eliminate Socrates as the source of his dialogue (Benardete 1984, 1–86).

17. See Schultz (2013, 73–100) for a more in-depth articulation of these issues.

18. The only Socratically narrated dialogue where the auditor questions Socrates during the course of the narration is the *Euthydemus*.

19. I realized this possible counterexample when reading Sara Ahbel-Rappe's (2018) *Socratic Ignorance and Platonic Knowledge in the Dialogues of Plato*. It is a fascinating, highly nuanced reading of Socratic aporia and the ways in which it provides a foundation for the more esoteric aspects of Plato's thought.

Chapter Two

Socratic Self-Disclosure in Plato's *Symposium*

In this chapter and the one following, I offer a reading of the *Symposium* in light of the self-disclosive dimensions of Socrates' speech. In this chapter, I focus on how he describes himself, his emotional states, and his thought process throughout the dialogue and then turn to his autobiographical account of the lessons of love he learned from Diotima. In the following chapter, I look at three imitations of Socratic autobiography that Alcibiades, Apollodorus, and Aristodemus provide. This chapter unfolds in the following manner. First, I place Socrates' autobiographical narrative in the overall dramatic context of the S*ymposium*.[1] Second, I examine several instances of Socratic self-disclosure that occur in the *Symposium* before we hear Socrates' account of his encounters with Diotima. Third, I turn to the center of the dialogue with Socrates' presentation of his conversations with Diotima. I briefly consider various scholarly perspectives on the historicity of Diotima in order to enhance our understanding of the significance of her being Socrates' teacher in Socrates' account. Then I explore Socrates' self-presentation in the four major sections of his autobiographical account of the lessons he learned from Diotima. Finally, I explore how Socrates uses Diotima's view of generation and creativity to attempt to provoke the symposiasts into deeper self-reflection and communally minded philosophical practice.

PLACING SOCRATIC AUTOBIOGRAPHY
IN THE CONTEXT OF THE *SYMPOSIUM*

Socrates tells the story of Diotima at a dinner party at Agathon's house in 416 BCE. The *Symposium* does not begin with this narrated account. Rather, we hear Socrates' narrative voice through a series of nested autobiographical narratives that frame the dialogue. The *Symposium* opens with Apollodorus' boastful claim: "I am not unprepared to tell the account you ask of" (*Symp.*, 172a). Apollodorus, the narrator of the entire dialogue, offers us an imitation of Socratic storytelling by including his own role as narrator of the story in the story itself. The *Symposium* begins with Apollodorus telling a friend about his preparation as storyteller, as a keeper of the Socratic legacy.[2] His story depends on another autobiographical account, namely, Aristodemus' version of the events that occurred when he met Socrates on the road to Agathon's house and accompanied him there. Apollodorus makes clear that he checked the story with Socrates (*Symp.*, 173b). Apollodorus preserves the autobiographical aspect of the transmission by telling his friend that he would rather tell the story "just as Aristodemus told the story to him" (*Symp.*, 174a). Apollodorus' decision to include Aristodemus' part in the story enhances our ability to trust him as an authoritative source of information. It increases his reliability because he is not obscuring the source of his information or presenting himself as the sole narrative authority.

Through this layered narrative filter, we learn how Aristodemus and Socrates arrive at Agathon's house for a victory celebration party (*Symp.*, 174a–175e). We hear of the symposiasts' collective decision not to drink heavily (*Symp.*, 176b–176e) and their proclamation to throw out the flute girls (*Symp.*, 176e). They resolve to entertain themselves by giving speeches in praise of love instead (*Symp.*, 177a–177e). Apollodorus recounts how Phaedrus, Pausanias, Eryximachus, Aristophanes, and Agathon each define love (*Symp.*, 178b–198b).[3] After Agathon's speech, Socrates questions him about his speech (*Symp.*, 199d–201c). Agathon admits, perhaps a bit too readily, that "he really didn't know what he was talking about in his speech" (*Symp.*, 201c). After Agathon admits aporia, Socrates reports his encounters with Diotima, "I shall try to go through for you the speech about Love I once heard from a woman of Mantinea, Diotima—a woman who was wise about many things besides this: once she even put off the plague for ten years by telling the Athenians what sacrifices to make" (*Symp.*, 201d). Seth Benardete makes the fascinating observation that Diotima's forestalling the plague for ten years actually "served to multiply its virulence when all the country people had been jammed into Athens at the start of the Peloponnesian War" (2000b, 179). Under this view, Socrates' reference to her political effectiveness in helping Athens seems to be undermined. Anderson makes note of this complication to Socrates' description of Diotima as well. Anderson suggests if the plague had happened earlier, "the Athenians might have taken steps to avoid the war altogether" (1993, 53). While one can recognize this irony at the level of the reader, it is not clear that Socrates expects that the symposiasts would recognize the historical tension in his description of Diotima's political wisdom. Socrates goes on to explain how he will narrate the account: "I think it will be easiest for me to proceed the way Diotima did and tell you how she questioned me" (*Symp.*, 201e). Socrates emphasizes his affinity with Agathon: "I had told her almost the same things Agathon told me just now; that Love is a great god and that he belongs to beautiful things" (*Symp.*, 210e). Just as he tells the Myth of Er to benefit Glaucon, he tells the story of himself and Diotima to benefit Agathon and by extension, the other symposiasts.[4] Socrates begins his account of the lessons of love by presenting a younger image of himself who shared Agathon's views. His subsequent narrative conveys how Diotima changes his philosophical perspective on love by exhorting him to undertake a journey to ascend to the beautiful itself, where he comes to understand what it means to give birth to true virtue (*Symp.*, 212b). Throughout his account, Socrates presents himself as an eager student, perhaps the sort of student that he wishes he had found among the symposiasts gathered at Agathon's house.

SOCRATIC SELF-DISCLOSURE AS PEDAGOGICAL ENTICEMENT

Having Become So Beautiful

Socrates' account of Diotima's teachings about love is the most sustained example of his autobiographical practice in the *Symposium*. However, there are many other examples of Socrates' self-disclosive speech that bear close consideration. These self-disclosive remarks resemble the kinds of comments Socrates makes in the dialogues that he narrates and should be considered as part of his overall narrative practice. For example, consider Socrates' very first words that Apollodorus preserves in the account that he tells to the unnamed friend. Socrates explains to Aristodemus why he is unusually dressed up: "I'm going to Agathon's for dinner. I managed to avoid yesterday's victory party—I really don't like crowds but I promised to be there today. So, naturally, I took great pains with my appearance. I'm going to the house of a good-looking man; I had to look my best" (*Symp.*, 174a). While this comment is not a fully developed autobiography in the way that Socrates' account of his lessons with Diotima is, it is a remarkable instance of self-disclosure. He explains his current situation to Aristodemus. He focuses on his state of mind and emotional state. He explains his dislike of crowds, his promise to Agathon, and the reason behind his unusual decision to make himself beautiful. This moment of self-disclosure seems to have a good pedagogical effect. By revealing his own state of mind, Socrates sets the stage to invite Aristodemus to join him. Socrates goes on to explicitly ask Aristodemus to join him: "But let me ask you this . . . I know you haven't been invited to the dinner; how would you like to come anyway?" (*Symp.*, 174b). Aristodemus responds, "I'll do whatever you say" (*Symp.*, 174b). I mention this brief moment of disclosure because it illustrates one intended purpose of Socratic self-disclosure. He reveals things about himself strategically in order to bring people into philosophical community with him. He is choosing to be vulnerable about how he feels and uses that vulnerability as a means to draw Aristodemus into a shared experience with him. Note Socrates' enthusiastic response to Aristodemus' willingness to come along to the party with him: "Come with me then, and we will prove the proverb wrong" (*Symp.*, 174b).[5] Steven Berg views Socrates' motivation somewhat differently. He writes, "He reattaches himself to the ugly appearance he has been forced to discard in decking himself out for the poet's party, and does so despite the fact that the poet himself has left Aristodemus off the guest list" (2010, 6). Socrates then explains his meaning by referring to a proverb by Eupolis, "Good men go uninvited to an inferior man's feast" (*Symp.*, 174b). Socrates justifies his revision of the proverb by mentioning an episode in the *Iliad* where Menelaus appears uninvited to Agamemnon's table.[6] By alluding to this well-known episode from Homer, Socrates implicitly asks Aristodemus to think more expansively about his current situation. At this point, Aristodemus seems less willing to follow along with Socrates' philosophical revision of Homer. Aristodemus claims Homer is more accurate than Socrates' rereading of him with respect to their current situation (*Symp.*, 174d). Nonetheless, Aristodemus is willing to go along anyway. Despite this willingness to go to the party, he charges Socrates with the responsibility of thinking up a good excuse for bringing Aristodemus along. Socrates responds to Aristodemus' worry about not being invited to the party by affirming the community between them: "We'll think about what to say 'as we proceed the two of us along the way'" (*Symp.*, 174d). Unfortunately, their philosophical community is rather short lived. Socrates soon lags behind. Aristodemus is forced to go to Agathon's house without him.

If Wisdom Were Like Water

The next instance of Socratic self-disclosure occurs when Socrates comes into Agathon's house after spending some time on his neighbor's porch (*Symp.*, 175c). He responds to Agathon's enthusiastic invitation to join him on the couch so that he might gain Socrates' newfound wisdom by touching him (*Symp.*, 175d). Socrates chastens Agathon, "How wonderful it would be, dear Agathon, if the foolish were like water, which always flows from a full cup into an empty one when we connect them with a piece of yarn" (*Symp.*, 175d). Socrates professes to wish this sort of inner transformation through touch if that were possible. He says, "I would consider it the greatest prize to have the chance to lie down next to you. I would soon be overflowing with your wonderful wisdom" (*Symp.*, 175d). Socrates refers to his mental and emotional state of mind, albeit ironically, by expressing his desire to lie down next to Agathon and receive his overflowing wonderful wisdom. On this point, Steven Berg notes, "The distinction between the public wisdom of the poet and the private nature of Socrates' thought and his erotics is the real issue at stake in what Agathon understands to be Socrates' crudely ironical and insulting 'praise' of his wisdom" (2010, 11). However, immediately after this ironic moment, Socrates seems quite sincere in what he says about his own wisdom. He tells Agathon and the others, "My own wisdom is of no account—a shadow in a dream" (*Symp.*, 175e). Socrates gives a clue about what this shadow in a dream might involve when he responds to Eryximachus' proposal to give speeches in praise of love, "How could I vote 'No' when the only thing I say I understand is the art of love?" (*Symp.*, 177e). Whatever his shadowy wisdom is, it involves the art of love. Socrates also notes that the other symposiasts share his interest in the art of love. He tells Eryximachus that neither Agathon nor Pausanias nor Aristophanes would vote against him (*Symp.*, 177e). This moment illustrates how Socrates uses self-disclosive commentary to draw others into community with him. He creates an environment where others can self-disclose as well. Differently put, Socrates professes his own interest in the subject of love and then invites others to share experience. Socrates fosters the possibility of a shared intellectual community between himself and the symposiasts. For example, Socrates expresses some hesitancy about Eryximachus' proposal, saying, "It is not quite fair to those of us who have to speak last, if the first speeches turn out to be good enough and to exhaust our subject" (*Symp.*, 177e). However, he immediately softens this potential objection, saying, "I promise we won't complain" (*Symp.*, 177e). Socrates then endorses Eryximachus' proposal and tells Phaedrus to begin. Apollodorus' narrative commentary emphasizes the shared affective philosophical community that Socrates' words create: "They all agreed with Socrates, and pressed Phaedrus to start" (*Symp.*, 187a). Steven Berg emphasizes the importance of this moment, "Socrates will eagerly seize upon Eryximachus' proposal to make eros the topic... it is precisely on this terrain that a contest between Aristophanes' poetic wisdom and Socrates' philosophy must be waged" (2010, 9). Let us now see how this contest unfolds.

Socrates' Response to Aristophanes and Agathon

Phaedrus, Pausanias, and Eryximachus both give their speeches without the auditor/reader learning anything about Socrates' thoughts about them. While Apollodorus reports numerous important details about the interactions between the interlocutors after each speech, he does not mention anything about Socrates' own responses. After Aristophanes gives his speech, he expresses his desire to hear what the two remaining speakers will say, "I'd prefer to hear what all the others will say—or rather what each of them will say, since Agathon and Socrates are the only ones left" (*Symp.*, 193e). Eryximachus pronounces Aristophanes' speech "delightful" and describes the first four speeches, which includes his own, as a "rich feast of speeches on love" (*Symp.*, 193e). He then remarks, "If I couldn't vouch for the fact that Socrates and Agathon are masters of the art of love, I'd be afraid that they'd have nothing left to say. But as it is I have no fears on this score" (*Symp.*, 193a). After these direct mentions of his upcoming speech by both Aristophanes and Eryximachus, Socrates responds, "That is because you did beautifully in the contest, Eryximachus. But if you ever get in my position, or rather the position I'll be in after Agathon's spoken so well, then you'll really be afraid. You'll be at your wit's end, as I am now" (*Symp.*, 194a).[7] Socrates overstates the depth of his nervousness here. However, it is worth noting that he finds it necessary to offer some account of his current state of mind to the symposiasts. Agathon claims his disclosure is strategic, aimed at making him feel afraid: "You are trying to bewitch me, Socrates, by making me think the audience expects great things of my speech, so I'll get flustered" (*Symp.*, 194a).

Socrates responds to Agathon. He shares his own observations of him the preceding day at the festival where he won the prize. "I saw how brave and dignified you were." "After seeing that, how could I expect you to be flustered by us, when we are so few?" (*Symp.*, 194b). When Agathon responds that he knows it is more daunting to speak to an intelligent audience than "a senseless crowd" (*Symp.*, 194c), Socrates admits, "It wouldn't be very handsome of me to think you crude in any way." He continues, "I'm sure that if you ever run into people you consider wise, you'll pay more attention to them than to ordinary people" (*Symp.*, 194c). This comment reveals a bit more about Socrates' views about Agathon than something about Socrates' internal state in and of itself. However, this exchange also illustrates another way that Socrates reveals his state of mind strategically. Here, Socrates seems to be sharing what he thinks in order to goad Agathon into engaging in elenchus. At this point, Socrates almost succeeds in engaging Agathon, but Phaedrus, who has seen Socrates in action many times, prevents it (*Symp.*, 194d). However, Socrates will not remain thwarted for long.

The next extended set of self-disclosive remarks occur just after Agathon gives his speech, which everyone applauded, "so becoming to himself and to the god did they think the young man's speech" (*Symp.*, 198a). Socrates returns his gaze to Eryximachus, saying, "Now do you think I was foolish to feel the fear I felt before: Didn't I speak like a prophet a while ago when I said that Agathon would give an amazing speech and I would be tongue-tied?" (*Symp.*, 198a). Eryximachus refuses to believe Socrates would have nothing to say. Socrates proceeds to give a lengthy account of his own inner response to Agathon's speech (*Symp.*, 198b–199b). Socrates asks Eryximachus incredulously, "How am I not going to be tongue-tied, I or anyone else, after a speech delivered with such beauty and variety?" (*Symp.*, 198b). He asks again, "Who would not be dumb-struck hearing the beauty of the words and phrases?" (*Symp.*, 198b). In addition to expressing his worry about being tongue-tied and dumbstruck, he also shares, "I was worried that I'd not be able to say anything that came close to them in beauty, and so I would almost have run away and escaped if there had been a place to go" (*Symp.*, 198c). Socrates' responses here are reminiscent of how he describes his responses to Protagoras' great speech and the sophistic displays of Euthydemus and Dionysodorus. Socrates makes this link with sophistic speech clear when he says, "the speech reminded me of Gorgias so that I actually experienced what Homer describes. I was afraid that Agathon would end by sending the Gorgian head" (*Symp.*, 198c). As he did in his initial exchange with Aristodemus, Socrates refers to Homer to describe his internal state. Socrates expresses his regret that he was willing to participate at all: "I realized how ridiculous I'd been to agree to join with you in praise of Love and to say that I was a master of the art of love when I knew nothing whatever of this business of how anything whatever ought to be praised" (*Symp.*, 198d). Socrates admits that he misunderstood what was expected of him. He explains his misconception, "In my foolishness, I thought you should tell the truth about whatever you praise that this should be your basis, and that from this a speaker should select the most beautiful truths and arrange them most suitably" (*Symp.*, 198d). He makes a similar admission of his own limitation, saying, "I was quite vain, thinking that I would talk well and that I knew the truth about praising anything whatever" (*Symp.*, 198e). He emphasizes his lack of understanding one last time; "but I didn't even know the method for giving praise; and it was in ignorance that I agreed to take part in this" (*Symp.*, 199a).

By sharing his own lack of understanding about the contest he was engaging in, Socrates accomplishes several things. First, it is clear that he is collectively dismissing all of their speeches, saying they are ungrounded in truth. These admissions about his own misunderstanding also explain some of his earlier references to being afraid. Second, though his critiques may seem harsh, by sharing so much of his internal discomfort with the symposiasts, it softens the potentially dismissive aspects of his refusal to participate. Socrates does go on to explain under what circumstances he would be willing to participate. He makes clear that "I'm not giving another eulogy using that method, not at all, I wouldn't be able to do it—but if you wish, I'd like to tell the truth my way. I want to avoid any comparison with your speeches so as not to give you a reason to laugh at me" (*Symp.*, 199b). Socrates distinguishes his mode of discourse, which will be autobiographical, from theirs. He sets the context for his account with Diotima to be an act of truth telling, a moment of parrhesia. In other words, he presents autobiography as a mode of parrhesia. Parrhesia is free or frank speech. According to Arlene Saxonhouse, it involved a practice of citizens "speaking their own minds—not on attempting to incorporate the views of others in one's own speech nor on the shading of one's convictions with the art of rhetoric" (2006, 87). All of these numerous references to his own internal state of mind in response to the speeches of Aristophanes and Agathon set the ground for his more extended self-revelation in his account of his encounters with Diotima.

While one could dismiss these self-reflective remarks as disingenuous because of their obvious irony, doing so dismisses the importance of the depth of how Socrates describes his inner experience. Also, he may really feel that true philosophical discourse has been endangered by the discursive practices of speech that Socrates has engaged in. Much like Socrates repents after giving the speech of the nonlover in the *Phaedrus* (242c–d), Socrates refuses to play the game on the terms that they have been playing it. He tells Phaedrus, "I'd like to tell the truth my way. I want to avoid any comparison with your speeches, so as not to give you a reason to laugh at me. So look, Phaedrus, would a speech like this satisfy your requirement? You will hear the truth about Love, and the words and phrasing will take care of themselves" (*Symp.*, 199b). Socrates characterizes his forthcoming speech as the "truth about love" (*Symp.*, 199b). Having gotten that approval, Socrates also gets his way cleared to ask Agathon a few questions. Socrates starts his refutation of Agathon with references to his own state of mind. "I thought you led the way beautifully into your speech" (*Symp.*, 199c), and he says, "I much admire that beginning" (*Symp.*, 199c), but, after sharing his opinions about the beautiful beginning of the speech, Socrates proceeds to get Agathon to admit, "I didn't know what I was talking about in that speech" (*Symp.*, 201c). On this point Mitchell Miller notes, "by exposing the two-fold contradictions in these claims, he subjects Agathon to a transformative reorientation" (2015, 292). Miller's references to a transformative reorientation are a helpful way of thinking about the intended effect of Socrates' self-disclosive speech. The passages we have examined in this section make clear that Socrates regularly discloses things about his thoughts and feelings to the symposiasts. This consistent practice of self-disclosure sets the stage for the possibility of their own transformation.

SOCRATES AS A STUDENT OF DIOTIMA

Agathon and Aporia

Socrates is set to speak just after Agathon. However, as I mentioned in the previous section, Socrates wants to engage Agathon in conversation about his speech he has just given. He asks Phaedrus for permission to "allow me to ask Agathon a few little questions, so that, once I have his agreement I may speak on that basis" (*Symp.*, 199c). Socrates proceeds to point out the numerous conceptual difficulties associated with his definition of love in terms of all its beautiful qualities. He starts by asking "Is love such as to be a love of something or of nothing" (*Symp.*, 199d), and in short order (*Symp.*, 199d–201c), he forces Agathon to admit that "I didn't know what I was talking about in that speech" (*Symp.*, 201c). This reduction to aporia is often seen as the hallmark of the "Socratic method."[8] The placement of Socrates' account of his lessons on love just after the elenchus suggests that we should regard autobiographical narrative as part of Socrates' philosophical method as well. This placement also contrasts the intended pedagogical effect of Socrates' autobiographical activity with the intended effect of the elenchus. Unlike the elenchus, its aim is not reductive, but rather generative of a new way of thinking about self and other in political community.

Did Diotima Exist?

I mentioned in the introduction that whether these autobiographies Socrates tells are meant to be taken as true accounts of things that happened to the historical Socrates is not my primary interest. Nonetheless, the question whether Diotima is a real person receives considerable attention in the secondary literature. It is worth mentioning the current views on this matter before delving into how Socrates presents himself as her student. In the *People of Plato*, Nails notes, "There is a current and widespread assumption that Diotima is the one named character Plato certainly invented" (2002, 137). Zuckert typifies this view. She writes, "The likelihood that Diotima is a fictional creation suggests that Socrates' account of his erotic education cannot be taken literally" (2009, 190n21). On this point, Anderson reasons, "There seems to be little reason to believe that Diotima is anything but fictional, and there seems to be some reason to believe that Sokrates (rather than Plato) intends for his listeners to regard her as fictional" (1993, 51). His primary reasons for thinking so are the references to the speeches of the symposiasts in her speech. Elsewhere, Nails argues persuasively against this mode of reasoning and concludes that "the reasons to regard a Mantinean priestess known to Socrates as having actually existed outweigh those for treating her as Plato's invention" (2015, 74). Other scholars agree with her assessment that Diotima could well have existed. For example, Ausland notes that she was widely regarded as historical until the modern era (2000, 186 n11). Connelly discusses a stele marker found in Mantineia: "Interpreters have been unable to resist associating this memorial with the famous female prophet of Mantineia, Diotima. The wise and thoughtful priestess . . . would be appropriately honored with such an impressive stele in her city's marketplace" (2007, 240). Connelly continues, "the relief from Mantineia stands on its own as an important testament to the role of women in divination and the high value that communities placed on the special agency of these women" (2007, 240). In *Socrates and Diotima*, Nye argues for the existence of Diotima by exploring questions like, "What if Diotima's lessons in love were exactly what they purport to be: religious teaching that places eros at the very heart of spiritual life as a privileged access to virtue and immortality?" (2015, xi). My own view is that the historical Socrates might well have learned from a historical Diotima. I find Nails' reasoning particularly persuasive, along with the observation that she is a named character and would be the only named character in Plato's dialogues that does not have a historical existence. Although I believe this is possible, my interest here lies more in how Plato's Socrates presents himself as having been taught by her and in ascertaining what he hopes to gain pedagogically by doing so. Simply put, the fact that Plato's Socrates chooses to tell this autobiography at this particular pedagogical moment provides a useful model for contemporary philosophers to consider incorporating into their classrooms and in their public philosophical practices as well. Like Socrates, we should tell stories of our own intellectual conversions to philosophy to our students, colleagues, and fellow citizens.

Socrates' Self-Presentation in Diotima's Speech

The dramatic date of Agathon's party is 416 BCE. The dramatic date for his encounters with Diotima would be in the 440s. Nails notes that "Socrates was an unattached man of thirty" (2002, 137), about the same age that Agathon would have been at the party. Socrates emphasizes his affinity with Agathon at the beginning of his speech, saying, "I had told her almost the same things Agathon told me just now: that love is a great god and belongs to beautiful things" (*Symp.*, 201d). At the same time, he emphasizes his affinity with Diotima: "She used the very same arguments against me that I used against Agathon" (*Symp.*, 201e). On this point, Zuckert observes, "Readers of Plato should be struck by the similarity between Diotima's way of leading the young Socrates step by step to see the truth by asking him a series of questions about his own opinions and the way in which he later interrogates his interlocutors" (2009, 195). In this way, Socrates presents himself in a dual manner.[9] He becomes both a student and a teacher of love as he begins to tell the symposiasts about his encounter with Diotima. Blondell sees a "kaleidoscopic presentation" of Socrates in the *Symposium*, where "Socrates can be viewed more or less plausibly as occupying all of the steps on the 'ladder of love'" (2006, 174).

Socrates structures his retelling of the ascent to the beautiful itself in four basic movements. He starts with the refutative exchange (*Symp.*, 201e–203b). During this exchange, Diotima presents Socrates with the idea that love is between mortal and immortal and should be regarded as a great daimon (*Symp.*, 202e). Second, Socrates recounts the story Diotima tells about the birth of Eros at Aphrodite's birthday party and the implications of its unusual dual parentage of Poros (resource) and Penia (lack) (*Symp.*,

203b–206b). Third, he recounts her teachings about the importance of reproduction and giving birth in beauty (*Symp.*, 206b–208b). Finally, he recounts the famous ascent passage where Diotima discusses a progressive account of love beginning with the love of beautiful bodies and culminating in a vision of the beautiful itself (*Symp.*, 208b–212b). Throughout his account, Socrates presents himself as an eager, engaged student whose understanding of love is transformed through his encounters with his powerful teacher.

There are three aspects of Socrates' presentation of himself as Diotima's student that I will focus on in the remainder of this chapter. First, he consistently asks her questions throughout the four phases of the story. Second, he is willing to admit aporia. Third, he calls attention to the affective dimensions of the learning process. I consider each of these in turn. First, Socrates presents himself as a relentless asker of questions. The questions involve finding out the truth about the nature of love. Socrates asks things like, "What do you mean, Diotima? Is Love ugly and bad?" (*Symp.*, 201e). He asks what is between wisdom and ignorance (*Symp.*, 202a). He inquires, "Who believes that Love is not a god?" (*Symp.*, 202c). Learning that love is not a god, Socrates asks, "What is it then?" (*Symp.*, 202d). When Diotima answers that love is a great daimon, Socrates asks about the function of such beings (*Symp.*, 202e). When she explains the function of love (*Symp.*, 203a), Socrates asks yet another question: "Who are its father and mother?" (*Symp.*, 203a). Once he learns that love involves being a lover, he implores, "what use is Love to human beings?" (*Symp.*, 204d). Through the constant use of questioning, Socrates presents himself as an eager student, perhaps the sort of student that he wishes he had. Indeed, Nails notes that Agathon does not ask Socrates any questions during the refutative exchange (*Symp.*, 199d–201c). She observes that "Socrates turns Diotima's statement and questions into questions of his own fifteen times" (2015, 80). His constant questions seem in no way aimed at undermining her authority. Rather, they reveal his willingness to listen to her and learn from her. In this way, these questions reveal Socrates' inner state of mind as a student. They illustrate his eagerness to learn. Deborah Nails also mentions more personal motivations: "Given the segregation of sexes in upper-class Athens, he would have had little opportunity to mix with females. At the time of the lessons, he was close to the age when he would be expected to marry" (2015, 7). Zuckert also recognizes the link between these two autobiographies. She writes, "In the *Symposium* Plato indicates more clearly what Socrates hoped to find by means of such investigations, why he had to extend his investigations from the arguments of philosophers about the character of being or the beings to the opinions human beings have about the beautiful and the good, and how limited the results of his investigations necessarily were" (2009, 189).

Second, Socrates readily admits that he does not know things. He makes clear that he does not understand all the dimensions of her teaching. Socrates emphasizes his aporetic state at numerous junctures. Here are some examples: "I said there was no way I could give a ready answer to that question" (*Symp.*, 204e); "I wonder about that myself" (*Symp.*, 205b); "If I could, I wouldn't be your student filled with admiration for your wisdom, and trying to learn these very things" (*Symp.*, 206b); "It would take divination to figure out what you mean. I can't" (*Symp.*, 206c); "And I said that I didn't know" (*Symp.*, 207c). And he emphasizes, "All this she taught me, on those occasions when she spoke on the art of love" (*Symp.*, 207a). Socrates appears to hold his teacher, Diotima, in the highest regard. His emotional responses to Diotima reveal his respectful, even reverent, attitude toward her. He is "filled with admiration for her wisdom" (*Symp.*, 206b), and he was "amazed" by her speech (*Symp.*, 208c). He also asks questions like "Most wise Diotima, is this really the way that it is?" (*Symp.*, 208c) and offers comments like "It would take divination to figure out what you mean" (*Symp.*, 206c).[10] Socrates emphasizes his eagerness to learn again, exclaiming, "But that's why I came to you, Diotima, as I just said. I knew I needed a teacher" (*Symp.*, 207c). He laments, "If I could, I wouldn't be your student filled with admiration for your wisdom, and trying to learn these very things" (*Symp.*, 206b). Socrates' willingness to listen to Diotima is important. It shows his ability to inhabit a vulnerable state of learning. He can inhabit the state of not knowing but being willing to learn and being willing to learn from a woman.

In addition to portraying admirable aspects of his own studentship, Socrates conveys Diotima's attitude toward him as well. Sometimes, she seems dismissive of his ability. For example, she laughs at him (*Symp.*, 202b) and remarks, "A child could tell you" (*Symp.*, 204b). Berg describes her tone here as "Xanthippian irascibility" (2010, 110). She finds "no surprise" in his confusion about love "as being loved rather than being a lover" (*Symp.*, 204c). She corrects him at numerous places such as "How do you think you'll ever master the art of love, if you don't know that?" (*Symp.*, 207c). At other times, she has some minimal regard for his intellectual abilities. Here are some other examples: "Even you, Socrates, could probably come to be initiated into these rites of love" (*Symp.*, 210a); "I don't know if you are capable of it: (i.e., the final and highest mystery)" (*Symp.*, 210a); "You must try to follow if you can" (*Symp.*, 210a); she exhorts him to "Try to pay attention to me as best you can" (*Symp.*, 210e). She reminds him, "Or haven't you remembered that in that life alone, when he looks at Beauty in the only way that Beauty can been seen" (*Symp.*, 212a). Socrates ends his account. Socrates says he is persuaded by her speech (*Symp.*, 212c). He explains how his changed point of view affects his relations with others; "And once persuaded, I try to persuade others too that human nature can find no better workmate for acquiring this than love. That's why I say that every man must honor Love, why I honor the rites of Love myself and practice them with special diligence, and why I commend them to others" (*Symp.*, 212c).

Simply put, Socrates tells the story to turn the symposiasts toward philosophy. He wants to persuade them to take the philosophical journey for themselves. According to Zuckert, this recounting of his lessons from Diotima also conveys his movement toward becoming a "teacher." She writes, "Before his 'instruction by Diotima' (or, to speak non-metaphorically, his discovery of the nature and significance of human eros), Socrates seems to have investigated the *logoi*, the accounts other human beings gave of things in general, and of the excellence of human life or the virtues in particular, but he did not seek young associates. He did not try to 'beget in the beautiful by implanting a notion of virtue in noble youth and seeing whether it would grow'" (2009, 198). He uses this narrative autobiography to show how he became motivated to exhort others toward philosophical inquiry. On this point, Adams writes, "If there is something 'conservative' in Socrates' focus on traditional values, then there is something 'liberal' in his attempt to turn his initiates into their own hierophants. Each us must make a good-faith effort to discover what is true, lawful, right and holy" (2017, ix).

Some scholars regard Diotima's speech as advocating a philosophical practice that removes one from everyday real-life concerns and into some state of ongoing contemplation of the beautiful and the good.[11] However, Socrates' decision to repeat this story suggests that he sees philosophical contemplation as a practice that exists alongside human social and political engagement with others. Nails writes, "Both Socrates and Plato chose to conduct their lives as engaged philosophers, guiding actual human beings where they had the opportunity to do so, and creating further opportunities when they could" (2015, 78). Sheffield concurs, noting that "placing the ascent within the larger context of the dialogue and its concerns suggests that Socrates has not lost sight of the nature and goals of interpersonal love relationships; rather, he is providing an account of the sorts of values that should inform such relationships" (2008, xxvi). With this broader context in mind, let us now consider what Socrates wants Agathon and the other symposiasts to learn. While their speeches are self-oriented, they do not exhibit the self-reflection needed to practice philosophy. On the social and political level, their self-orientation keeps them from truly caring for one another and from the possibility of sustaining philosophical community with each other. Sheffield suggests that "it is only when one has some sense of where human happiness resides that one can be a proper educator and muse to the young. The end of Socrates' speech is the beginning, not the end of a truly beneficial love relationship." (2008, xxvi). Socrates tries to exhibit this self-reflection needed to practice philosophy by telling this story about a younger version of himself and how he came to be the philosopher he is now. Sara Ahbel-Rappe has a fascinating reading of the process of involution that Socrates undergoes through his encounters with Diotima. Ahbel-Rappe regards Diotima as a shamanistic figure who destroys Socrates' limited understanding of himself.

She writes, "Self-identity ebbs away in the flow of memory while consciousness disappears without a trace of its previous contents" (2018, xxxv). Socrates has to reconstruct a new identity for himself after Diotima's presentation of the ladder of love and he retells this story of his old self to articulate the transformative path that the others can follow through a sustained practice of introspection. Ahbel-Rappe writes, "Socrates' message to his interlocutor is literally, 'shed your skin'; in other words, let your soul appear, and behold yourself in the mirror of wisdom" (2018, xxxviii). Viewed in light of her compelling reading, Socrates' practice of sustained self-disclosure that I explore throughout this book is ultimately aimed at overcoming the self. She describes his "ethics of wisdom that fundamentally calls into question the nature of what the self is by investigating the boundaries between self and not-self" (Ahbel-Rappe 2018, 7). It is curious that if she is right, Socrates uses the focus on himself through self-disclosive practices as the means to get beyond himself.

The second main lesson that Socrates' self-presentation imparts is a call for communal engagement. This challenge arises in a variety of ways in the story he tells about himself and Diotima. First, that he chooses to tell about a dialogical exchange rather than give a speech in praise about the nature of love illustrates something important about the nature of love, namely, that it occurs between people. Second, he mentions Diotima's care for the citizens of Athens by mentioning that "once she even put off the plague for ten years by telling the Athenians what sacrifices to make" (*Symp.*, 201d). The reproduction metaphors throughout also convey a strong political component to her view of eros. She explains, "It's because reproduction goes on forever; it is what mortals have in place of immortality" (*Symp.*, 207a). We also have the production of new citizens. Diotima also emphasizes the need that animals have for intercourse and nurturing the young and the willingness to care for one another, even to die for another (*Symp.*, 207b); they along with humans have some desire to "live forever and be immortal" (*Symp.*, 207e).

On this point, McCoy writes, "Diotima's account of eros is generously and even lavishly productive and re-productive; these relations between lover and beloved, the things created in love and the longing for more creation to find one's immortality, are more fundamental to the nature of love than static qualities in the object of the beloved. The creative nature of eros, in these penultimate stages on the ladder of love, begins with individual lack and need, but results in the lover's reorientation of his energy and focus on the beloved, outside of himself" (2013, 125). Finally, the references to "ideas that make the young better" and the subsequent interest in "activities and laws" illustrate he political aim of philosophical education (*Symp.*, 210c). Forging a pedagogically oriented, philosophically grounded community would perhaps help the symposiasts overcome their infatuation with, and hence vulnerability to, sophists, poets, and the political ambitions of those seeking to influence Athens. Berg writes that Socrates' recounting of Diotima's speech "has been devoted to showing not only the falsehood of Agathon's and Aristophanes' understandings of eros, but the falsehood of their understanding of poetry as well . . . it is precisely in the city of Athens in which these partial and distorted versions of eros and poetry rule" (2010, 121). Miller extends the political provocation to the dialogue as a whole. When discussing the dating narrative retelling, Miller writes, "Hence the retelling should be dated as late as after 408 as possible while still preceding the period of Socrates' trial" (2015, 287). Miller reminds us that "these were abysmal times for the city, as dark as the period around 416 was bright." He argues further that the *Symposium* was 'published in the early 370s when Athens was experiencing some revitalization. Miller concludes, "This gives Plato's gift of remembrance to the reviving Athens of the early 370s the character of critical challenge" (2015, 287). In the following chapter, I will explore how well Socrates' philosophical and political provocation achieves its aims of provoking "critical challenge" in those who care about him most. To this end, I will now examine the three imitations of Socratic autobiography offered by Alcibiades, Apollodorus, and Aristodemus.

NOTES

1. I use the following translation of the *Symposium*. 'Symposium." In *Plato: Complete Works*, edited by John M. Cooper, translated by Alexander Nehamas and Paul Woodruff, 457–505. Indianapolis: Hackett.

The secondary literature on the *Symposium* is vast. I am particularly influenced by the following readings of this work listed in alphabetical order: Anderson (1993); Benardete (2000a); Berg (2010); Corrigan and Glazov-Corrigan (2004); Destrée and Giannopoulou (2017); Halperin (1990b); Irigaray (1988); Lesher, Nails, and Sheffield (2006); Nussbaum (1986); Nye (1989); Rosen (1987); Scott (2000); and Leo Strauss (2001).

2. I am grateful to Emily Glass of Baylor University for drawing my awareness to the importance of the theme of preparation in the opening of the *Symposium*. See Glass (2015).

3. As is often noted in the secondary literature, each of these speakers define love in such a way that it benefits them. See Rosen (1987) and Anderson (1993).

4. See Howland (2019).

5. See Berg (2010, 6).

6. Socrates paraphrases Homer to express his own views. It supports Howland's reading of Socrates as a new philosophical Homer. See Howland (1993). On the presentation of Homer in the Platonic dialogues, see Mulhern (2015).

7. On the affinities between Erxyimachus' speech and Socrates' account of Diotima's speech, see McPherran (2006).

8. On the elenchus and important reconsiderations of it, see Scott (2004).

9. On the numerous appearances of the dyad in the *Symposium*, see Hopkins (2011).

10. Other examples of Socratic questioning occur at *Symp.* 201e, 202a, 202c, 202d, 202e, 203b, and 204b.

11. See most famously Vlastos (1981). He accuses Plato of developing a theory of Eros that "does not provide for love of whole persons, but only for love of that abstract version of persons which consists of a complex of their best qualities" (Vlastos 1981, 31). Mitchell Miller (2015) regards her teaching on the Beautiful itself as a new form of divinity.

Chapter Three

Three Imitations of Socratic Narration

This chapter unfolds in the following manner. First, I briefly reconsider the overall dramatic structure of the *Symposium* to emphasize that Socrates presents his autobiographical account as a means of philosophical provocation. This philosophical provocation offers us the opportunity to assess three other autobiographical accounts that frame the dialogue as a whole: Alcibiades, Aristodemus, and Aristodemus. Second, I examine Alcibiades' speech, which shares many elements of Socrates' autobiographical account of his lessons on love. The self-disclosive aspects of Alcibiades' speech offer an opportunity to reassess how much he truly understood Socrates' philosophical teachings. Third, I consider Apollodorus' and Aristodemus' accounts of the events that transpired at Agathon's house. Each of these narrators also imitate the Socratic practice of philosophical self-disclosure. I explore these three imitations of Socratic autobiography for several reasons. First, they illustrate the pervasiveness of self-disclosive narratives in the *Symposium*. Second, they allow us to see all three characters in a more favorable light than is generally the case in the secondary literature. Third, they provide examples of narratives about philosophical practice that we can examine as instances of public philosophy.

DRAMATIC STRUCTURE AND PHILOSOPHICAL PROVOCATION

Although unique in terms of its dual narrative frame, the *Symposium* exhibits many structural similarities with other dialogues. Some scholars describe the dialogical structure as a "pyramid" or "pediment."[1] For a variety of reasons, I prefer the imagery of a mountain better than either a pyramid or a pediment. It conveys a naturalness to the philosophical process and resonates with the philosophical journey as Plato describes it in the Allegory of the Cave, where the former prisoner is "dragged along the rough steep upward way" (*Rep.*, 515e). Most dialogues begin at the bottom of the mountain with Socrates and his interlocutors discussing some topic that is not particularly philosophical. Socrates inevitably turns the conversation in a philosophical direction by asking his interlocutors to consider what some philosophical concept means in and of itself. The interlocutor proceeds to offer a series of definitions, and Socrates refutes them. The interlocutor then admits aporia. At that point, Socrates drags them up the philosophical mountain. At the top of the philosophical mountain, Socrates offers his interlocutors a new way of looking at the subject under discussion.[2] After this philosophical provocation, Socrates, either explicitly or implicitly, offers his interlocutors what Mitchell Miller calls "a test for philosophical kinship."[3] The reader, then, has the opportunity to see how the interlocutors respond to Socrates' philosophical provocation. Generally speaking, the interlocutors fail the test, and the reader has a new opportunity to see what the interlocutors did not recognize. Almost all of the dialogues follow this general structure. Within the reported events that Apollodorus conveys to his friend, the *Symposium* does so as well. It begins at the bottom of the mountain as Socrates and Aristodemus walk toward Agathon's house and join with the other symposiasts (*Symp.*, 174b–177e). The conversation turns in a philosophical direction as at Eryximachus' suggestion (with Socrates' support) that they each give a speech in praise of love (*Symp.*, 177e) . Each of the five speeches present a definition of love (*Symp.*, 178b–197e). When Socrates refutes Agathon, he is symbolically refuting all the symposiasts (*Symp.*, 198a–201c). Socrates then offers the symposiasts a new way of looking at love by giving his reported account of the lessons he learned from Diotima (*Symp.*, 201d–212c).

There are two indications in the text that suggest we will hear how the symposiasts respond to Socrates' philosophical provocation. First, Socrates' speech finishes to "loud applause" (*Symp.*, 212c). This comment suggests that their initial response was enthusiastic. Second, Apollodorus tells us, "Meanwhile, Aristophanes was trying to make himself heard over their cheers in order to make a response to something Socrates had said about his own speech" (*Symp.*, 212c).[4] At this point, things seem philosophically promising. Aristophanes appears ready to apply Socrates' account of his lessons on love to his own speech. Unfortunately, we never hear how the symposiasts themselves respond to Socrates because Alcibiades arrives at the gate (*Symp.*, 212c). Apollodorus tells the unnamed auditor, "All of a sudden, there was even more noise. A large drunken party had arrived at the courtyard door and they were rattling it loudly accompanied by the shrieks of some flute-girl they had brought along" (*Symp.*, 212c). As Rosen (1987, 283) notes, Alcibiades' arrival and subsequent actions and speech should be regarded as a replacement for the response of the symposiasts. Several aspects of the text support this reading. First, Agathon asks the slave to go see who it is. Second, the word *exphaines* (all of a sudden) links his appearance with the appearance of the beautiful itself (*Symp.*, 210e) and also with his realization that Socrates is sitting next to him on Agathon's couch (*Symp.*, 213c). Third, they respond favorably to Alcibiades' two requests to join their gathering (*Symp.*, 213a). Apollodorus reports, "Naturally they all made a big fuss, they implored him to join, they begged him to take a seat" (*Symp.*, 213a). In fact, it seems that they are eager not to have to respond to Socrates themselves. Fourth, Agathon, the host of the party, calls Alcibiades to his side (*Symp.*, 213a) and has his slaves take off Alcibiades' shoes. Agathon's actions serve to make Alcibiades one of the symposiasts. So even though Alcibiades has not actually heard Socrates' account of his conversations with Diotima this particular evening, these numerous elements of the text suggest that we should regard his speech in praise of Socrates as representing the response of all the symposiasts.

ALCIBIADES AND THE IMITATION OF SOCRATIC SELF-DISCLOSURE

Alcibiades, both as a historical personage, and as a character in the world of the Platonic dialogues, attracts a great deal of attention in the secondary literature.[5] Despite this abundant coverage in the literature, examining his practice of autobiographical self-disclosure has not been sufficiently detailed. Careful attention to Alcibiades' remarks both before he gives the speech in praise of Socrates and during his speech exhibit many of the same qualities of Socratic self-disclosing narrative commentary. Like Socrates, Alcibiades' self-disclosive commentary reveals his mental and emotional state to the symposiasts. He speaks to draw them into an understanding of his experience of Socrates, much like Socrates uses strategic self-disclosure to draw people toward the practice of philosophy. After assessing these aspects of Alcibiades' speech, I then argue that his imitation of the Socratic practice of autobiographical self-disclosure suggests that he understood much more of Socrates' teaching than is often acknowledged in the secondary literature. The fact that Plato portrays Alcibiades as having understood so much about Socrates' philosophical aims and practices further heightens the tragic dimensions of the dialogue as a whole.[6] Miller explains, "The Athenian auditor in the mid-370s can hardly hear the poignant words of the city's rising young star without being moved to recognize in the trajectory of his life-to-come a cautionary tale: that his lifelong attempt to make himself leader of the city collapsed in his two betrayals, first to Sparta and then to Persia" (2015, 305).

We should read Alcibiades' speech in its proper political context—with the knowledge that Alcibiades would betray Athens. In addition, Alcibiades' turns from philosophy to politics raises the ongoing possibility of philosophical pedagogical failure. The possibility that our pedagogical endeavors may not be successful is something that we have to acknowledge as we think about how to best share our philosophical stories in the public sphere.

Alcibiades' first words in the *Symposium* describe his current state of being. Though no doubt obvious to the symposiasts, Alcibiades announces his drunken condition: "Good evening, gentlemen. I'm plastered" (*Symp.*, 212e). Helfer remarks, "Everything about Alcibiades' appearance in the *Symposium* . . . reminds us that his eros continues to be directed toward the common, finite, and familiar objects that Diotima insists are pursued in vain" (2017, 188). He asks if he can join the party and then reveals his purpose in arriving there: to crown Agathon for his victory. He asks whether, even if he is not allowed to join the party, he be allowed to crown Agathon, "which is all I came to do anyway" (*Symp.*, 212e). Like Socrates, he could not make it to the festivities last night, but he tells the symposiasts, "nothing could stop me tonight" (*Symp.*, 212e). He tells them, "See, I'm wearing the garland myself. I want this crown to come directly from my head to the head that belongs, I don't mind saying to the cleverest and best-looking man in town" (*Symp.*, 212e). At this point, Alcibiades acknowledges how out of place he might appear to them. He emphasizes his inebriated state, saying, "Ah you laugh: you think I'm drunk" (*Symp.*, 213a). He asks again to join the party and, after they all enthusiastically agree, makes his way to Agathon's couch where Socrates had moved over to make room for him (*Symp.*, 213b).

Once he realizes Socrates is sitting right beside him, Alcibiades reacts rather dramatically. He reveals his inner state of mind to the symposiasts by addressing Socrates with a string of accusations and pointed questions: "By Heracles, what's going on here? It's Socrates! You've trapped me again! You always do this to me—all of a sudden—you'll turn up out of nowhere where I least expect you! Well what do you want now? Why did you choose this particular couch? Why aren't you with Aristophanes or anyone else we could tease you about? But no, you figured out a way to find a place next to the most handsome man in the room!" (*Symp.*, 213c). Socrates, for his part, matches the drama that Alcibiades has brought into the scene. Socrates describes Alcibiades' jealousy and violent outbursts (*Symp.*, 213d). He asks Agathon to "control him," and, if he cannot protect him from Alcibiades' jealous and potentially violent outbursts, Alcibiades declares, "I shall never forgive you!" and tells Socrates, "I promise you, you'll pay for this!" but then he decides to follow a different course of action. He takes some of the ribbons from Agathon's crown and places them on Socrates' "wonderous head" (*Symp.*, 213e). Alcibiades explains his reasoning for this action: "Otherwise I know, he'll make a scene" (*Symp.*, 213e). It is interesting that he claims to have insight into Socrates' own state of mind here: "He'll be grumbling that, though I crowned you for your first victory, I didn't honor him even though he has never lost an argument in his life" (*Symp.*, 213e). His claim to know Socrates' thought process is one of the many instances in the text that emphasize strong affinities between Alcibiades and Socrates.[7]

After crowning Socrates, he leans back. He expresses surprise that they are not drinking heavily, and begins to move the party in that direction (*Symp.*, 213e–214b). Eryximachus then objects to the descent into chaotic drinking. He explains how they have entertained themselves this evening. Alcibiades agrees to participate in their speechmaking contest. However, at Eryximachus' instigation, he chooses to praise Socrates instead of love (*Symp.*, 214d). When Socrates begins to object, "Are you going to praise me only in order to mock me?" Alcibiades says, "I'll only tell the truth," and Socrates gives his permission (*Symp.*, 214e). Just before he begins his speech, Alcibiades asks for Socrates' help to attest to the truth of his story. He tells Socrates to interrupt if he says anything not true. After requesting Socrates' help, Alcibiades offers another self-descriptive assessment of his current state: "At worst there there'll be mistakes in my speech, not lies. But you can't hold it against me if I don't get everything in the right order—I'll say things as they come to mind. And even a sober and unclouded mind would find it hard to come to terms with your bizarreness" (*Symp.*, 215a). To a degree, he is admitting aporia before he begins his speech. He is doing genuinely what Agathon feigned to doing earlier (*Symp.*, 210c).

Alcibiades begins his speech. C. D. C. Reeve describes its overall effect in this way, "It is so vivid, so entertaining, so alive, in fact, that we almost forget it had any predecessors" (2006, 124). Alcibiades starts by explaining his intent—"I'll try to praise Socrates, my friends"—and also how he will proceed, "I'll have to use an image" (*Symp.*, 215b). Again, Alcibiades claims to have insight into Socrates' inner state of mind: "And though he may think I'm trying to make fun of him I assure you my image is no joke" (*Symp.*, 215b). Alcibiades describes the effect that Socrates has on him at several junctures. After comparing Socrates to the satyr Marsyas, Alcibiades notes, "let anyone—man, woman, or child—listen to you or even to a poor account of what you say—and we are all transported, completely possessed" (*Symp.*, 215d). He continues, "If I were to describe for you what an extraordinary effect his words have always had on me (I can feel it this moment even as I'm speaking), you might actually suspect that I'm drunk!" (*Symp.*, 215e). Alcibiades reveals even more about how he feels around Socrates: "Still, I swear to you, the moment he starts to speak, I am beside myself, my heart starts leaping in my chest, the tears come streaming down my face" (*Symp.*, 215e). Alcibiades elaborates further, saying that the Corybantes "seem sane" compared to him under Socrates' spell (*Symp.*, 215e). Alcibiades makes clear that Socrates' speech reaches his soul: "My very own soul started protesting that my life—my life! Was no better than the most miserable slaves'" (*Symp.*, 216a). Alcibiades focuses on the words of Socrates. Socrates' words force him into unwanted self-reflection about the nature of his life: "He makes me admit that my political career is a waste of time" (*Symp.*, 216a). Rather than acknowledge his "personal shortcomings," Alcibiades claims that he "refuses to listen to him" (*Symp.*, 216b). He confesses that only Socrates makes him feel shame (*Symp.*, 216b). He emphasizes this point again, "Yes, he makes me feel ashamed" (*Symp.*, 216b) and again, saying he feels "deeply ashamed" (*Symp.*, 216c).

Alcibiades goes on to explain what happens when he is not with Socrates. Even though he agrees with Socrates about improving himself: "I go back to my own ways. I cave into my desire to please the crowd" (*Symp.*, 216c). Alcibiades describes his existential misery in great detail. He complains, "My whole life has become one constant effort to escape from him and keep away" (*Symp.*, 216c). However, his attempts fail: "When I see him, I feel deeply ashamed because I'm doing nothing about my way of life, though I have already agreed with him that I should" (*Symp.*, 216c). He even claims he would be happier with Socrates dead, though he immediately acknowledges that then he would be even more miserable (*Symp.*, 216c). Alcibiades tells the symposiasts, "I can't live with him. I can't live without him" (*Symp.*, 216c). Even though his speech is ostensibly about Socrates, it is remarkable how much Alcibiades discloses about himself. His emotional turmoil is palpable. His willingness to share his inner thought process and emotional states with the symposiasts mirrors Socrates' self-disclosive practices. Alcibiades seems very vulnerable. However, as Marina McCoy notes, he "is unable to transform his vulnerability from awareness into action. Plato's inclusion of this Alcibiades—who possesses some self-knowledge, yet is unable to transform his life accordingly—suggests Plato's sensitivity to the tragic" (2013, 117).

In the next section of his speech, Alcibiades compares Socrates to Silenus (*Symp.*, 216e–217a). Alcibiades claims to have a great deal of insight into Socrates' internal experience. He calls him "sober and temperate" and uninterested in "whether a person is beautiful, or rich, or famous in any other way that most people admire" (*Symp.*, 216e). He tells the symposiasts that Socrates' life is a "game of irony" (*Symp.*, 216e). Alcibiades' insight into Socrates' motivations suggests that he feels a deep affinity with Socrates. His use of self-disclosive speech is also another indication of his affinity for Socrates. As he attempts to describe Socrates' inner experience, Alcibiades also describes his own: "I once caught a glimpse of the figures he keeps hidden within: they were so godlike-so bright and beautiful, so utterly amazing that I no longer had a choice—I just had to do whatever he told me" (*Symp.*, 217a). Alcibiades continues to describe his state of mind, "I thought at the time . . . that what he really wanted was me, and that seemed to me the Luckiest coincidence" (*Symp.*, 217a). Alcibiades reveals more details about his thought process, "All I had to do was to let him have his way with me, and he would teach me everything he knew" (*Symp.*, 217a). Alcibiades emphasizes this point by addressing the symposiasts directly, "Believe me, I had a lot of confidence in my looks" (*Symp.*, 217a). Alcibiades notes that they had never been alone together, but now discloses his new aim, "With this in mind, I sent the attendant away, and met Socrates alone" (*Symp.*, 217b). At this point, he interrupts the story to address the symposiasts again, exhorting them to pay attention, much like how Diotima exhorts Socrates to pay attention (*Symp.*, 210e). Alcibiades also addresses Socrates by name, again telling him to correct anything that is untrue. In fact, Alcibiades says quite emphatically, "And, Socrates, if I say anything untrue, I want you to correct me" (*Symp.*, 217b).

Alcibiades continues to reveal his emotional and mental states to the symposiasts. He is confident that Socrates will take advantage of the moment: "My idea, naturally, was that he'd take advantage of the opportunity to tell me whatever it is that lovers say when they find themselves alone" (*Symp.*, 217b). He also reveals his emotional state: "I relished the moment" (*Symp.*, 217b). Alcibiades tells the symposiasts that nothing happened; "Socrates had his usual sort of conversation with me and at the end of the day he went off" (*Symp.*, 217b), much like Socrates goes off at the end of the party (*Symp.*, 223d). Despite his struggles with achieving his aim, Alcibiades does not give up. He reports, "My next idea was to invite him to the gymnasium with me." He discloses his confidence: "I was sure that this would lead to something" (*Symp.*, 217c). Alcibiades admits that nothing happened despite exercising together alone many times (*Symp.*, 217c). Alcibiades describes how he changes his strategy once this plan fails to work. First, he explains his reasoning process, "When I realized that my ploy had failed, I decided on a frontal attack. I refused to retreat from a battle I myself had begun, and I needed to know just where matters stood" (*Symp.*, 217c). Alcibiades relates the next stage of his seduction plan: "So what I did was to invite him to dinner, as if I were his lover and he my young prey" (*Symp.*, 217d). Alcibiades conveys a great deal of vulnerability by revealing his willingness to reverse the typical roles in the lover-beloved relationship.[8] However, this strategy seems not to work at first. Alcibiades notes that Socrates took a long time to accept the invitation. When Socrates finally accepts one of Alcibiades' invitations, he leaves right after dinner. Alcibiades again shares his emotional state. He admits, "I was too shy to try to stop him" (*Symp.*, 217d). Alcibiades remains persistent. He adapts to Socrates' seeming lack of interest in him and explains his new plan. The next time Socrates arrives, Alcibiades is prepared. Just as dinner is ending, Alcibiades engages him in discussion "and kept him talking late into the night" (*Symp.*, 217d). When Socrates wants to leave, Alcibiades "used the lateness of the hour" as an excuse to get him to stay. Alcibiades reports, "I managed to persuade him to spend the night at my house. Socrates agrees to remain there with Alcibiades and starts to sleep on the couch where he had his meal" (*Symp.*, 217d).

Alcibiades interrupts the story again. He notes that the story thus far has been "perfectly decent" and claims that he would not tell the rest of the story if he were not under the influence of wine (*Symp.*, 217e). He also admits that he feels a shared affinity with the symposiasts because they understand what it is like to suffer the "snakebite" of philosophy (*Symp.*, 218a).[9] Alcibiades discloses the depth of his existential despair, "Well, something much more painful than a snake has bitten me in my most sensitive part, I mean my heart, or my soul, or whatever you want to call it, which has been struck and bitten by philosophy" (*Symp.*, 218a). He reaffirms his shared affinity with the symposiasts by calling each of the speakers by name, and, interestingly, he also includes Aristodemus in the group, along with Socrates (*Symp.*, 218b). They "have all shared in the madness, the Bacchic frenzy of philosophy" (*Symp.*, 218b). He also asks for their understanding of, and forgiveness for, "what I did then and what I say now" (*Symp.*, 218b). He warns those who are not similarly initiated to close their ears (*Symp.*, 218b). Most scholars suggest this is a reference to the profanation of the mysteries.[10] I agree, but it also raises an important point about the appropriate audience for self-disclosive narration. We have to be judicious in narration of experience and discerning about who we tell stories to and in what context. Alcibiades' direct address to the symposiasts and his appeal to them sharing his experience suggests that he is aware that he is verging on telling a story that is perhaps not appropriate to tell. He says, "as for the house slaves and for anyone else who is not an initiate, my story's not for you; block your ears" (*Symp.*, 218c). Alcibiades seems to only want a very small, select group to hear this story. This seems to suggest that his narrative self-disclosure is appropriate for this context but not a broad public context. After this warning, he gets back to the story. "The lights were out; the slaves had left; the time was right, I thought, to come to the point and tell him freely what I had in mind" (*Symp.*, 218c).

At this point, Alcibiades simply relates the encounter between himself and Socrates without adding commentary about his internal state of mind or inner feelings. This mimics Socrates' own narrative practice as his self-referential remarks typically fall away as the action of the dialogues he narrates progresses. Without Alcibiades' narrative intervention, it is as if they are there in the room listening or watching the conversation unfold between them. However, as a character in his own narration, Alcibiades continues to reveal his inner states. Alcibiades shakes Socrates and asks if he is up. He tells Socrates that he's the "only worthy lover, I have ever had" (*Symp.*, 218c). He accuses Socrates of being "shy" with him. Alcibiades confesses that he plans to submit to Socrates because he realizes that no one can help him more in his endeavors to become the best man he can be other than

Socrates. He explains his reasoning process to Socrates: "Nothing is more important to me than becoming the best man I can be, and no one can help me more than you to reach that aim. He also reveals, perhaps unconsciously, how much he is concerned about his social reputation, "With a man like you, in fact, I'd be much more ashamed of what wise people would say if I did not take you as my lover, than I would of what all the others, in their foolishness, would say if I did" (*Symp.*, 218d). This is much like his earlier admission that he submit to the crowds when he is away from Socrates (*Symp.*, 216b). Alcibiades describes Socrates' "absolutely inimitable ironic manner" (*Symp.*, 218d). Socrates, at first, seems to affirm Alcibiades' aims (*Symp.*, 218e), but then accuses him of wanting to exchange the gold of Socrates' own inner virtue for the bronze of his mere physical beauty. Socrates also warns Alcibiades that he may not be of any help to him and that he is not yet at a stage to see the true inner beauty of Socrates and how Alcibiades might transform his own soul and turn it around to the good. Nonetheless, Socrates tells him, "We'll always do what seems the best to the two of us" (*Symp.*, 219b).

Alcibiades describes his state of mind: "His words made me think that my own had finally hit their mark, that he was smitten by my arrows. I didn't give him a chance to say another word. I stood up immediately and placed my mantle over the light cloak which, though it was the middle of winter, was his only clothing" (*Symp.*, 219c). Alcibiades reports how he slips beneath the cloak and embraces Socrates. Alcibiades calls attention to this moment by addressing Socrates directly: "you can't deny a word of it" (*Symp.*, 291c). He then tells the symposiasts that Socrates turned him down; "he spurned my beauty of which I was so proud" (*Symp.*, 219c). He then addresses the symposiasts as "members of the jury." He tells them their job is to sit in judgment of "Socrates' amazing arrogance and pride" (*Symp.*, 219d). On this point, Helfer notes, "The theme of hubris is intriguing; Alcibiades' accusation of Socratic hubris in the context of an account of their relationship suggests the possibility that Alcibiades' own hubristic political ambition may be the result of some Socratic influence" (2017, 13). After swearing to all the gods and goddesses, he attests to them that nothing occurred on that night; "my night with Socrates went no further than if I had spent it with my own father or older brother!" (*Symp.*, 219d).

Alcibiades again describes his state of mind, emphasizing both his emotions and his thought processes, "Of course I was deeply humiliated, but also I couldn't help admiring his natural character, his moderation, his fortitude—here was a man whose strength and wisdom went beyond my wildest dreams! How could I bring myself to hate him? I couldn't bear to lose his friendship." (*Symp.*, 219d). At this point, it seems that Alcibiades realizes that their relationship would not be sexual. However, the next sentence reveals that Alcibiades still desires the physical dimension of a relationship with Socrates: "But how could I win him over?" (*Symp.*, 219e). He describes his existential angst as "the only trap by means of which I had thought I might capture him had already proved a dismal failure. I had no idea what to do, no purpose in life; ah, no one else has ever known the real meaning of slavery" (*Symp.*, 219e).

Some self-disclosing discourse continues as Alcibiades reports Socrates' behavior in the battles of Potidaea and Delium. He tells how Socrates saves his life and his armor. He addresses Socrates directly at this point: "For my part, Socrates, I told them right then that the decoration really belonged to you and you can blame me neither for doing so then nor for saying so now" (*Symp.*, 220e).[11] Alcibiades describes his actions during the retreat from Delium: "I was there with the cavalry, I happened to see them (Socrates and Laches) just by chance and the moment I did I started shouting encouragements to them, telling them I was never going to leave their side, and so on. That day I had a better opportunity to watch Socrates than I ever had at Potidaea, for, being on horseback, I wasn't in very great danger (*Symp.*, 221a).

As his account ends, Alcibiades' narrative voice shifts to address the symposiasts directly. He draws the symposiasts into the story by mentioning Aristophanes by name and by quoting *The Clouds* to describe Socrates (*Symp.*, 221b). Alcibiades describes Socrates' "calmness," his keen observation of the enemy, and his bravery (*Symp.*, 221c). He ends his account by emphasizing Socrates' uniqueness, saying there is no one else to compare him to: "This man here is so bizarre, his ways and ideas are so unusual that, search as you might, you'll never find anyone else, alive or dead, who's even remotely like him" (*Symp.*, 221d). Alcibiades ends, saying, "this is my praise of Socrates, though I haven't spared my reproach, either. I told you how horribly he treated me and not only me but also Charmides, Euthydemus, and many others. He has deceived us all; he presents himself as your lover, and before you know it, you're in love with him yourself. I warn you Agathon, don't let him fool you. Remember our torments" (*Symp.*, 222c). Apollodorus tells his auditor that "Alcibiades' frankness provoked a lot of laughter, especially since it was obvious that he was still in love with Socrates" (*Symp.*, 222c). The fact that the symposiasts laugh at Alcibiades' speech raises the question whether we should regard Alcibiades as speaking truthfully about his feelings and his relationship with Socrates. Apollodorus mentions his "frankness," at 222c. Socrates never protests, and Alcibiades gives him several opportunities to do so (*Symp.*, 217a).[12]

In sum, Plato presents Alcibiades' autobiographical account as a response to the autobiographical account Socrates has just given to the symposiasts. In this way, Alcibiades demonstrates an affinity with Socrates that the other symposiasts lack. Alcibiades' narrative offers a model for all the symposiasts to follow. Like Alcibiades, they should reflect on love and its manifestation in their lives. They should reflect on this question and share their stories with each other. While they have all given speeches that praise both love and themselves, they have not yet shared how love or the love of philosophy transforms them. If they can learn to tell their own tales of beauty, they will be following Diotima's advice to make the young better (*Symp.*, 210c). They will begin the journey toward a life lived in true beauty (*Symp.*, 212a). They should begin to philosophize in that manner, in a manner that will enable them to care for themselves and for one another.

THE NARRATIVE FRAMES AS IMITATIONS OF SOCRATIC SELF-DISCLOSURE

As I mentioned in the previous chapter, the bulk of the *Symposium* is contained within a doubly nested narrative frame where Apollodorus decides to tell his unnamed friend about the party at Agathon's "just as Aristodemus told it to him" (*Symp.*, 174a). However, the *Symposium* actually begins with a direct conversation between Apollodorus and an unnamed friend. The dialogue starts with Apollodorus responding to a question that his friend has asked (*Symp.*, 172a). Apollodorus immediately tells the friend how he came to be prepared to answer his question. He tells the friend how Glaucon approached him to hear the speeches about love that happened at Agathon's house with Socrates and Alcibiades present (*Symp.*, 172a). Apollodorus admonishes Glaucon for thinking that the party happened recently and believing that Apollodorus was there himself (*Symp.*, 172c). He explains, "You know very well Agathon hasn't lived in Athens for many years, while it's been less than three that I've been Socrates' companion and made it my job to know exactly what he says and does each day" (*Symp.*, 173a). This remark is fascinating to consider in light of Socratic autobiographical practice because Apollodorus would have been privy to many of Socrates' own accounts of his philosophical practice. Corrigan's treatment of the nested prologue is excellent. Of particular interest is his observation that it is an "imitation of an imitation" (2004, 11). He argues, "the basic narrative structure of the *Symposium* is at least analogous to that thirdhand imitation of reality examined in the *Republic*" (2004, 12). If it is only three years, that is also about the time that Phaedo came into Socrates' circle (Nails 2002, 231). It appears that there is a shared affinity for Socrates' autobiographical imitation with these recent philosophical converts. Apollodorus emphasizes his knowledge of what Socrates says first, further emphasizing his interest in the words of Socrates. When viewed with this statement in mind, we can perhaps begin to think of the opening lines of the dialogue, "In fact, your question does not find me unprepared" (*Symp.*, 172a) in a different light. The word "preparation" is important in the context of autobiographical practice. Apollodorus presents autobiography as a mode of philosophical preparation and of philosophical care for Socrates. Furthermore, Apollodorus shares his own philosophical experience as an imitation of Socrates sharing his experience with others. Apollodorus places himself in the story from the beginning. Viewed in this way, he makes the opening of the *Symposium*, and, by extension, nearly all of the *Symposium*, his own autobiographical discourse. In doing so, he imitates both the words and deeds of Socrates. He makes the story of Socrates his own.

Apollodorus

Apollodorus begins his account, telling his friend, "I was walking to the city from my home in Phaleron when a man I know, who was making his way behind me, saw me and called from a distance, 'The gentleman from Phaleron!' he yelled, trying to be funny, 'Hey Apollodorus, wait!' So, I stopped and waited" (*Symp.*, 172a).[13] Several scholars have noted the parallels to the *Republic*, a dialogue that Socrates narrates. The parallels are numerous. Apollodorus is walking to Athens from a port city, just as Socrates walks back to Athens from the Piraeus. He is stopped, though not by force, though the person is "yelling" at him to get his attention. There are significant differences though. Apollodorus seems willing to stop and wait, whereas Socrates is "forced" to remain in the Piraeus (*Symp.*, 327e). Also, Apollodorus is originally alone, whereas Socrates is with Glaucon. However, the person who yells at him and stops him shares Glaucon's name, and, hence, Apollodorus, like Socrates, is with a Glaucon. There are some difficulties with the assumption that this Glaucon is the same Glaucon of the *Republic*. Debra Nails explains that if we give a dramatic date of 421 to the *Republic*, "The Glaucon of the *Republic* cannot be the Glaucon of the *Symposium* frame because a Glaucon born by 444 would no child in 416" (2002, 155). Also, if Mark Munn is correct about Glaucon's death in the battle of Munychia in 404, he would not be alive when the narrative frame of the *Symposium* is likely to taken place (2003, 239). Jacob Howland's recent book, *Glaucon's Fate*, offers a transformational reassessment of the *Republic* in light of this information about Glaucon (2019). Despite these historical difficulties, the name clearly carries an association with the *Republic*. When thinking about the similarity between these two dialogues in terms of autobiographical practice, Plato may have constructed this account in such a way that Apollodorus is specifically imitating elements of the account of the *Republic* he may well have heard from Socrates.[14] Apollodorus certainly could have heard Socrates retelling the events of the *Republic*. Socrates probably told it more than once. There were probably many "yesterdays" for Socrates' retelling of the events at Cephalus' house. Indeed, Apollodorus' "just the other day" temporal marker is another implicit link to Socrates' autobiographical retelling of the *Republic*.

Apollodorus reports Glaucon's urgent questioning and his desire to hear the story about the party at Agathon's. In doing so, even before he explicitly mentions it, Apollodorus makes clear to the unnamed friend that he is an authority, someone with valued knowledge about Socrates' comings and goings. Several aspects of his account underscore that he has thorough knowledge of Socratic practice. For example, Apollodorus' retelling emphasizes the practicing of questioning and asking. Glaucon avers that he has been "looking for" Apollodorus. He "wants to ask him about the speeches they made on Love" (*Symp.*, 172b). He asks a specific question, "What were they?" He notes that the man he heard the account from said "you were the one to ask." He asks three questions in a row: "So please, will you tell me all about it?" and another, "Who has a better right than you to report his conversation?" and finally, "Were you there yourself" (*Symp.*, 172c). A little later, Glaucon asks two more questions, wanting to know who told him the story and if Socrates was the source of the story (*Symp.*, 173a). Apollodorus may just be presenting Glaucon's eagerness as a way of emphasizing his own authority, but I think the decision to preserve the urgent questioning also tells us something important about autobiographical inquiry and the sharing of that inquiry. Autobiography is part of an interrogative stance with respect to one's self, a mode of questioning that is part of living the examined life. At the same time, Glaucon's questions reveal some limitations of narrative retelling as a mode of knowledge. He tells Apollodorus, "He heard about it from a man who heard it from Phoenix, Philip's son, but it was badly garbled" (*Symp.*, 172b). Apollodorus emphasizes the inaccuracy of the account by chastising Glaucon for his thinking that the party happened recently (*Symp.*, 173a). The fact Alcibiades is named along with Agathon and Socrates in his initial query also puts the focus squarely on Alcibiades from the beginning.[15] Helfer remarks, "We are thus given the impression that Athens is at present abuzz with the telling and retelling of more or less precise versions of this story" (2017, 149).

Thus far, I have been painting Apollodorus in a rather favorable light. He is often regarded rather harshly in the literature. O'Connor calls him "a distorting mirror of Socrates, too manly in speech, too womanly in deed" (2015, 22). Corrigan observes that "Apollodorus is oppressed by his lack of true philosophical insight compared to that of his master" (2004, 11). He compares him to "a Homeric rhapsodist" (2004, 12), but acknowledges that he is "presented as a necessary precondition for the preservation of the historical memory that makes the dialogue possible" (2004, 12). Giannopoulou observes, "Upon scrutiny, Apollodorus' zeal has little, if anything, to do with an understanding of the good encapsulated by Socrates' words" (2017, 20). In *On Plato's Symposium*, Strauss regards him more favorably terms calling him "an enthusiast for philosophy" (2001, 20), but notes despite this love of philosophy he is "cursed, most unhappy" (2001, 22). Also, in his favor, he is depicted along with Crito and Critobulus as being willing to pay a fine on Socrates' behalf in the *Apology* (*Ap.*, 38b). Apollodorus is engaged in an imitation of Socrates' narrative practice, and, in that way, is attempting to bring both Glaucon and the friend he tells the story to into some level of philosophical self-reflection. However, his attempts are not without some negative aspects. For example, he chastises Glaucon, which might damper Glaucon's enthusiasm to hear the account and apply its lessons to his own life. He chastises him not just for thinking the party happened recently but goes so far as to call him "worthless" (*Symp.*, 173a).

Apollodorus also has a negative view of himself that he feels compelled to include in his account. He used to regard himself as "the most worthless man on earth." He also admits that he "used to think philosophy was the last thing a man should do" (*Symp.*, 173a). Apollodorus' negativity also extends to Aristodemus, his narrative source of the information. He calls Aristodemus "a real runt of a man, who always went barefoot. He went to the party because, I think, he was obsessed with Socrates—one of the worst cases at the time" (*Symp.*, 173b). Glaucon, for his part, seems undismayed by Apollodorus' negativity. He acknowledges his joking and insists that Apollodorus tell "when the party took place" (*Symp.*, 173a). Apollodorus' response suggests he has a friendly relationship with Glaucon. He says the party took place while they were children. He dates the party as having occurred after Agathon's first victory celebration. Glaucon remains focused on the story. He asks, "Then who told you about it? Was it Socrates himself?" (*Symp.*, 173a). Apollodorus presents himself as quite knowledgeable in response. He knows that Aristodemus was the source of Phoenix's account. He also checks the account with Socrates and conveys the Socratic approval of the account (*Symp.*, 173b). Glaucon echoes his continued enthusiasm: "Please tell them then. You speak and I'll listen as we walk to the city. This is the perfect opportunity" (*Symp.*, 173b). Apollodorus' inclusion of this level of detail about his preparation suggests some things about appropriate audience for autobiographical self-disclosure. He tells the story of himself to someone he knows somewhat well. There are strong indications that this is Socrates' practice as well.[16]

Apollodorus' negativity continues as he returns to converse with his friend directly. First, he expresses negativity toward the friend who asks him to tell the story. Then he says, "all other talk, especially the talk of rich businessmen like you, bores me to tears and I'm sorry for you and your friends because you think your affairs are important when really they're totally trivial" (*Symp.*, 173d). He continues, "Perhaps in your turn, you think I'm a failure, and, believe me, I think that what you think is true. But as for all of you, I don't just think you are failures—I know it for a fact" (*Symp.*, 173d). It seems like an odd way to treat someone who just presented him with the opportunity to do what he loves best, namely, engage in philosophical conversation. However, the friend seems not to be particularly insulted, responding, "You'll never change, Apollodorus. Always nagging, even at yourself" (*Symp.*, 173d). So, perhaps all of this negativity is just a way of joking, but it still seems to run the risk of turning some potential audience away from philosophy. Apollodorus' negative self-image also arises in his exchange with the friend. Apollodorus agrees with the judgment of himself as a "failure" (*Symp.*, 173d), affirming that he thinks that is true. The friend attests to Apollodorus' negative self-image: "I do believe you think everybody—yourself first of all—is totally worthless, except, of course, Socrates" (*Symp.*, 173d). He goes even further, referring to his nickname "the maniac" and emphasizes the fittingness of this nickname: "you certainly talk like one, always furious with everyone, and including yourself—but not with Socrates" (*Symp.*, 173d). However, it is possible to view his negative self-description along with his previous self-deprecating remarks to Glaucon in a different light. When Apollodorus mentions that he "simply drifted aimlessly" and that he "thought what he was doing was important" and that he was "totally worthless" (*Symp.*, 173a), he is also attesting to the transformative power of the practice of philosophy in general and the transformative power of listening to philosophical autobiography in particular. Nonetheless, it doesn't seem to change his own self-image.

When he turns to address the friend, Apollodorus emphasizes his own part in the story again, saying, "So this is what we talked about on our way, and that's why as I said before, I'm not unprepared" (*Symp.*, 173c). He then explains that "If I'm to tell you about it too, I'll be glad to." Apollodorus is more than willing to launch into another retelling of the story and place himself at the center of it. Apollodorus explains to the friend, "After all, my greatest pleasure comes from philosophical conversation, even if I'm only a listener" (*Symp.*, 173c). Here, he reinforces the fact that he previously told Glaucon that he had spent the last three years listening to Socrates. He then goes on to insult the friend who has asked him to tell the story (*Symp.*, 173d). The friend, like Glaucon, seems to know Apollodorus rather well and doesn't seem all that put off by Apollodorus' rant. He also provides some additional insight into Apollodorus' character, "You'll never change, Apollodorus! Always nagging, even at yourself! I do believe you think everybody-yourself first of all—is totally worthless, except, of course, Socrates. I don't know exactly how you came to be called 'the maniac,' but you certainly talk like one, always furious with everyone, including yourself—but not with Socrates" (*Symp.*, 173d).

Despite all the dismissive things that Apollodorus says about Aristodemus' character and his memory, Apollodorus does decide to tell his friend "the whole story from the very beginning, as Aristodemus told it to me" (*Symp.*, 174a). In this way, he preserves another autobiographical narrative, namely, that of Aristodemus. This preservation emphasizes the importance of autobiographical discourse from the very beginning of the dialogue and cues us to look for other instances of it as the retelling of the dialogue unfolds. His decision itself reflects an imitation of Socrates' own narrative decision to tell the symposiasts what happened just as Diotima taught him, "I think it will be easiest for me to proceed the way Diotima did and tell you how she questioned me" (*Symp.*, 201e). His willingness to tell Aristodemus' story overcomes some worries scholars and readers may have about his reliability. For example, Marina McCoy articulates this worry about Apollodorus: "Apollodorus narrates the discussion to an unnamed friend. We are not even certain that the story is entirely faithful to the reality, as Apollodorus admits that he has forgotten some parts" (2013, 118). Furthermore, Apollodorus acknowledges the limitation of his narrative source and his narrative ability. He admits to the friend, "Of course, Aristodemus couldn't remember exactly what everyone said" (*Symp.*, 178a). He readily acknowledges that "I myself don't remember everything he told me. But I'll tell you what he remembered best, and what I consider the most important" (*Symp.*, 178a). In doing so, Apollodorus asserts his narrative authority over his narrative source. He chooses the most important points to convey to his friend. It is worth considering whether he preserved Aristodemus' voice in the original telling to Glaucon. The text does not indicate that he did. In fact, that Apollodorus begins his response to his friend by focusing on the speeches suggests that he did not. He starts off, "Well, the speeches went something like this" (*Symp.*, 174a). His inclusion of Aristodemus suggests that he is trying to improve his account on this retelling of the events.

Aristodemus

It is a difficult interpretive task to sort out exactly what Aristodemus told Apollodorus from what Apollodorus reports about it. Nonetheless, aspects of the retelling give us some indication of how Aristodemus told the story of the party. For example, Aristodemus certainly could have just reported the speeches on love to Apollodorus. However, Aristodemus places himself in the narrative he tells Apollodorus about Socrates; "He said that one day he ran into Socrates who had just bathed and put on his fancy sandals—both very unusual events. So he asked where he was going and why he was looking so good" (*Symp.*, 174a). Admittedly, the focus of Aristodemus' narrative is primarily Socrates, but he tells the story by starting with his own encounter and extended conversation with Socrates rather than just telling the speeches to Apollodorus. After Socrates explains that he has made himself beautiful because he has agreed to go to Agathon's victory party, Socrates asks Aristodemus if he would like to come along, despite the fact that he has not been invited (*Symp.*, 174b). Aristodemus reports his willingness to go: "I'll do whatever you say" (*Symp.*, 174b). Socrates seems pleased and says that they will remake the proverb by having "Goodmen go uninvited to the Goodman's feast." Socrates likens them to Homer, who also disregarded the proverb by having the weak Menelaus arrive uninvited at his superior's table" (*Symp.*, 174c).

Aristodemus reports his response to this Socratic provocation. Although he initially expresses willingness to do whatever Socrates says, he does not agree with Socrates' positive assessment of their situation. Rather, Aristodemus says, "Socrates, I am afraid Homer's description is bound to fit me better than yours. Mine is a case of an obvious inferior arriving uninvited at the table of a man of letters" (*Symp.*, 174c). He then places the responsibility on Socrates to figure out something to explain this difficult social situation: "I think you'd better figure out a good excuse for bringing me along, because, you know, I won't admit I've come without an invitation" (*Symp.*, 174c). All Aristodemus can think of is this, "I'll say I'm your guest" (*Symp.*, 174d). At this juncture, Aristodemus has centered his narrative around his own experience of his inadequacy. Scholars typically view Aristodemus in a negative light partly because of his emphasis on his own inadequacy. For example, David O'Connor remarks, "that the short in stature Aristodemus wanted to imitate Socrates. But Shorty falls short of Socrates. He is too small, not of physical stature, but too small of soul. There is a side of Socrates that he is too short to see" (2015, 23). But, I think it is possible to regard Aristodemus in more favorable terms. To explain, his remarks to Socrates illustrate two important qualities of Socratic self-disclosure, namely, the inclusion of his emotional states and his reasoning processes. Aristodemus tells Apollodorus how he feels and how he thinks about the situation he finds himself in with Socrates. Socrates, for his part, seems unwilling to accept Aristodemus' view of the situation. He says, "Let's go. We'll think about what to say 'as we proceed the two of us along the way" (*Symp.*, 174d).

It is worth noting the parallels between how Apollodorus has crafted his initial narrative about his preparation to tell the story with Aristodemus' narrative he is now recounting. Apollodorus seems to be imitating an aspect of Aristodemus' account, but with a certain reversal. He casts himself in the role of Socrates. To explain further, Aristodemus runs into Socrates. Apollodorus is hailed from behind by Glaucon. Glaucon and Apollodorus walk on the road to Athens together. Aristodemus and Socrates walk on the road to Agathon's house together.

At this point, Apollodorus summarizes Aristodemus' account (*Symp.*, 174d–174e). We learn of Aristodemus' story partly through his own voice that appears in places like this conversation with Socrates. Other times, Apollodorus specifically mentions that Aristodemus said something.[17] Apollodorus sometimes preserves Aristodemus' own voice. At times, his own voice reports what was told to him by Aristodemus. Often these voices intermingle. For example, Apollodorus describes what happens between

Aristodemus and Socrates as they walk toward Agathon's house (*Symp.*, 174d–174e). Things start out in a philosophically promising manner. They walk together, ostensibly discussing their plans, though Apollodorus only mentions they were walking, not that they were talking. Socrates starts to think about something and lags behind "lost in thought" (*Symp.*, 174d).[18] This is a fascinating moment to consider. If Socrates and Aristodemus were talking about something, perhaps the conversation stimulated Socrates' internal reflection. Another way of reading the moment is that their conversation was not sufficiently engaging for Socrates to stay involved with it.[19] From an autobiographical perspective, this moment shows that Socrates keeps some things to himself. He does not disclose everything that happens to him. Aristodemus waits for him, but Socrates tells him to go ahead (*Symp.*, 174e). Apollodorus reports that Aristodemus arrives at Agathon's house in "a very embarrassing situation" (*Symp.*, 174e). The slave brings him into the dining room just as dinner is being served" (*Symp.*, 174e). Agathon, for his part, greets him (*Symp.*, 174e). Then Apollodorus says, "So I turned around (Aristodemus said) and Socrates was nowhere to be seen. And I said that it was actually Socrates who had brought *me* along as his guest" (*Symp.*, 174e). When Agathon asks where Socrates is, Aristodemus responds, "He was directly behind me, but I have no idea where he is now" (*Symp.*, 175a).[20] Agathon tells Eryximachus to sit on Eryximachus' couch, leaving his own couch free for Socrates to sit next to him. Aristodemus interferes in Agathon's attempt to send his slaves to bring Socrates in: "Leave him alone. It's one of his habits: every now and then he just goes off like that and stands motionless, wherever he happens to be. I'm sure he'll come in very soon, so don't disturb him; let him be" (*Symp.*, 175b). Aristodemus' intervention is rather forceful, and Agathon acquiesces for the time being, but Agathon continues his attempt to disturb Socrates. Apollodorus reports what Aristodemus said, "So they went ahead and started eating, but there was still no sign of Socrates. Agathon wanted to send for him many times, but Aristodemus wouldn't let him" (*Symp.*, 175d).

Other places that Aristodemus must have mentioned himself in the story occur when Eryximachus refers to him as a weak drinker (*Symp.*, 176c); when he cannot remember the speeches after Phaedrus, so he "skipped over them" (*Symp.*, 180c); and when Alcibiades includes him in those who share in the snake bite of philosophy (*Symp.*, 218b). Aristodemus also includes the fact that he falls asleep "and slept for a long time" (*Symp.*, 223c). Aristodemus must have mentioned that "He woke up just as dawn was about to break; the roosters were crowing already" (*Symp.*, 223c). In addition, Aristodemus admits that could not remember what Agathon, Aristophanes, and Socrates were discussing (*Symp.*, 223d). Aristodemus must have explained to Apollodorus that he had "missed the first part of their discussion, and he was half-asleep anyway" (*Symp.*, 223d). He does remember that "the main point was that Socrates was trying to prove to them that the authors should be able to write both comedy and tragedy" (*Symp.*, 223d). And, finally, Aristodemus includes himself in the conclusion of his narrative: "Socrates got up and left and Aristodemus followed him. Apollodorus notes that Aristodemus said that Socrates went directly to the Lyceum, washed up, spent the rest of the day just as he always did, and only then as evening was falling, went home to rest" (*Symp.*, 223d). This observation seems to imply that Aristodemus followed Socrates around for the whole next day. Otherwise how would Aristodemus know what Socrates did? Though the final scene of the dialogue focuses on Socrates, Apollodorus preserves Aristodemus' role in the ending of his account as well. He offers no final summing up of Socrates' character as Phaedo gives to Echecrates at the end of the *Phaedo* (*Symp.*, 118a). In doing so, he leaves the focus on Socrates explicitly and implicitly on Aristodemus.

Aristodemus, like Apollodorus, generally receives negative treatment in the secondary literature.[21] However, this focus on his self-inclusive speech paints him in a more favorable light. In sum, Aristodemus could have left out his own role in the story. He does not. Apollodorus sees his role as narrator of the account important enough to include in his own story that he tells to his friend. In doing so, he provides the opportunity for us to see a disciple of Socrates engaging in the practice of placing himself in the story of Socrates. He makes Socratic discourse his own as he shares the story with others. Again, it is a model we can reflect upon as we think about how best to share our own philosophical stories in the public sphere.

NOTES

1. See Thesleff (1993; 2015, 121–22). See also Tejera (1999). For an excellent account of similar modes of reading Plato have gained a great deal of traction over the past two decades, see Press (2018).
2. I am currently at work on an article that explores mountain and cave imagery in Plato's dialogues. See also Kingsley (1995) and Corcoran (2016).
3. See the introduction to Mitchell Miller (2004) and the introduction to Plato's "Parmenides" (1997c). When talking about this moment in the dialogues with my students, I often refer to it as a "philosophical pop quiz."
4. Miller (2015, 301) suggests that the references to laws on the ladder of love refers directly to Pausanias, and the move toward sciences is a reference to Eryximachus, but neither of them are depicted as desiring to make a response.
5. As a historical figure, see Thucydides (1998, 6:8–26). See Nails (2002, 2006b) and Ellis (1989). For a thought-provoking reading of Alcibiades' place in the Platonic Cosmos as a whole, see Helfer (2017). Helfer (2017, 7) remarks, "No character aside from Socrates receives such sustained attention in Plato's dialogues." Of interest also is Altman (2018). On Alcibiades' role in the *Symposium* specifically, see Rosen (1987, 278–327), Reeve (2006), Nichols (2007), and Scott (2000).
6. On the tragedy of the dialogue, see Nails (2006b).

7. There are numerous parallels between himself and Socrates. There are significant disparities as well. Alcibiades is drunk. Alcohol does not affect Socrates. Alcibiades demands to see Agathon right away when he arrives. Socrates seems to be in no hurry to arrive at the party.

8. On the lover-beloved relationship, see Dover (1978) and Halperin (1990a). See also Brisson (2006), Hubbard (2003), Nussbaum and Sihvola (2002), and Winkler (1990).

9. Helfer (2017, 161) notes the narrative interruption calls attention to the importance of the moment.

10. See Reeve (2006, 131) and Edmonds (2017).

11. Helfer (2017, 171) sees this point as indicating that Socrates does still have some attachment to how others view him.

12. For a contrasting view, see Helfer (2017, 154) and Lutz (1998, 138).

13. On the nature of the joke, see Cotter (1992) and Hopkins (2011, 287).

14. On Socrates' role as narrator of the *Republic*, see Schultz (2013), Howland (2004, 2019), Rosen (2005), and Roochnik (2003). See also Moore (2018) and Altman (2012).

15. See Nussbaum (1986).

16. See Schultz (2013).

17. For another good account of the complexities of the narrative frame and prologue, see Giannopoulou (2017). Blondell's (2006, 147–151) "Ladder of Love" also offers good insights.

18. For an exploration of what Socrates might be doing in this moment, see Schultz and Carron (2013). See also Naddaff (2019) and Blondell (2006, 158).

19. For this view, see Blondell (2006, 149).

20. On the narrative structural complexities of this passage and the dialogue as a whole see Corrigan and Glazov-Corrigan (2004), Halperin (1992), and Rosen (1987).

21. On negative views of Aristodemus, see Frosolono (1993).

Chapter Four

Socratic Self-Disclosure in Plato's *Apology*

INTRODUCTION

The *Apology* present a compelling image of Socrates as a philosopher engaged in living the examined life and defending the purpose and value of that life to his fellow citizens. The dialogue takes place in Athens, in 399 BCE. Socrates faces charges of impiety and corrupting the youth. Plato constructs the *Apology* as a direct account of this event. I do not mean to assert that Plato constructs the *Apology* as a factual record of a historical event.[1] Rather, I call attention to the fact that Plato consciously writes the *Apology* as if it were a direct report of Socrates' own words and actions at the trial. Scholars have often observed the highly rhetorical nature of the dialogue. For example, Plato places it in conversation with other texts of the Greek philosophical and literary tradition.[2] James Barrett, for instance, underscores its affinities with Gorgias' *Defense of Palamedes*. Within this complex dialogue, scholars have also explored Plato's multifaceted portrait of Socrates. Ann Michelini calls Socrates the "paradigm exemplar of the scorned underestimated intellectual who turns the tables on his on adversaries" (2003, 57). Robert Metcalf (2009, 62–84) explores how Plato presents Socrates as an Achilles figure.[3] Jake Howland (2018, 89–100) considers how Socrates presents himself as Heracles. In this chapter, I draw attention to another aspect of Plato's construction of the image of Socrates in the *Apology* that has largely gone unnoticed. Just as he does in the *Theaetetus* and the *Symposium*, Plato presents Socrates as an autobiographer of his own life story throughout the *Apology*.

There are four autobiographical accounts that Plato's Socrates offers as part of his defense in the *Apology*.[4] The first autobiography, and the one most often commented on in the secondary literature, is Socrates' lengthy report of how he tests the Delphic oracle (*Ap.*, 21a–23a). Working in the order that they appear in the text, the next autobiographical moment occurs when Socrates describes his conflict with the Athenian Council concerning their attempt to try ten generals for war crimes en masse (*Ap.*, 32a–c). The third autobiographical reflection occurs almost immediately following. Socrates refers to his protest of the actions of the Thirty regarding the recall of Leon from Salamis (*Ap.*, 32c–33d). The fourth autobiographical narrative revolves around Socrates' account of the daimon, a divine voice that has spoken to him since childhood (*Ap.*, 32d–e). Each of these passages has, of course, received significant scholarly attention.[5] However, to my knowledge, they have not been explored together as part of Socrates' self-disclosive narrative practices. Regarding the passages in this way enhances our ability to embrace the Socratic injunction "to care more for the good than the things of themselves and the city" (*Ap.*, 29d) in the complexities of our contemporary American civic landscape.

This chapter unfolds in the following manner. First, I explore each of these autobiographical narratives on their own terms. I then suggest that Socrates consistently appropriates moments of his life story to illustrate how his philosophical commitments intertwine with his political commitments. These stories are an important part Socrates' ongoing commitment to exhort his fellow citizens to care about the good. Finally, I offer a preliminary sketch of how Socrates' presentation of his own story offers a model for public autobiographical self-disclosure.

INTERROGATING THE ORACLE

Socrates tells the jurors about the Delphic oracle's pronouncement as a way of explaining why he, and, by extension, the philosophy that he practices, has garnered such a bad reputation.[6] Socrates makes it clear that he is less concerned about the current charges he faces from "Anytus and his friends" (*Ap.*, 18b). Rather, he regards the earlier accusations about his wisdom as more pernicious. Socrates tells the jury, "[T]hey got hold of most of you from childhood, persuaded you and accused me quite falsely, saying that there is a man called Socrates, a wise man, a student of all things in the sky and below the earth, who makes the worse argument the stronger" (*Ap.*, 18b). Simply put, these older accusations paint him as a natural philosopher and a sophist. Socrates addresses the causes of these misperceptions (*Ap.*, 18d–20c). He blames Aristophanes' comedy for promulgating the image that he is a natural philosopher. He directly challenges the view that he charges a fee for teaching wisdom as the sophists do (*Ap.*, 20c).[7] Robert Metcalf notes that it is only after he dismisses the charges of the first accusers, "somewhat cursorily," (2004, 144) that Socrates presents the account of the oracle.

Socrates then imagines a hypothetical auditor asking him, "But Socrates, what is your occupation? From where have these slanders come? For surely if you did not busy yourself with something out of the common, all these rumors and talk would not have arisen unless you did something other than most people?" (*Ap.*, 20c). Much like he imagines a conversation with the Laws in the *Crito* (*Crt.*, 50a–54e), Socrates sets up the auditory context for the narrative he will tell. He imagines an engaged auditor that will listen to his narrative. Rather than answer this hypothetical auditor's questions, Socrates addresses the jurors sitting before him with the words "Listen then" (*Ap.*, 20d). With these words, Socrates turns the jurors into auditors for the narrative he is about to tell. Just as he regularly does in the dialogues he narrates, Socrates seems highly attuned to the auditors' mental and emotional states. Despite the fact that his own life is on trial, Socrates appears sympathetic to his audience. He imagines their mindset of doubt: "Perhaps some of you will think I am jesting, but be sure that all I shall say is true" (*Ap.*, 20d). Socrates attempts to assuage their apparent doubts about him, saying, "What has caused my reputation is none other than a certain kind of wisdom. What kind of wisdom? Human wisdom perhaps" (*Ap.*, 20d). Socrates allows that he may possess this sort of wisdom, but, if anyone claims he has any other sort of wisdom, "they are lying and speak to slander me" (*Ap.*, 20e). All of a sudden, there is a disturbance among the jurors. Socrates' remarks provoke an emotional response in the audience. We learn about this disturbance from Socrates himself when he tells them, "Do not create a disturbance, gentlemen" (*Ap.*, 20e). This address to the audience functions like many of the asides that Socrates makes to his auditors in the dialogues he narrates. Christopher Long explores the four references to audience disturbances. He writes, "In each of these four moments of injunction, we hear something of the idiosyncratic, provocative, and subversive dimensions of Socratic politics" (2014, 107). When Socrates switches to direct address, it often gives the auditor he is speaking to in the text (along with the contemporary reader) more information about what is going on at the dramatic level of the text.[8] Just when the audience's emotions are running high, Socrates offers his autobiographical account about his quest to understand the Delphic oracle's pronouncement on his wisdom. He offers his account to correct the false impressions that his fellow citizens have of him: "The story I shall tell does not originate with me, but I will refer you to a trustworthy source" (*Ap.*, 20e–21a). He also swears to the veracity of the narrative he is about to convey; "I shall call upon the god at Delphi as witness to the existence and nature of my wisdom" (*Ap.*, 21a).

Socrates begins, "You know Chaerephon. He was my friend from youth, and the friend of most of you, as he shared your exile and your return. You surely know the kind of man he was, how impulsive in any course of action"

(*Ap.*, 21a).⁹ Socrates offers us glimpses into Chaerephon's character in the Socratically narrated dialogue *Charmides*. Upon his return to the Athenian Palestra after a long battle at Potidaea, Socrates describes the enthusiastic welcome he receives: "I was immediately hailed at a distance by people coming up from all directions and Chaerephon, like the wild man he is, sprang up from the midst of a group of people and ran towards me and seizing me by the hand, exclaimed, 'Socrates, how did you come off in the battle?'" (*Char.*, 153b). Here, Socrates explains that Chaerephon went to the oracle and "ventured" (*Ap.*, 21a) to ask the question if anyone were wiser than Socrates. Just as Socrates begins this account, we learn that another uproar arises in the courtroom. Socrates addresses the jurors directly, much like he would address the auditor of his narratives.¹⁰ He tells them, " as I say, gentlemen, do not make a disturbance" (*Ap.*, 21a). After reporting the oracle's response, Socrates refers to Chaerephon's brother as a means of verifying his account because Chaerephon is dead. Why are the jurors responding in such emotional terms to Socrates' contextualization of the story he is about to tell? Socrates' reference to the exile under the Thirty and his reference to Chaerephon's death provide us with two clues.¹¹ Barry Strauss explains that when the Thirty began killing prodemocratic citizens, "those who survived financed an anti-oligarchic movement in the mountains outside Athens, with help from Sparta's rivals abroad. Within a year, the movement grew into an army. The democrats defeated the oligarchs in battle" (2013, 32). This is the battle in which Chaerephon loses his life. This happened only four short years before Socrates' trial. Socrates' remark challenges the current political peace by reminding them of how tenuous political self-governance is. No doubt, no one in the courtroom liked to be reminded of how recently democracy has been restored and the jurors would have been highly attuned to Socrates' reference in this context. On this point, Raaflaub notes, "Trained for decades in the skills of recognizing political allusions, the Athenians would have picked up hints of tyranny much more frequently and easily than we suspect" (2003, 72). In this highly charged context, Socrates proceeds to tell his autobiographical narrative. Socrates emphasizes that he is telling a story with the words "I am going to tell you" and with his reminder that this story is based on the account he heard from Chaerephon about the oracle's pronouncement.

Socrates relates his own response to the story that he has heard from Chaerephon about the oracle. Much like he does throughout the narrated dialogues, Socrates conveys his internal state of mind by focusing his questioning process: "When I heard of this reply I asked myself: 'Whatever does the god mean? What is his riddle? What then does he mean by saying that I am the wisest?'" (*Ap.*, 21b). Socrates underscores his awareness of his lack of wisdom—"I am very conscious that I am not wise at all" (*Ap.*, 21b)—and his aporetic state of mind: "For a long time I was at a loss as to his meaning"

(*Ap.*, 21b). Socrates describes how he moved away from this aporia: "I very reluctantly turned to some such investigation as this" (*Ap.*, 21b). He approaches someone with a reputation for wisdom, "one of our public men" (*Ap.*, 21c). Socrates explains his motivation for doing so, "thinking that there, if anywhere, I could refute the oracle" (*Ap.*, 21c). He reports: "I thought that he appeared wise to many people and especially to himself, but he was not. I then tried to show him that he thought himself wise, but that he was not" (*Ap.*, 21d). Socrates is keenly aware that his inquiry causes a negative emotional response in his community. Socrates reports the result of his investigation, "he came to dislike me, and so did many of the bystanders" (*Ap.*, 21d). Socrates describes his thought process in some detail.

> So I withdrew and thought to myself, "I am wiser than this man; it is likely that neither of us knows anything worthwhile, but he thinks he knows something when he does not, whereas when I do not know, neither do I think I know so I am likely to be wiser than he to this small extent, that I do not think I know what I do not know." After this I approached another man, one of those thought to be wiser than he, and I thought the same thing, and so I came to be disliked both by him and by many others. (*Ap.*, 21d–e)

Eventually, Socrates emerges from this aporetic state and recovers from his despair over how his fellow citizens dislike him. Some might be tempted to dismiss or discount Socrates' level of suffering. Perhaps Socrates is being ironic and is not really concerned by how people view him. However, I think Socrates is being sincere. He is conveying the depth of his commitment to the city and its citizens. Remember that Socrates is much younger at the time he is recounting, and he is trying to portray the perspective of his younger self to them. He might have been much more affected by the hostility of his fellow citizens. Nonetheless, he proceeds. Furthermore, even at the time of the trial, it is reasonable to think that Socrates still regards his fellow citizens as potential interlocutors with whom he attempts to engage philosophically. This desire depends on a certain level of friendly feeling on his part. Also, based on how Plato portrays Socrates' narrative activity in other dialogues, Socrates does generally narrate to people he is on friendly terms with. This practice of narrating stories about himself to friends suggests that even at the time of his trial he felt some friendship toward his fellow citizens.

Socrates describes how his investigation affected his reputation: "I realized to my sorrow and alarm that I was getting unpopular" (*Ap.*, 21e) and emphasizes how this decline in reputation affected him. Despite the emotional upheaval he experiences, despite his sorrow and despite his alarm, Socrates proceeds with the investigation: "I thought that I must attach the greatest importance to the god's oracle so I must go to all those who had any reputation for knowledge to examine its meaning" (*Ap.*, 22a). Robert Metcalf (2004, 145) suggests that Socrates presents himself as a passive recipient of both the oracle's command and how he receives the effects of the interrogation. While I agree that Socrates presents himself passively, in retelling these events at his trial, Socrates becomes an active participant in his own story. Even if as a character in his narrative, he was a passive actor, qua teller of his own story, he is active. Also, though Socrates was passive in the sense of being acted on by the oracle, even within the confines of the story he tells, Socrates does the interrogating of his fellow citizens. Having questioned the politicians and finding them lacking in wisdom, Socrates calls attention to the fact that he turns to an investigation of the poets by directly addressing the jurors as "gentlemen" and by claiming to report "the truth." According to Socrates, the poets "are like seers and prophets who also say many fine things without any understanding of what they say" (*Ap.*, 22c). Socrates attests that they thought they were wise men in other respects, which they were not. He reports: "So there again I withdrew, thinking that I had the same advantage over them as I had over the politicians" (*Ap.*, 22e). Socrates' inquiry into finding wisdom in the public sphere might strike people as odd. Why would he expect to find wisdom here? He may well not expect to find any. Nonetheless, he engages in this public inquiry to test the oracle's pronouncement that no one is wiser than Socrates.

Socrates turns to the craftsmen. As he recounts this part of the story, Socrates emphasizes his thought process, his aporia, and his emotional states: "I was conscious of knowing practically nothing, and I knew that I would find that they had knowledge of many fine things" (*Ap.*, 22d). Socrates finds some satisfaction with the craftsmen: "They knew things I did not know, and to that extent they were wiser than I" (*Ap.*, 22d). Again, he addresses the jury directly as he concludes, "The good craftsmen seemed to me to have the same fault as the poets. This error of theirs overshadowed the wisdom they had" (*Ap.*, 22e). Socrates relates his response to this insight: "So I asked myself, on behalf of the oracle, whether I should prefer to be as I am, with neither their wisdom nor their ignorance or to have both. The answer I gave myself and the oracle was that it was to my advantage to be as I am" (*Ap.*, 22e). Socrates eloquently describes his emotional response to this process. He laments: "I acquired much unpopularity of a kind that is hard to deal with and is a heavy burden" (*Ap.*, 23a).[12] Misunderstanding and slander follow. Not only does the story about the oracle offer explanation of the hatred he incurred, but it also demonstrates his piety in that he continues his quest to understand the oracle's meaning despite the consequences.

Socrates alludes to his allegiance to the divine as he ends this account. Socrates offers his conclusion about what he learned as student of the oracle: "What is probable, gentlemen, is that in fact the god is wise and that his oracular response meant that human wisdom is worth little or nothing" (*Ap.*, 23a). Socrates uses this story to help the jurors see why he has lived his life in the way that he has. He is still a student of the oracle. He tells them, "So even now I continue this investigation as the god bade me and I go around seeking out anyone, citizen or stranger, who I think wise. Then if I do not think he is, I come to the assistance of the god and show him that he is not wise" (*Ap.*, 23b). Socrates acknowledges that his autobiographical disclosure will not have its intended effect (*Ap.*, 24a). Nonetheless, he presents this image of himself to the jurors. Socrates ends this first autobiographical reflection about his engagement with the oracle saying, "Let this suffice as a defense against the charges of my earlier accusers" (*Ap.*, 24b). That Socrates goes to such lengths to describe his actions with respect to understanding the oracle may not simply be part of his defense strategy. It suggests that Socrates regards the autobiographical retelling itself as an important part of the Delphic injunction to know one's self. As William Altman notes, "Particularly in narrating his response to the oracle, Socrates makes us privy to his private thoughts, and the passage that begins 'What is the God saying, and what is he riddling?' (*Ap.*, 21b3–4), should be understood as a narrated inner dialogue, thus giving unparalleled access to the mind of Plato's Philosopher" (2016b, 525). Socrates gives the jurors access to the inner workings of his mind at several other junctures in the *Apology* as well. I turn to those now.

TWO MOMENTS OF CONFLICT WITH THE CITY

The next autobiographical moment occurs when Socrates describes his time as a member of the Council.

> I have never held any other office in the city, but I served as a member of the Council, and our tribe Antiochis was presiding at the time when you wanted to try as a body the ten generals who had failed to pick up the survivors of the naval battle. This was illegal, as you all recognized later. I was the only member of the presiding committee to oppose your doing something contrary to the laws, and I voted against it. The orators were ready to prosecute me and take me away, and your shouts were egging them on, but I thought I should run any risk on the side of law and justice rather than join you for fear of prison or death, when you were engaged in an unjust course. (*Ap.*, 32b–c)

Scholars often refer to this passage as a way of showing how Socrates' philosophical practice puts him in conflict with the political rule of the city.[13] It is not generally regarded as an autobiographical account in the way that the account of the oracle is. However, when we examine this brief passage in autobiographical terms, it enhances our ability to connect it to the Delphic account. It also shows that Socrates did engage in the political affairs of his democratic city. Although this story is highly compressed, it shares many of the features of the narrative that he tells about his encounter with the oracle. First, it illustrates Socrates' philosophical activity, putting him in conflict with the city. Second, it refers to Socrates' internal states and moral commitments. He describes own actions and internal deliberations. Third, it is directly told to the jurors as a story about his past, just as the story of the oracle is. Fourth, we see the pedagogical intent of the autobiographical disclosure. Socrates tells this story about his own life to remind the city of its collective moral failings.

Because this narrative is so concise, one might not even recognize it as a moment of self-disclosive speech. As he reports this moment from his life, Socrates draws upon the implicit knowledge of the jurors to fill out the overall storyline. Socrates places this story in a particular temporal context. It occurs in 406 BCE, seven years before Socrates' trial. Although Socrates lives the majority of his life without engaging in public political practice, this moment aligns with his overall mission to exhort people to care for justice more than the material comforts of the world and the demands of political expediency. Barry Strauss notes, "Although the Athenian assembly generally behaved in a responsible and law-abiding manner, even in its adolescent period, it fumbled egregiously from time to time" (2013, 31). Socrates refers to one of these egregious moments where the assembly did not provide the generals with their legal right to have an individual trial. This moment of Socratic autobiography reflects the very situation he now finds himself in—again at odds with the city. By recounting this short moment from his life, Socrates suggests to the jurors that law and justice are on his side, not theirs.

As I mentioned earlier, scholars often seize on Socrates' conflict with the democratic regime as an indication of Socrates' and Plato's anti-democratic feelings. However, Socrates also runs into conflict with the city when it is ruled by the Thirty.[14]

> When the oligarchy was established, the Thirty summoned me to the hall, along with four others, and ordered us to bring Leon from Salamis, that he might be executed. They gave many such orders to many people, in order to implicate as many as possible in their guilt. Then I showed again, not in words but in action, that if it were not rather vulgar to say so, death is something I couldn't care less about, but that my whole concern is not to do anything unjust or impious. The government, powerful as it was, did not frighten me into any wrongdoing. When we left the Hall, the other four went to Salamis and brought in Leon, but I went home. I might have been put to death for this, had not the government fallen shortly afterwards. There are many who will witness to these events. (*Ap.*, 32c–e)

Socrates places this story in a particular temporal moment, 404 BCE, when the reign of the Thirty was established. Barry Strauss describes the Thirty in this way: "In 404 BCE, Athens lost the war and Sparta made common ground with Athenian oligarchs. Together they imposed on Athens a new and more narrowly-based oligarchy led by only thirty men, and so known as 'The Thirty.' The regime began to kill prominent, wealthy pro-democrats in Athens" (2013, 32). Socrates' story emphasizes how the Thirty operated by ordering people to participate in their injustices.

In the *Hellenica*, Xenophon mentions the death of Leon as well: "Leon of Salamis, a man of high and well-deserved reputation, was put to death, though he had not committed the shadow of a crime" (Book II, 3, 39). As in the preceding autobiographical accounts, Socrates presents his words and deeds in contrast to the general citizenship of Athens. Socrates here emphasizes his *action* of protest more than his *words* of protest. He notes, "My whole concern is not to do anything unjust or impious" (*Ap.*, 32e). Peter Krentz also points out that Socrates' protest was perhaps not as robust as one might hope. For instance, "He did not try to prevent others from arresting Leon, nor did he endeavor to warn Leon himself. He went home" (1982, 83). Socrates' main concern seems to be his own actions more than the unjust actions of the regime. Nonetheless, Krentz asserts that "Socrates must have been unusual in opposing the government even this much" (1982, 83). As he does in the story of testing the Delphic oracle, Socrates mentions his emotional states here. He is "not frightened" (*Ap.*, 32d). He also notes his awareness that his actions came with great potential risk. Indeed, he mentions the possibility of his own death but notes that he is unconcerned about death (*Ap.*, 32d). Instead, his "whole concern is not to do anything unjust or impious" (*Ap.*, 32d). Like his previous reference to the Thirty, this self-disclosive moment emphasizes the tenuousness of political power. That Plato and Adeimantus are mentioned here in support of Socrates would call attention to Glaucon's death in support of the Thirty in the minds of the jurors. By underscoring the shift of political power in Athens, Socrates suggests that he upholds a view of justice that is independent of the particular political regime that may hold power at any particular time.

SOCRATES AND THE DAIMON

Socrates mentions the daimon just after he has told these two stories about his antagonism with the governmental regimes of Athens. Socrates attempts to explain why he has continued to follow the philosophical path that he started when interrogating the oracle. In doing so, he offers a brief account of his inner life by describing his daimon.

> I have a divine or spiritual sign. This began when I was a child. It is a voice, and whenever it speaks it turns me away from something I am about to do, but it never encourages me to do anything. This is what has prevented me from taking part in public affairs and I think it was quite right to prevent me. (*Ap.*, 32d–e)

While he does not offer an exhaustive narrative account of the role that the daimon plays in his life as he did when describing how he tested the Delphic oracle, it is, nonetheless, a striking moment of Socratic self-disclosure. It is striking how much he insists that the philosophical practice is a private matter and yet he practices it in public. The literature on Socrates' daimon is vast, but it generally overlooks the fact that we often learn about Socrates' encounter with the daimon in moments of self-report such as this. Consider the *Euthydemus*, where Socrates tells Crito that his daimon kept him from leaving the wrestling room, and, as a result, he stayed for a lengthy conversation with Euthydemus and Dionysodorus.[15] We depend on Socrates' narrative accounting of his own inner experience to know how the daimon affects him.[16] Socrates uses his experiences with the daimon to shape the public conception of his commitment to philosophy. He tells this final narrative about himself to show the Athenians who he really is. As he does in the two accounts about his discord with the governmental regimes of Athens, Socrates places his encounters with the daimon in a temporal context. This is something that has happened to him since childhood. The daimon's silence has power, just as the cryptic Delphic utterance does. Socrates interprets it as a justification to act in the way he does. Naddaff writes, "The daimonion thus forces Socrates to enter into a spiritual relationship with himself and with the city. Attending to silence, Socrates cares for himself and creates a new form of philosophy discourse and legal-political practice" (2019, 58). Through these moments of self-disclosure, Socrates offers what Claudia Barachi calls "a reflection on the task and danger of the philosophical endeavor—indeed of the philosophical life" (2006, 269).

Surely it is not a rhetorical accident that the autobiographical dimensions of the *Apology* are so pronounced. Plato's Socrates shares these four moments of his life to illustrate how he carried out the oracles' command. The process of self-knowledge simply could be regarded as a private interior task. However, Socrates crystalizes his own moral and philosophical identity by telling tales about himself in the public sphere. While these practices can be private, Socrates' autobiographical self-disclosure at his trial brings out the public dimensions of living the examined life. The autobiographical dimensions of Socrates' work give voice to the work of the philosopher in the public sphere. Socrates' narrative self-disclosure also becomes another means, besides the elenchus, by which he interrogates others. Like the *Apology* itself, Socratic autobiography should provoke us into philosophical reflection and beyond that into the public expression of our private philosophical lives. As such, Socratic autobiography presents us with a model of how we might practice public philosophy. Socratic autobiography should provoke us to tell our individual story of philosophy in our own lives. It should compel all of us to transform the public sphere through sustained philosophical self-reflection. In *Plato's Philosophers*, Zuckert upholds a strong distinction between Socrates' private work, exhibited in dialogues like the *Phaedo*, and Socrates' public work. In the public sphere, Zuckert sees Socrates as stimulating the Athenians to become good by giving them a new version of their own collective history. Zuckert writes, "A philosopher might shape public opinion by offering his fellow citizens a just account of their own history" (2009, 816).

The autobiographical dimensions of the *Apology* offer us a way to bridge this strong distinction between public and private. Through his self-disclosive practices, Socrates makes the private discourse of philosophy a public practice of edification. Socrates shows the juror how he became who he is.[17] He leaves a pedagogical trail for others who wish to follow this path and develop their own inner resources just as Socrates developed his. The audience might well expect him to talk about his own political formation and influences—to argue that he's been shaped by the community into the person who he has become, as a means to exonerate himself. But when he brings his story to the people, he recreates his own philosophical formation for them. His autobiography is a counter story, against the stories being told against him.[18] Of course, the *Apology* is an exceptional dialogue. After all, most of the time, we are not on trial for our philosophical practices. We would do well not to model our practices on this dialogue alone. We should take these examples and put them alongside the moments of Socratic self-disclosure in the *Theaetetus*, the *Symposium*, and the *Phaedo* as well as the five dialogues that Socrates narrates as we decide how to craft our own philosophical stories in the public sphere.

NOTES

1. On the historicity of the trial, see Colaiaco (2013) and Guthrie (1965).
2. See Michelini (2003) and Barrett (2001).
3. Barrett also notes affinities with Achilles as does Angela Hobbs (2000).
4. All references to the *Apology* are from Cooper (1997a).
5. The literature on the *Apology* is immense. See Brickhouse and Smith (2002) for a standard overview of the issues. See also Nails (2006a). The entire *Companion to Socrates* is an invaluable resource. I find the following sources particularly helpful: Altman (2016b), Fagan and Russon (2009), and Leibowitz (2010).
6. For a good overview of the issues involved with Socrates and his daimon, see Bussanich (2006). I find the following sources most helpful for my own thinking. See also Brickhouse and Smith (1983), Colaiaco (2013), Corey (2005), Leibowitz (2010), Dorion (2012), Howland (1998), Lara (2007), and Ranasinghe (2012).
7. That Socrates is regularly taken to be a sophist by the Athenian populace is clear in a number of dialogues, most especially the opening of the *Protagoras* and the end of the *Euthydemus*. David Corey (2015) explores the relationship between Socrates and the sophists at length in *The Sophists in Plato's Dialogues*. See also Gagarin (1969) and Thomas Chance (1992).
8. Examples of this narrative interruption occur throughout the Socratically narrated dialogues. See Schultz (2013).
9. On the historical Chaerephon, see Nails (2002, 86–87).

10. See Schultz (2013).

11. On the Thirty, see Krentz (1982). On tyranny in the Classical Greek world in general, see Morgan (2003b). On Athens specifically, see Kurt Raaflaub (2003). See also Kasimis (2018).

12. He mentions his unpopularity again (*Ap.*, 28b).

13. See Nussbaum (1997).

14. See Bowery and Beaty (2003).

15. See Schultz (2013).

16. See Schultz and Carron (2013).

17. See Lampert (2013).

18. Thank you to Sabrina Little for helping me draw out the implications of this observation.

Chapter Five

Socratic Self-Disclosure in Plato's *Phaedo*

Plato's *Phaedo* offers an inspirational account of Socrates' final hours. On the day that Socrates must drink the poison hemlock, his companions "foregathered at daybreak at the court where the trial took place" (*Phd.*, 59d). As they pass the time of this last day together, Socrates responds to several challenging objections raised by Simmias and Cebes with respect to Socrates' apparently unwavering belief in the immortality of the soul. Even in the face of his own death, by and large, Socrates seems unafraid of whatever fate awaits him. His countenance in the face of death offers a profound model of what it means "to die well."[1] In addition to being one of Plato's most emotionally resonant dialogues, the *Phaedo* is also one of his most intricately crafted narrative works. It begins with a conversation between Echecrates and Phaedo (*Phd.*, 57a–59d). Phaedo is visiting Echecrates and the others in the town of Phlius. Echecrates laments that they have heard little from Athens lately (*Phd.*, 57b). We learn of the events of Socrates' death through Phaedo's evocative recounting of them to this group of eager Pythagorean listeners. In this way, the narrative structure of the *Phaedo* is not that different from the *Symposium* where we learn of Socrates' activities through the narrative filter of others. As I did in the exploration of the *Symposium* in chapter 2, I focus on how the character Socrates uses self-disclosive speech and autobiographical narrative within the reported events of this dialogue. This chapter unfolds in the following manner. First, I focus on several important moments of Socratic self-disclosure near the beginning of his conversations in the prison cell. I consider Socrates' reinterpretation of his ongoing dreams that have commanded him to make and practice music. The result is that he sets Aesop and the Homeric hymns to verse (*Phd.*, 60b–61b). I also examine his reference to being like Apollo's swans (*Phd.*, 84d–85b) and his self-disclosive remark that he is in danger of not having a philosophical attitude in the face of death (*Phd.*, 91a–c). Second, I turn to the famous "second sailing" passage where Socrates tells his intellectual autobiography about his encounters with Anaxagoras' writings, his subsequent disillusionment with them, and his turn away from natural philosophy to the development of his own linguistic mode of inquiry into the fundamental nature of reality (*Phd.*, 96a–100a). Third, I suggest that Socrates may be presenting a different understanding of immortality through his autobiographical self-disclosure that is aimed not at personal glory but at communal obligation. His self-disclosive speech and autobiographical narrative help create a new communal space for future philosophical dialogue. Fourth, I examine Phaedo's narrative retelling of the events of Socrates' last day as an example of using self-disclosive speech to create philosophical community. Finally, I offer an autobiographical reflection about my mother's recent passing and how the *Phaedo* shaped my experience of it.

THREE MOMENTS OF SOCRATIC SELF-DISCLOSURE: AESOP, THE SWANS, AND FEAR OF DEATH

Although the most extended example of autobiographical discourse in the *Phaedo* is the story that Socrates tells about how he becomes disillusioned with Anaxagoras' conception of nous (*Phd.*, 96a–100a), there are other important moments of Socratic self-disclosure in the *Phaedo*.[2] The first occurs early in Phaedo's report of the events surrounding Socrates' death. Socrates shares his reinterpretation of his ongoing dreams that have commanded him to "practice and cultivate the arts" (*Phd.*, 60b–61b). After Phaedo reports how they gathered early on the morning after the ship returned from Delos, he describes how Xanthippe responds to their appearance in the prison for their last day with Socrates. He makes note of her mournful departure after Socrates' insistence that Crito's people take her away.[3] Phaedo then reports how Socrates describes his current situation. As Socrates rubs his leg, he talks about the strange interrelationship between pleasure and pain.

> What a strange thing, my friends, that which men call pleasure. How astonishing the relation it has to what is thought to be its opposite, namely pain! A man cannot have both at the same time. Yet if he pursues and catches the one, he is almost always bound to catch the other also, like two creates with one head. I think, if Aesop had noted this, he would have composed a fable that a god wished to reconcile their opposition but could not do so, so he joined their two heads together, and therefore when a man has the one, the other follows later. (*Phd.*, 60b–c)

He concludes this observation about the interrelationship of opposites by making clear that he is describing his own current situation. Socrates links this hypothetical fable to his own experience: "This seems to be happening to me. My bonds caused pain in my leg, and now pleasure seems to be following" (*Phd.*, 60c). Kathryn Morgan calls this passage "an Aesop-like mythos on the mutual dependence of pleasure and pain" (2000, 192).[4] Morgan also notes an autobiographical parallel between Aesop and Socrates: "We might remember also that Aesop was lynched by a mob of outraged Delphians who disliked his particular way of interacting with their community" (2000, 193n18). This moment of self-disclosure causes Cebes to ask for even more details about Socrates' personal experience. Cebes asks about the poems and hymns that Socrates has been composing. Phaedo characterizes Cebes' questioning as "intervening" (*Phd.*, 60c) or as an interrupting. Cebes exclaims, "By Zeus, Socrates, you did well to remind me. Evenus asked me the day before yesterday, as others had done before, what induced you to write poetry after you came to prison, you who had never composed any poetry before, putting the fables of Aesop into verse and composing the hymn to Apollo" (*Phd.*, 60d). By characterizing Cebes' question as an interruption, Phaedo intimates to his audience that Socrates was getting ready to reveal more about his current mental and emotional state before Cebes asked him about Evenus' question.

It is interesting to note that Socrates' activities in the prison appear to be well known even by those who have not been visiting him regularly. This suggests that the people who meet with Socrates each day have been talking to others about what they are experiencing and observing in the prison. Evenus probably heard about Socrates' practice from Cebes, for example. However, Evenus is confused by what he hears about Socrates' newfound poetic practices. Cebes, in turn, asked Socrates for clarification that he might share with Evenus in turn. Cebes goes to the Socratic source just as Apollodorus did when he checks Aristodemus' account with Socrates (*Symp.*, 173b). Cebes implores Socrates, "If it is of any concern to you that I should have an answer to give Evenus when he repeats his question, as I know he will, tell me what to say to him" (*Phd.*, 60d). Cebes wants to understand why Socrates engages in this activity. Perhaps he wants to have the authority to tell his own story of Socrates' last days just as Phaedo does by narrating the account of Socrates' final days to Echecrates and the others in Phlius.

As Socrates responds to Cebes, he begins to reveal his motivation for his poetical turn: "Tell him the truth, Cebes, that I did not do this with the idea of rivalling him or his poems, for I knew that would not be easy" (*Phd.*, 60d). At this point, Socrates explains his motivation in more detail, "Because I wanted to find out the meaning of certain dreams, and to satisfy my conscience in case it was this kind of art they were frequently bidding me to practice" (*Phd.*, 60d). Socrates' remarks here describe another second sailing, like the one Socrates will describe later (*Phd.*, 96a–100a). Socrates makes clear that he is willing to reassess his lifelong understanding of what it means to practice philosophy by composing poetry. Much like he is willing to question the meaning of the oracle's pronouncement in the *Apology*, he interrogates his own interpretation of his dreams.

Socrates continues with this self-disclosure: "The dreams were something like this: The same dream often came to me in the past, now in one shape now in another, but saying the same thing: 'Socrates,' it said, 'practice and cultivate the arts'" (*Phd.*, 60e). Socrates explains how he reevaluates his thinking to Cebes and the others. He describes his reasoning process, "In the past I imagined that it was instructing and advising me to do what I was doing, such as those who encourage runners in a race, that the dream was thus bidding me to do the very thing I was doing, namely, to practice the art of philosophy, this being the highest kind of art, and I was doing that" (*Phd.*, 61a). Socrates describes his previous willingness to listen to the ongoing commands of the dreams. Indeed, Socrates structures his life around the command of the dreams. However, now Socrates is willing to reconsider his lifelong understanding. He acknowledges that the dreams may be saying something else. He chooses to listen to their command differently, so much so that he changes his actions accordingly (*Phd.*, 60d).[5] On this point, Christopher Long notes, "Already here in his first response to Kebes, Socrates demonstrates a willingness to call even his deepest convictions, the very convictions for which he was condemned to die, into question" (2014, 74). Socrates reassesses his total life work: "But now, after my trial took place, and the festival of the god was preventing my execution, I thought that in case my dream was bidding me to practice this popular art, I should not disobey it but compose poetry" (*Phd.*, 61b). Socrates emphasizes his own state of mind during this process of reevaluation. He explains, "I thought it was safer not to leave here until I had satisfied my conscience by writing poems in obedience to the dream" (*Phd.*, 61b). Socrates describes his new plan of action: "So first I wrote in honor of the god of the present festival. After that I realized that a poet, if he is to be a poet, must compose fables not arguments" (*Phd.*, 61b). Socrates claims that he is "not a teller of fables," so he turns to the fables of Aesop and puts them into verse (*Phd.*, 61b). Though Socrates does not tell fables, he does tell a different kind of story. Socrates tells the story of his own experience in reinterpreting his dreams. He offers philosophical self-disclosure and reflection on his experience in addition to his new poetic recreations of Aesop. He ends this evocative moment of self-disclosure by telling Cebes to bid Evenus farewell and to follow as quickly as he can (*Phd.*, 61b).

Simmias and Cebes respond to this exhortation to Evenus by asking why it is wrong to take one's own life, and Socrates asserts that we are possessions of the gods and that it would be wrong to leave a good master before the master desires it (*Phd.*, 62a–62e). Simmias and Cebes both challenge his reasoning (*Phd.*, 62e). In response, Socrates says, "Let me try to make my defense to you more convincing than it was to the jury" (*Phd.*, 63c). As he begins to make his case, Socrates explains his reasoning process to them. He gives Simmias, Cebes, and the others access to his inner state of mind, both his reasoning and the variety of emotions he feels at the prospect of going to his death. He begins by explaining his reasoning process: "I should be wrong not to resent dying if I did not believe that I should go first to the other wise and good gods" (*Phd.*, 63c). He continues, "I expect to join the company of good men" (*Phd.*, 63c). Socrates also emphasizes his belief "that I shall come to gods who are very good masters" (*Phd.*, 63c). Socrates then includes his emotional state at the prospect of joining these good masters: "I am not so resentful, because I have good hope that some future awaits men after death" (*Phd.*, 63c). At this point, Simmias asks Socrates to share his belief with them. Before Socrates responds, he calls their attention to the fact that Crito has been trying to get his attention for some time. Crito relays the warning that the person administering the poison has conveyed. They should not talk too long because talking will heat the body. If that happens, the poison may need to be administered "two or three times" (*Phd.*, 63e). Socrates tells Crito: "Take no notice of him; only let him be prepared to administer it twice, or if necessary three times" (*Phd.*, 63e).

After this brief exchange with Crito, Socrates continues with his defense. He even calls those gathered around him "my judges" (*Phd.*, 63e). The direct references to the trial here and also the preceding one (*Phd.*, 63c) are interesting to consider in light of Socrates' self-disclosive practices. Just as he does in the *Apology*, Socrates reveals his inner state of mind and his emotional states to his audience in his attempts to justify his life of philosophy. He continues his defense, "I want to make my argument before you, my judges, as to why I think that a man who has truly spent his life in philosophy is probably right to be of good cheer in the face of death and to be very hopeful that after death he will attain the greatest blessings yonder" (*Phd.*, 64a). He addresses Simmias and Cebes directly then continues with his reasoning, "I am afraid that other people do not realize that the one aim of those who practice philosophy in the proper manner is to practice for dying and death. Now if this is true it would be strange indeed if they were eager for this all their lives and then resent it when what they have wanted and practiced for a long time comes upon them" (*Phd.*, 64a). Socrates' reasoning is filled with references to emotional states: fear, eagerness, resentment, desire. The emotional aspects of Socrates' remarks have an emotional effect on Simmias. Simmias laughs and then discloses his own inner state, "By Zeus, Socrates, you made me laugh though I was in no laughing mood just now" (*Phd.*, 64b). Simmias explains why he thinks Socrates' remark was so humorous: "I think the majority, on hearing this will think that it describes the philosophers very well, and our people in Thebes would thoroughly agree that philosophers are nearly dead and that the majority of men is well aware that they deserve to be" (*Phd.*, 64b). Socrates tells Simmias not to worry about what other things and leads them to "talk amongst ourselves" (*Phd.*, 64c). Christopher Long characterizes the importance of this moment nicely. He writes, "Socrates performs the central political act of the dialogue: to create a community of friends animated by a healthy erotic relationship to truth in the wake of the ineluctable finitude that conditions all human life" (2014, 78).

Socrates begins to lead them through a consideration of death being a separation of the soul from the body (*Phd.*, 64d–69e). Throughout this passage, Socrates shares his reasoning processes, his beliefs, and his emotional states. For example, he refers to his "love of learning" (*Phd.*, 67b) and his "good hope that on arriving where I am going, if anywhere, I shall acquire what has been our chief preoccupation in our past life, so that the journey that is now ordered for me is full of good hope (*Phd.*, 67c). He also reminds Simmias, "As I said at the beginning, it would be ridiculous for a man to train himself in life to live in a state as close to death as possible, then to resent it when it comes" (*Phd.*, 67d). Socrates goes on to emphasize the importance of living in true virtue, having moderation and courage in order to become purified for the next life: "he who arrives purified and initiated will dwell with the gods" (*Phd.*, 69b). Indeed, Socrates describes Bacchant initiates as those who have practiced philosophy correctly. He concludes this next stage of his defense, saying, "I have in my life left nothing undone in order to be counted among these as far as possible, as I have been eager to be in every way. Whether my eagerness was right and we accomplished anything we shall, I think know for certain in a short time, god willing, on arriving yonder" (*Phd.*, 69e). Despite Socrates' enthusiastic good hope, Cebes remains unconvinced and they have a long conversation about whether or not the soul has existence after the body or whether it will be scattered like the wind (*Phd.*, 70a–84b). Throughout this passage, Socrates emphasizes the importance of being a philosopher and a lover of learning. He explains, "this is how the soul of the philosopher would reason; it would not think that while philosophy must free it, it should while being freed surrender itself to pleasures and pains and imprison itself again, thus laboring in vain like Penelope at her web." He explains further, "The soul of the philosopher achieves a calm from such emotions; it follows reasons and ever stays with it contemplating the true, the divine, which is not the object of opinion" (*Phd.*, 84b). Socrates describes the philosopher as being "nurtured" by this path and that nurturing overcomes the fear that the soul will scatter after death" (*Phd.*, 84b).

At this point, Phaedo's narrative voice intervenes and reports that there was a long silence except for Simmias and Cebes "whispering to each other" (*Phd.*, 84c). They continue to express doubt, but they do not want to disturb

Socrates on their final day. Socrates "laughs quietly" (*Phd.*, 84e), and again emphasizes that he is untroubled by his present state. Socrates now compares himself to Apollo's swans.[6] He challenges Simmias, "You seem to think me inferior to the swans in prophecy" (*Phd.*, 85a). He explains how the swans sing at the moment of their death: "They sing before too, but when they realize that they must die they sing most and most beautifully, as they rejoice that they are about to depart to join the god whose servants they are" (*Phd.*, 85a). Socrates explains that humans project their own fear of death onto the swans and do not understand the nature of their singing. Socrates explains what he believes about the swans, "As they belong to Apollo, they are prophetic, have knowledge of the future and sing of the blessings of the underworld, sing and rejoice on that day beyond what they did before" (*Phd.*, 85b). Socrates goes on to compare himself to the swans, "I believe myself to be a fellow servant with the swans and dedicated to the same god, and have received from my master a gift of prophecy not inferior to theirs, I am no more despondent than they on leaving life" (*Phd.*, 85b). Kathryn Morgan links this compassion to the swans with Socrates' earlier explanation of his appropriation of Aesop's fables. She writes, "As Apollo's philosophical swan who sings that this life is a prelude to a disincarnate afterlife and who speculates on transmigration into and out of animal bodies, he recomposes his prelude to Apollo and his Aesopic mythoi as the dialogue progresses" (Morgan 2000, 196). She notes further that Socrates implies that he spins out the myth for the sake of its emotional force" (Morgan 2000, 201). But Morgan also notes that he fails to persuade Cebes and Simmias, but at least he manages to convince them to continue voicing their philosophical difficulties with Socrates' good hope in the face of death (*Phd.*, 85c).

Simmias and Cebes then offer objections of their own. Simmias raises questions about what he views as Socrates' harmony model of understanding the relationship between the soul and the body (*Phd.*, 85c–86d). Socrates acknowledges his concerns are fair and asks Cebes to articulate his objection that the soul eventually will wither away much like a cloak that is no longer in use (*Phd.*, 87b–88c). Socrates warns all of them about the dangers of misology and misanthropy, telling them, "We should not allow into our minds the conviction that argumentation has nothing sound about it; much rather we should believe that it is we who are not yet sound and we must take courage and be eager to attain soundness, you and the others for the sake of your whole life still to come and I for the same of death itself" (*Phd.*, 91a). At this point, Socrates discloses his own fears about the value of argument in the face of death. He remarks, "I am in danger at this moment of not having a philosophical attitude about this, but like those who are quite uneducated, I am eager to get the better of you in argument, for the uneducated, when they engage in argument about anything, give no thought to the truth about the subject of discussion but are only eager that those present will accept the position they have set forth" (*Phd.*, 91b). It is not so much that Socrates is fearing death, but he is fearing the temptation of argument and his own desire to convince them through persuasive means rather than truthful content. Despite his concerns, Socrates tells Simmias and Cebes that he is willing to address their concerns: "Thus prepared, Simmias and Cebes, I come to deal with your argument. If you will take my advice, you will give but little thought to Socrates but much more to the truth. If you think that what I say is true, agree with me; if not, oppose it with every argument and take care that in my eagerness I do not deceive myself and you and, like a bee, leaving my sting in you when I go" (*Phd.*, 91c). Jill Gordon offers insight into Socrates' motivation to continue helping Simmias and Cebes. She writes, Socrates' cure for the anxiety of the interlocutors amounts to an admonition never to tire of the pursuit of an argument and, furthermore, when philosophy fails, never to blame the argument, but to see the failing in ourselves" (1999, 145).

SOCRATES' SECOND SAILING

On Socrates' last day, as Phaedo tells the story, those present discuss several arguments for the immortality of the soul; all are philosophically problematic. They discuss a promising view, the harmony model, at length (*Phd.*, 86a–95a). However, just before Socrates offers his extended autobiographical account about how he moves from natural philosophy to his own method, the harmony model is abandoned as well. Socrates tells Simmias, "my good friend, it is quite wrong for us to say that the soul is a harmony, and in saying so we would disagree both with the divine poet Homer and with ourselves" (*Phd.*, 95a).[7] Socrates distills the essence of Simmias' and Cebes' concern about the fate of the soul (*Phd.*, 95b–e). That the soul has endured many incarnations does not suffice: "It makes no difference whether it enters a body once or many times as far as the fate of each of us is concerned" (*Phd.*, 95d). If we cannot prove the soul immortal, there is good reason to fear death. He challenges Cebes. "This I think is what you maintain, Cebes: I deliberately repeat it often, in order that no point may escape us, and that you may add or subtract something if you wish" (*Phd.*, 95d). Cebes affirms that he wishes to add or subtract nothing.[8]

At this juncture, Phaedo's narrative voice breaks in. He recounts this poignant moment, "Socrates paused for a long time, deep in thought" (*Phd.*, 96a). After this long silence, Socrates continues, "This is no unimportant problem that you raise, Cebes, for it requires a thorough investigation of the cause of generation and destruction" (*Phd.*, 96a). At this aporetic impasse, Socrates offers his autobiographical account, "I will, if you wish, give you an account of my experiences in these matters" (*Phd.*, 96a). Socrates begins, "When I was a young man, I was wonderfully keen on that wisdom which they call natural science, for I thought it splendid to know the causes of everything, why it comes to be, why it perishes, and why it exists at all" (*Phd.*, 96a). Socrates presents himself as being concerned with generation and destruction of all things, the soul included. As he tells this story, Socrates emphasizes his thought process. For example, he remarks, "I was often changing my mind in the investigation" (*Phd.*, 96b), reports "that is what I thought then" (*Phd.* 96d), and affirms, "I thought my opinion was satisfactory" (*Phd.*, 96d).

Socrates relates the next stage of his journey: "Then again, as I investigated how these things perish and what happens to things in the sky and on the earth, finally I became convinced that I have no natural aptitude at all for that kind of investigation, and of this I will give you sufficient proof" (*Phd.*, 96b). Socrates emphasizes the depth of his ignorance, "this investigation made me quite blind to those things which I and others thought that I clearly knew before, so that I unlearned what I thought I knew before, about many other things and specifically about how men grew" (*Phd.*, 96c). Socrates then asks Cebes, "Do you not think it was reasonable?" (*Phd.*, 96d). Socrates draws Cebes into the story with these questions. I suggest that he does so because he wants Cebes to feel his confidence and then the despair of aporia that follows, and, finally, the solace in the solution that Socrates adopts. Socrates' strategy seems to work. Cebes asks him his current thoughts on such matters (*Phd.*, 96e). Socrates responds, "That I am far, by Zeus, from believing that I know the cause of any of those things." He discusses his rejection of units of measure, addition and subtraction, and emphasizes: "nor can I any longer be persuaded about division. Being the cause of becoming two" (*Phd.*, 97b).[9] Socrates summarizes the effect of his engagement with natural philosophy: "I do not any longer persuade myself that I know why a unit or anything else comes to be, or perishes or exists by the old method of investigation and I do not accept it" (*Phd.*, 97b).

Socrates now describes how he developed "a confused method of my own" (*Phd.*, 97b). He begins, "One day I heard someone reading, as he said, from a book of Anaxagoras, and saying that it is Mind that directs and is the cause of everything. I was delighted with this cause and it seems to be good, in a way, that Mind should be the cause of everything" (*Phd.*, 97c). It is interesting to note that Socrates learns that Anaxagoras is the author from the person reading the book. Socrates preserves this detail about the transmission of knowledge through oral recitation of the written word. This small fact calls to mind the opening of the *Theaetetus* where Euclides and Terpsion hear a slave read Euclides' written text of the encounters Socrates has with Theaetetus and Theodorus (*Tht.*, 143c)

Socrates uses emotional language to describe his response to Anaxagoras: He is delighted and "glad to think that I had found in Anaxagoras a teacher about the cause of things after my own heart" (*Phd.*, 97e). In addition to characterizing his thought process in highly emotional terms here, Socrates presents himself as an eager, responsible learner. Then, he conveys his expectations: "He would tell me, first whether the earth is flat or round and then he would explain why it is so saying which is better, and that it was better to be so . . . If he showed me those things I should be prepared never to desire any other kind of cause" (*Phd.*, 98a). Simply put, Socrates assumed that Anaxagoras had a teleological dimension to his teaching.

> I never thought that Anaxagoras, who said that those things were directed by Mind, would bring in any other cause for them than that it was best for them to be as they are. Once he had given the best for each as the cause for each and the general cause of all, I thought he would go on to explain the common good for all, and I would not have exchanged my hopes for a fortune. I eagerly acquired his books and read them as quickly as I could in order to know the best and the worst as soon possible. (*Phd.*, 98c)

Several things are striking about this passage. First, Socrates describes his own involvement in the learning process. He does not merely listen to someone else reading. He himself reads. In fact, he eagerly acquires the books as quickly as possible. Again, Socrates includes descriptions of his emotional states. In this way, he underscores the affective dimensions of the learning process. He—like Augustine centuries later—is on fire to know.[10] Second, he offers an emotional accounting of his learning process. He eagerly acquires the books and reads them quickly. He expresses his despair when Anaxagoras' book disappoints him: "This wonderful hope was dashed as I went on reading and saw that the man made no use of Mind nor gave it any responsibility for the management of things" (*Phd.*, 98c). Third, Socrates reveals what he came to believe. He explains that Anaxagoras was no different from any of the natural philosophers. Socrates suggests that this lack of interest in ethical grounding is the cause of so much disagreement of causes and principles (*Phd.*, 99c). He summarizes what is lacking in their approach: "they do not believe that the truly good and 'binding' binds and holds them together" (*Phd.*, 99c). Unlike the teacher Socrates found in Diotima, Anaxagoras offers Socrates no vision of the beautiful itself, noting that it is the ultimate aim of all previous efforts.

Socrates eloquently articulates his desire for the teacher he imagined Anaxagoras to be: "I would gladly become the disciple of any man who taught the workings of that kind of cause" (*Phd.*, 99d). However, no such teacher exists. At this juncture, he asks Cebes if he would like to know what Socrates did in the absence of just such a teacher. The uneven parallels of their position are abundantly apparent. Socrates could not find the teacher that he desired. Cebes worries how he will exist without the teacher he has found. Socrates offers Cebes his own solution, "Since I was deprived [of such a teacher] and could neither discover it myself nor learn it from another, do you wish me to give you an explanation of how, as a second best, I busied myself with the search for the cause, Cebes?" (*Phd.*, 99d). Cebes eagerly responds, "I would wish it above all else" (*Phd.*, 99d). Socrates complies.

> When I had wearied of the investigation of things, I thought that I must be careful to avoid the experience of those who watch an eclipse of the sun, for some of them ruin their eyes unless they watch its reflection in water or some such material. A similar thought crossed my mind, and I feared that my soul would be altogether blinded if I looked at things with my eyes and tried to grasp them with each of my senses. (*Phd.*, 99e)

Socrates evocatively describes his emotional state. For example, he feels "deprived" and "weary" of investigating. He "fears" his soul would be blinded. Even more important, Socrates describes the philosophical process he developed as a result of his fear. First, he explains, "I thought I must take refuge in discussions and investigate the truth of things by means of words" (*Phd.*, 99e). He elaborates further, "I started in this manner; taking as my hypothesis in each case the theory that seemed to me the most compelling, I would consider as true, about cause and everything else whatever agreed with this, and as untrue whatever did not so agree" (*Phd.*, 100a). Socrates describes how he becomes his own teacher. He becomes his own trusted guide. He holds his own life up for analysis. James Crooks describes the importance of this autobiography nicely: "He makes explicit the mature ground of his confidence in moral discourse, the argument behind the whole of his investigation here and elsewhere. This takes him beyond Anaxagoras" (2000, 168). In addition, Socrates offers this story of pedagogical transformation to teach others. In this way, his narrative practice demonstrates his commitment to personal philosophical freedom and his pedagogical responsibility toward others. He recognizes that his avid pupil, Cebes, has no idea what he is talking about. Socrates turns to Cebes and says, "But I want to put my meaning more clearly, for I do not think that you understand me now" (*Phd.*, 100b). Cebes affirms that he does not. Socrates explains again.

> This is what I mean. It is nothing new, but what I have never stopped talking about, both elsewhere and in the earlier part of our conversation. I am going to try to show you the kind of cause with which I have concerned myself. I turn back to those oft-mentioned things and proceed from them. I assume the existence of a beautiful, itself by itself, of a Good and a Great, and all the rest. If you grant me these and agree that they exist, I hope to show you the cause as a result, and to find the soul to be immortal. (*Phd.*, 100b)

Socrates describes his self-motivated inquiry. He charts his own course. He does not wait for others to give him the answers he seeks. He asks something of Cebes in return for the story that he tells. Socrates wants Cebes to invest more fully in the philosophical process. Cebes must stop waiting for proof to be given to him. Cebes qualifies his response: "Take it that I grant you this, and hasten to your conclusion" (*Phd.*, 100c). He still sees this process as something that belongs to Socrates. He has not taken the process to be his own. Socrates' account more or less ends here: the next pages of the dialogue are Socrates' interrogation with Cebes about what he really believes with respect to the forms (*Phd.*, 101b–107b). Socrates implicitly asks Cebes to take responsibility for his beliefs. He must take this next step to participate in the life of philosophy after the life of Socrates ends.

KLEOS RECONSIDERED

The Homeric sense of *kleos* is basically a narrative immortality in which human actions—more specifically, heroic deeds—will be remembered and glorified forever in words. In "The Homeric Narrator and His Own *Kleos*," Irene de Jong makes the compelling case that the Homeric poet (him or herself) aspires to a similar glory and perhaps even attains one. She offers several reasons in support of this view. For example, she notes that "calling on the Muses, whom Hesiod refers to as 'the daughters of Mnemosyne,' is also an indirect advertisement of the narrator's extraordinary ability to memorize long stories crammed with name" (De Jong 2006, 192). She argues further, "Assuming that the Homeric narrator thinks of his own poems as texts and is familiar with the phenomenon of re-performance, he may also be expected to foresee immortal *kleos* for his poems" (De Jong 2006, 204). She summarizes her overall argument, " the narrator indirectly promotes his own person and poems via the Muses, suggests that poetry, including his own, can itself attain that most coveted heroic asset kleos, makes his own work anticipated by his heroes, and hints that while monuments are subject to the ravages of time, his poems, made with divine assistance, are indestructible, indeed themselves partake in and thereby confer immortal kleos" (De Jong 2006, 206).

Jacob Howland and others have argued that Plato is involved in a sustained attempt to rewrite the Homeric epics with a new philosophical purpose, a new philosophical hero.[11] If so, it would not be surprising to see elements of both heroic and narrative *kleos* in the dialogues. Indeed, one could quite easily regard Plato as creating just such an immortality for his teacher. The dialogues have created a narrative *kleos* for Socrates though the immortalization of his words and deeds. But Socrates' own stories, at least the way they are told in Plato's words, are stories of a different sort. Socrates does not tell the story of Anaxagoras to preserve the works of Anaxagoras for posterity, nor does he tell the story to carve out a space of personal glory about the development of his own method. Rather he narrates this story for the care of the community of people that he loves. As Phaedo's account draws to a close, we see Socrates presenting his narrative struggles to "develop a confused method of his own" (*Phd.*, 97b) as a model for those surrounding him on this final day. They must find their own way a model for crafting and discovering their own philosophical narratives rather than use their philosophical energy to enshrine his immortality.

In my view, Socrates' autobiographical account meets with limited success.[12] He does not persuade them completely. Socrates concludes, "Therefore the soul, Cebes, is most certainly deathless and indestructible and our souls will really dwell in the underworld." Cebes does not quite say that he believes it, but rather, "I have nothing more to say against that Socrates, nor can I doubt your arguments" (*Phd.*, 107a). Cebes suggests that Simmias might have still more to say, which indicates that he too is not completely convinced (*Phd.*, 107b). Simmias admits he has "private misgivings" (*Phd.*, 107b). Socrates encourages them to analyze the arguments "adequately," and, if the conclusion is "clear," they should "look no further" (*Phd.*,107b). In my view, Socrates is suggesting that they not demand more precision than the subject matter allows. Rather, they should cultivate their own resources for the journey ahead and not let the desire for proof undermine the value of belief. After the autobiographical account, Socrates tells another story about the guides and the journey to the regions of the earth (*Phd.*, 109a–115a). His autobiographical account guides them to a place where they can accept this mythic explanation of what awaits them at the end. The autobiography begins where the arguments end. Perhaps a new model of understanding the immortality of soul can be found there.

Socrates' narrative about Anaxagoras speaks to their immediate challenge: to learn how to live and philosophize without their beloved guide. Socrates tells them how he became prepared to philosophize on his own so that they might have a model of how to philosophize on their own. Phaedo imitates, and thereby initiates, the process of philosophizing on his own by telling his story as a means of caring for the community in Phlius and helping them care for one another. The Pythagorean context has very much to do with legacy.[13] It is possible that Plato would have been aware of the different groups of Pythagoreans, the split after Pythagoras death.[14] The Philians are there as a group caring for each other. Surely, the followers of Socrates are expected to go forth and do likewise.

Phaedo's words and deeds indicate to us what a post–Socratic philosophical community might involve. As Pierre Hadot says, "the real problem (for Socrates) is therefore not the problem of knowing this or that, but *of being* in this way or that way" (1988, 29). The same problem confronts the students of Socrates in the absence of Socrates. As a way of finding a life beyond Socrates, they should take Socrates' cautions about misology and misanthropy to heart (*Phd.*, 89d). As Socrates explains the dangers of hatred of argument, he links the continuation of the practice of philosophy with their continued existence and with his death. He tells them, "we must take courage and be eager to attain soundness, you and the others for the sake of your whole life still to come, and I for the sake of death itself" (*Phd.*, 91d). Socrates admits, "I am in danger at this moment of not having a philosophical attitude about this" (*Phd.*, 91b), and he asks their help in continuing the argument forward (*Phd.*, 91b–d). Later, Socrates also tells them that they must comfort each other. They must use these arguments as incantations to quell the disquiet in their souls (*Phd.*, 114d). On this point, Christopher Long notes, "Socrates here turns the attention of those present to the community gathered there, implicitly encouraging them to become singers themselves and to care for the community once he is no longer with them" (2014, 83). Differently put, they must learn to see the practice of philosophy as a means by which they can support one another. They are not yet good at providing this care to each other. Phaedo tells Echecrates, "So we stayed, talking among ourselves questioning what had been said and then again talking of the great misfortune that had befallen us. We all felt as if we had lost a father and would be orphaned for the rest of our lives" (*Phd.*, 116b). However, all is not lost. They are talking together and questioning each other. Though they may not fully realize the benefits of their communal engagement, they are, nonetheless, in community with each other. The lamenting continues; Apollodorus, Phaedo, Crito, everyone present breaks down in tears (*Phd.*, 117d). Socrates exhorts them to change their behavior. Phaedo reports that "his words made us ashamed and we checked our tears" (*Phd.*, 118a). However, the fact that Phaedo tells the story to the Philians conveys a sense of hopefulness that he might meet Socrates' philosophical expectations. He does not just tell the story of Socrates, but he tells a story of himself and Socrates. He makes Socrates' story his own. In doing so, he abides in true virtue by caring for the legacy of Socrates. We must continue this practice as we craft our own philosophical narratives and share them with our students. It is our responsibility to uphold the Socratic legacy of philosophical freedom in our complex contemporary age. One way we can achieve this aim is by practicing public philosophy.

PHAEDO AND THE IMITATION OF SOCRATIC SELF-DISCLOSURE

The *Phaedo* is one of Plato's most intricately crafted narrative works. We learn of Socrates' last days through the mediation of Phaedo's narrative account to Echecrates and the other silent listeners in Phlius. The *Phaedo* is rather unusual in its narrative structure in that the temporality of the narrative outer frame intercedes at important junctures in the text. These moments in the narrative framing give us additional insight into what is happening at the dramatic level of the text. They also allow us to gain insight into Phaedo's own perspective on the events as they unfolded. However, one important aspect of Phaedo's narrative has been largely overlooked, namely, Phaedo's inclusion of himself in the story he tells about Socrates' last days. Phaedo does not simply tell the story of Socrates, but he places himself in the story he tells. In this way, he too, practices the art of Socratic self-disclosure. He makes the story of Socrates into his own story and, in doing so, provides one model for how we might think about sharing our own philosophical stories in the public realm.

In this section, I examine how Phaedo discloses aspects of himself and how those moments of self-disclosure function as a Socratic exhortation to Echecrates and the Phlians to continue to live out the examined life in community with each other. The opening line of the dialogue focuses our attention on the possibility that we will hear Phaedo's own account of Socrates' death. Echecrates asks Phaedo, "Were you there with Socrates yourself, Phaedo, on the day when he drank the poison in prison, or did you hear about it from someone else?" (*Phd.*, 57a). In fact, in Greek, the very first word of the dialogue is *Autos* (yourself), emphasizing still more that we will hear Phaedo's self-report. Phaedo affirms that he was indeed there himself. Phaedo expresses his initial affinity with Echecrates by echoing the same word back to Echecrates and calling him by name just as Echecrates has referred to him by name. Echecrates also refers to him by name at (*Phd.*, 58a), and Phaedo responds in turn. It happens again at 58c and 58e, with Echecrates calling Phaedo by name. Echecrates also emphasizes Phaedo's importance as narrator of the hours surrounding Socrates' death by asking him if he has time (*Phd.*, 58d) to tell the story and by assuring him that "he will have hearers who feel as [he] does" (*Phd.*, 58e).

Phaedo's inclusion of himself in this narrative about Socrates is, to some degree, a response to Echecrates' own questions about him. Like Socrates, Phaedo tethers his narrative to the philosophical interests and needs of the auditor. Phaedo makes clear that he was not the only one present (*Phd.*, 58c). His story is not his alone but belongs to all that were present. However, Phaedo distinguishes his own experience of the events before he lists the people who were present. Phaedo begins by describing his own experience in response to Echecrates eager prompting "to tell us every detail as exactly as you can" (*Phd.*, 58d). Phaedo seems to be suggesting that his own experience of the events is the best way to report accurately. As Socrates regularly does in his own narrations, Phaedo includes descriptions of his own emotional states and thought process. For example, "I certainly found being there an astonishing experience" (*Phd.*, 58e). The word he uses is *thaumasia*. Phaedo finds the experience wonderous. John Sallis emphasizes this point, "Even before Phaedo set about narrating to Echecrates the story of Socrates' last day, he begins in effect differentiating the story from tragedy. He speaks of the wondrous pathos he felt in the presence of the events of that day" (2004, 153).

Phaedo reports Socrates' emotional states as well, noting that he "appeared happy in both manner and words" (*Phd.*, 58e), and, as a result of this observation, Phaedo shares his thoughts about the overall situation. "So, it struck me that even in going down to the underworld he was going with the gods' blessing and that he would fare well when he got there, if anyone ever does" (*Phd.*, 59a). Phaedo emphasizes again that he "had no feeling of pity" as would be expected at the place of death (*Phd.*, 59a). He describes another aspect of the strangeness of his experience, the fact that he did not feel the normal "pleasure" in philosophical discourse but rather "a strange feeling, an unaccustomed mixture of pleasure and pain at the same time as I reflected that he was just about to die" (*Phd.*, 59a). This description mirrors Socrates' own description of the pain in his leg and its pleasure upon being released from his bonds (*Phd.*, 59e). Phaedo also attests that the other shared his experience. Sallis notes, "He recalls also the mixed condition in which all those present found themselves" (2004, 153). First, he describes philosophy as a shared communal experience: "we engaged in philosophical discussion as we were accustomed to do—for our arguments were of that sort" (*Phd.*, 59a) and that "all of us present were affected in much the same way, sometimes laughing, then weeping" (*Phd.*, 59a) Phaedo then mentions Apollodorus specifically and draws Echecrates into the experience directly by telling him "you know the man and his ways," and Echecrates affirms that he does (*Phd.*, 59b). Phaedo then mentions that Apollodorus was "quite overcome" but then returns to his own feelings and the others, "But I was myself disturbed as so were the others" (*Phd.*, 59b).

At this point, Echecrates appears to get a little tired of Phaedo's self-disclosure and asks him who was there (*Phd.*, 59b). Phaedo complies and lists the Athenians first and his own belief that Plato was ill (*Phd.*, 59b). After Phaedo accounts for the foreigners present, Echecrates asks if anyone else was there, and Phaedo reports, "I think these were about all" (*Phd.*, 59c). In response to Echecrates' continued urging to report the conversation, Phaedo emphasizes the fact that he is telling the story as it appeared to him. He avers, "I will try to tell you everything from the beginning" (*Phd.*, 59d). Phaedo explains how he and the others would meet at daybreak at the courthouse and talk before the prison opening and then, when the prison opened, they would pass the day talking with Socrates (*Phd.*, 59d). On the death day, they gathered earlier because they had heard the ship had arrived. At this point in recounting the story, Phaedo makes clear that this was a shared communal experience at several points. He tells Echecrates about their habitual practice, "We foregathered at day break and each day we used to wait around talking until the prison should open" (*Phd.*, 59d). He relates how their course of action for the day that Socrates would die was a communal decision: "On this day we gathered rather early, because when we left the prison on the previous evening we were informed that the ship from Delos arrived, arrived and so we told each other to come to the usual place as early as possible" (*Phd.*, 59e). Even when they arrive at the prison, Phaedo continues to report what happened to them as a group: "When we arrived the gatekeeper who used to answer our knock came out and told us to wait and not go in until he told us to" (*Phd.*, 59e). By describing his experience in these communal terms, Phaedo draws those listening to his account in Phlius not only into his personal experience but into a shared communal experience.

Phaedo also attunes his audience to listen carefully to Socrates' words by mentioning the highly saturated linguistic context of their habitual gathering at the prison. For example, he tells Echecrates that "Socrates seemed happy in both his manner and words" (*Phd.*, 58e). Phaedo emphasizes that each day they would gather "at daybreak at the court where the trial took place, for it was close to the prison, and each day we used to wait around talking until the prison should open, for it did not open early" (*Phd.*, 59d). Once the prison opened, Phaedo tells Echecrates that "we used to go in to Socrates, and spend most of the day with him" (*Phd.*, 59d). These references to ongoing conversation between them and Socrates makes clear that this was a shared communal endeavor. An important part of Phaedo's own experience is the fact that he is a member of the close group of those that surround Socrates at his death.

Phaedo continues to report what happened on the actual day of the death: "When we arrived the gatekeeper who used to answer our knock came out and told us to wait and not go in until he told us to" (*Phd.*, 59e). After they wait "a short time," they enter the jail (*Phd.*, 60a). He describes how Socrates has been released from his chains and that Xanthippe and their small son were sitting with him. He asserts that Echecrates knows her.[15] Phaedo includes Xanthippe's response to them in his narration, "When she saw us, she cried out and said the sort of thing that women usually say: 'Socrates this is the last time your friends will talk to you and you to them'" (*Phd.*, 60a). It is ironic that Phaedo characterizes her remark as something that women would say in that he has just previously reported his own feelings at the last day of talking to Socrates in some detail in rather similar terms (*Phd.*, 59a). After Socrates tells Crito to have people take Xanthippe home, Phaedo returns to his focus on Socrates, and here we also see how Phaedo has placed himself in his accounting of the story as a way of emulating Socrates. Either Phaedo is casting Socrates' words in light of his own previous remarks, or he is echoing Socrates' words in his own narrative. Either way, Phaedo makes himself a central part of the story of Socrates' death.

Phaedo continues the report without much interruption other than to mention that Socrates put his feet down on the ground and remained sitting in that way through the rest of the conversation (*Phd.*, 60d). He reports Cebes' discomfort with Socrates claiming that the wise are not troubled by dying. At this point, Phaedo offers his own reflection on this poignant moment, "I thought that when Socrates heard this he was pleased by Cebes' argument" (*Phd.*, 63a). Phaedo's assessment of the situation may well not be the same as Socrates' own assessment, but he still places his own perception and thought process into the events he narrates. Christopher Long describes Phaedo's description of Socrates as "editorializing" (2014, 82). Phaedo seems to be aware of the possibility intrusive aspects of his remarks. He does not disrupt his own narrative again until just after Socrates' emphatic assertion about a soul nurtured in true philosophy: "After such nurture there is no danger, Simmias and Cebes, that one should fear that, on parting from the body, the soul would be scattered and dissipated by the winds and no longer be anything anywhere" (*Phd.*, 84b). Phaedo tells Echecrates, "When Socrates finished speaking there was a long silence. He appeared to be concentrating on what had been said, and so were most of us" (*Phd.*, 84c). Phaedo includes himself in the collective experience of silence and also as one of them, like Socrates himself, who was absorbed in what had been said about the state of the soul of the true philosopher after death. Phaedo then tells Echecrates that Simmias and Cebes were conversing with each other and that Socrates saw them and asks, "Do you think there is something lacking in my argument?" (*Phd.*, 84c). Socrates then talks about Apollo's swans and exhorts Simmias to share his objections and not hold back. After this, Phaedo again includes himself in the collective: "Then Socrates, looking keenly at us, as he often used to do, smiled" (*Phd.*, 86e). Phaedo reports Simmias' and Cebes' challenge to Socrates as well, and, more important, Phaedo reveals how Cebes' objection affected them all. He explains, "When we heard what they said we were all depressed, as we told each other afterwards. We had been quite convinced by the previous argument and they seemed to confuse us again, and to drive us to doubt not only what had already been said but also what was going to be said" (*Phd.*, 88c). Phaedo again reports his inclusion in the group. He emphasizes how the group shares his emotional state of being uncomfortable, and his thought process, and how it changes to confusion, doubt, distrust, and fear. Their future discussions and trust in logos are undermined by the challenges Simmias and Cebes present. At this point, Simmias and Cebes seem separate, almost at odds with the rest of the group.

There are only two narrated dialogues where the auditor listening to the narrator breaks into the storytelling to ask a question or offer a response to the narrated events as they unfold. Crito does so in the *Euthydemus*, and Echecrates does so here in the *Phaedo*. The rareness of such occurrences should cause us to pay special attention to them. Echecrates breaks in, "By the gods, Phaedo, you have my sympathy, for as I listen to you now I find myself saying to myself, 'What argument shall we trust?'" (*Phd.*, 88d). Phaedo's inclusion of himself and his experience serves to draw his auditor into the experience of the narrative quite deeply. It is almost like Echecrates was there himself experiencing their collective aporia through the power of Phaedo's narrations of his own experiences. On this point, Jill Gordon remarks, "Not only do those witnessing the action first hand in the jail cell need reassurance, but so does Echecrates who is hearing the story . . . The reader is likewise provided with a respite from her anxiety by Plato's having created this interlude" (1999, 144).

Note that Echecrates also explains his thought process and emotional states. He says that the doctrine of soul harmony had a wonderful hold upon him and that Phaedo's recounting "reminded me that I had previously thought so" (*Phd.*, 88d). In this way, he seems to imitate Simmias and Cebes, who don't appear to have a strong memory of the teachings of Philolaus that involve memory (*Phd.*, 61d–e). Echecrates describes his aporia and the fact that he has to begin all over again (*Phd.*, 88d). He exhorts Phaedo, "Tell me then, by Zeus, how Socrates tackled the argument. Was he obviously distressed, as you say you people were, or was he not, but quietly came to the rescue of his argument, and did he do so satisfactorily or inadequately? Tell us everything as precisely as you can" (*Phd.*, 88e). Echecrates acts much in the way that he did in the opening narrative frame. He asked repeated questions about Socrates' state of mind along with his ongoing interest in the argument and its defense. He also reinforces the fact that there are a group of people listening to the narrative in Phlius as he does in the opening frame. In addition, he repeats his desire that Phaedo be as accurate as he can (*Phd.*, 58d).

Phaedo happily complies, saying, "I have certainly often admired Socrates, Echecrates, but never more than on this occasion. That he had a reply was perhaps not strange. What I wondered at most in him was the pleasant, kind and admiring way he received the young men's argument, and how sharply he was aware of the effect the discussion had on us, and then how well he healed our distress and, as it were, recalled us from our flight and defeat and turned us around to join him in the examination of their argument" (*Phd.*, 89a). Several things are important to note. There is the repeated use of the word *thauma* (wonder). Phaedo emphasizes Socrates' manner and ability to sense the group mood. Indeed, as he is in the narrated dialogues, Socrates is highly attuned to the emotional states of his interlocutors. Though Phaedo places himself in the story, what is more striking is Phaedo's continued inclusion of himself as a member of the group. He also emphasizes Socrates' ability to cure and turn them back to considering the argument at hand. Through his attentiveness to their emotional states, he heals them and prepares them for further philosophical reflection.

Echecrates asks eagerly, "How did he do this?" (*Phd.*, 89b). Phaedo responds. In doing so, he places himself and his dialogue with Socrates in the very center of the story he reports to Echecrates and the others listening in Phlius. "I will tell you. I happened to be sitting on his right by the couch on a low stool, so that he was sitting well above me. He stroked my head and pressed the hair on the back of my neck, for he was in the habit of playing with my hair at times, 'Tomorrow, Phaedo,' he said, 'you will probably cut this beautiful hair'" (*Phd.*, 89b).

Phaedo continues to report his conversation with Socrates. In doing so, he draws Echecrates and the others into the temporality of the prison scene:

> Likely enough, Socrates, I said.
> Not if you take my advice, he said.
> Why not, said I?
> What shall I do then? I asked.
> It is today, he said, that I shall cut my hair and you yours, if our argument dies on us, and we cannot revive it. If I were you, and the argument escaped me, I would take an oath, as the Argives did, not to let my hair grow before I fought again and defeated the argument of Simmias and Cebes. (*Phd.*, 89b–89d)

For Socrates the life of the argument is worthier of mourning through the cutting of the hair than his own life. Socrates includes Phaedo in his commitment to argument. He creates a strong sense of community between them. He tells Phaedo that he should also be more committed to the process of philosophical argument than any concerns that he has about Socrates' passing.

> But, I said, that they say not even Heracles could fight two people.
> Then call on me as your Iolaus as long as the daylight lasts.
> I shall call on you, but in this case as Iolaus calling on Heracles. (*Phd.*, 89c)

Phaedo is challenging Socrates' poetical references just as Aristodemus does in the *Symposium*.

Socrates responds to Phaedo's revision, saying, "it makes no difference" (*Phd.*, 89c). In doing so, he affirms the community between Phaedo and himself on the inner dramatic layer of the dialogue. This sense of community with Socrates is instantiated on the narrative level as Phaedo intertwines his own story with the story of Socrates. Then Socrates warns Phaedo that "there is a certain experience we must be careful to avoid" (*Phd.*, 89c). Phaedo asks what it is, and Socrates presents the dual dangers of misology and misanthropy. Socrates responds at length:

> That we should not become misologues, as people become misanthropes. There is no greater evil one can suffer than to hate reasonable discourse. Misology and misanthropy arise in the same way. Misanthropy comes when a man without knowledge or skill has placed great trust in someone and believes him to be altogether truthful, sound and trustworthy; then, a short time afterwards he finds him to be wicked and unreliable, and then this happens in another case; when one has frequently had that experience, especially with those whom one believed to be one's closest friend, then, in the end, after

many such blows, one comes to hate all men and to believe that no one is sound in anyway at all. (*Phd.*, 89d–e)

Phaedo responds that he understands Socrates' concern. Given Phaedo's own personal background of sexual slavery, it is not difficult to imagine that he has experienced precisely this sort of distrust and hatred.[16] It is important to note that this warning about misology and misanthropy arises while Socrates is in direct conversation with Phaedo. Phaedo actually overcomes both by telling the narrative about Socrates' last days to the people in Phlius.

In this next part of the exchange with Phaedo, Socrates talks about the necessity of knowing human nature and the rarity of extremes, and the examples between the extremes are many. Phaedo's responses are highly affirmative (*Phd.*, 90a–91c). There is a strong association between arguments and persons throughout this passage. Socrates reasons that he can't give up on soundness just because arguments appear at one time true, at another time untrue" (*Phd.*, 90d). Phaedo affirms that it would be "pitiable indeed" (*Phd.*, 90d). Socrates continues his exhortation about not allowing argument to be undermined completely: "This then is the first thing we should guard against, he said. We should not allow into our minds the conviction that argumentation has nothing sound about it; much rather we should believe that it is we who are not yet sound and that we must take courage and be eager to attain soundness, you and the others for the sake of your whole life still to come, and I for the sake of death itself" (*Phd.*, 90e–91a). Socrates' direct dialogue with Phaedo ends with his admission that he is "in danger at this moment of not having a philosophical attitude" about the truth of the matter (*Phd.*, 91a). As mentioned above, he is tempted by wanting to win the argument rather than seeking the truth of the matter (*Phd.*, 91b). At this point, Socrates turns his attention back to Simmias and Cebes within the inner dialogue. Phaedo continues to recount their argument along with their concern that, even though they have established that the soul may have existed for a very long time in some other place before embodiment, there is no good reason to believe that it will continue to exist after.

After Cebes affirms that Socrates has captured his argument exactly, Phaedo's narrative voice intercedes again. He describes Socrates' second silence. "Socrates paused for a long time, deep in thought" (*Phd.*, 95e). This is where the most famous autobiographical passage occurs (*Phd.*, 96a–100c). Socrates then proceeds to test Cebes understanding, "if you grant me these and agree that they exist, I hope to show you the cause as a result, and to find the soul to be immortal" (*Phd.*, 100c). Socrates proceeds to do just this and asserts, "I will not insist on the precise nature of the relationship but that all beautiful things are beautiful by the Beautiful. That, I think, is the safest answer I can give myself or anyone else. And if I stick to this I think I shall never fall into error'" (*Phd.*, 100e). Socrates continues the testing of the great and the small through 102a. Socrates ends, warning Cebes not to mix up various aspects of his argument, "but if you are a philosopher, I think you will do as I say" (*Phd.*, 102a). Simmias and Cebes respond together at this point, even though Socrates has been addressing his remarks primarily to Cebes.

After they both affirm the truth of what Socrates presented, Echecrates again interrupts Phaedo's narrative reporting. He exclaims, "Yes, by Zeus, Phaedo, and they were right, I think he made these things wonderfully clear to anyone of even small intelligence" (*Phd.*, 102a). Phaedo affirms, "Yes indeed, Echecrates, and all those present thought so too" (*Phd.*, 102a). Again, Phaedo associates himself with the group. His story is part of the communal story. The temporal move to the outer narrative frame in Phlius further emphasizes this shared communal ascent moving outward from the moment of Socrates' death to the moment of the retelling. Echecrates makes this point explicit. He emphasizes, "And so do we who were not present but hear of it now" (*Phd.*, 102a). In addition, in the act of reading, the philosophical community extends outward into the present temporal moment anytime someone reads the dialogue carefully.

Echecrates, is, however, wanting to hear still more. Phaedo responds, "As I recall it, when the above had been accepted, and it was agreed that each of the Forms existed, and that other things acquired their name by having a share in them, he followed this up by asking, If you say these things are so, when you then say that Simmias is taller than Socrates but shorter than Phaedo, do you not mean that there is in Simmias both tallness and shortness?" (*Phd.*, 102b). Phaedo's response to Echecrates initially emphasizes the shared communal agreement again. He also refers to his own memory. And then he reports how Socrates himself kept including Phaedo in the example as an object that Simmias could compare himself to. Phaedo goes onto report, "Then someone of those present—I have no clear memory of who it was—said, 'By the gods, did we not agree earlier in our discussion to the very opposite of what is now being said?'" (*Phd.*, 103a). Phaedo then tells Echecrates that "on hearing this, Socrates inclined his head towards the speaker and said, 'you have bravely reminded us but you do not understand the difference between what is said now and what was said then'" (*Phd.*, 103b) and corrects the interrupter. Phaedo reports, "At the same time, he looked to Cebes and said, 'Does anything of what this man says also disturb you?'" (*Phd.*, 103c). Socrates continues to argue for the immortality of the soul when he finally concludes, "Therefore for the soul, Cebes, is most certainly deathless and indestructible and our souls will really dwell in the underworld" (*Phd.*, 107b). Socrates talks again about the fate of the soul. Simmias and Cebes both admit that they cannot doubt the argument, but Simmias admits to "private misgivings" (*Phd.*, 107b). All this occurs without any additional narrative description on Phaedo's part or any interruption by Echecrates.

At this point, Socrates goes on to talk about the journey of the soul to the various regions of the earth (*Phd.*, 108a–115a). He ends this long account, addressing Simmias, Cebes, and the rest. "Now you, Simmias, Cebes and the rest of you, Socrates continued, will each take that journey at some other time but my fated day calls me now as a tragic character might say, and it is about time for me to have my bath, for I think it better to have it before I drink the poison and save the women the trouble of washing the corpse" (*Phd.*, 115a). Phaedo notes that Crito interrupts at this point to ask about how they should bury Socrates. Phaedo now reports the final events. Socrates leaves to take his bath.[17] Crito follows him. The others wait. Phaedo tells Echecrates, "So we stayed talking among ourselves, questioning what had been said and then again talking of the great misfortune that had befallen us. We all felt as if we had lost a father and would be orphaned for the rest of our lives" (*Phd.*, 116b). Phaedo again emphasizes how he is a member of the philosophical group. They are beginning the process of philosophizing without Socrates. They start out talking about philosophy and reflecting on the discourse. Nonetheless, they seem not to understand the message Socrates is trying to impart in that they still have questions. They quickly move onto the experience of their collective sorrow.

Phaedo now reports that Socrates has come back in from the bath and joins them after sending the women and children away (*Phd.*, 116b). Phaedo then focuses on the emotional response of the officer of the Eleven and Socrates' admiration of him. Socrates then reports that he is ready for the poison. Crito implores him not to as "the sun still shines about the hills and has not yet set" (*Phd.*, 116e). Socrates corrects him for his lack of understanding once more and says, "I do not expect any benefit from drinking the poison a little later, except to become ridiculous in my own eyes for clinging to life, and be sparing of it when there is none left. So, do as I ask and do not refuse me" (*Phd.*, 117a). Phaedo then tells Echecrates that Crito went to tell the slave to get the person who would administer the poison. Phaedo calls Echecrates by name at the moment that he reports how Socrates took the cup: "And he offered the cup to Socrates who took it quite cheerfully, Echecrates, without a tremor or any change of feature or color" (*Phd.*, 117a). Socrates then asks for directions, and the man tells Socrates to walk until his legs become heavy, and he should lie down. Socrates asks if he can offer a libation, but the man said, "We only mix as much as we believe will suffice." Socrates then offers his final prayer, "To the gods that the journey from here to yonder may be fortunate" (*Phd.*, 117c). Phaedo describes the scene, "While he was saying this, he was holding the cup, and then drained it calmly and easily" (*Phd.*, 117d). Phaedo continues to describe how they all respond.

> Most of us had been able to hold back our tears reasonably well up till then, but when we saw him drinking it and after he drank it, we could hold them back no longer; my own tears came in floods against my will. So, I covered my face, I was weeping for myself, not for him—for my misfortune in being deprived of such a comrade. Even before me, Crito was unable to restrain his tears and got up. Apollodorus had not ceased from weeping before, and at this moment his noisy tears and anger made everybody present break down. (*Phd.*, 117d)

Socrates chastises them, and Phaedo says, "His words made us ashamed and we checked our tears" (*Phd.*, 117e). He narrates the progress of the poison and the movements of Socrates and his final words. Phaedo reports, "And uncovering his face, which had been covered, he said, and these were his last words 'Crito, we owe a cock to Asclepius; make this offering to him and do not forget.' But there was no answer. Shortly afterwards Socrates made a movement; the man uncovered him and his eyes were fixed. Seeing this Crito closed his mouth and his eyes" (*Phd.*, 118a). Phaedo finishes his account, "Such was the end of our comrade, Echecrates, a man who, we would say, was of all those we have known the best and also the wisest and the most upright" (*Phd.*, 118a). We do not hear Echecrates' response to Phaedo's narration. Instead, we end with Phaedo's own assessment of Socrates. Nonetheless, Phaedo includes Echecrates in his assessment by addressing him by name with his repeated us of the plural "we." In doing so, Plato presents Phaedo as having created a new philosophical community in Phlius. Christopher Long eloquently explains the overall effect of Plato's work in crafting the *Phaedo* in this way: "Plato also invites us to think about the nature of political writing and the possibility, indeed, that such writing might need to take the form of a kind of storytelling, or muthologia" (2014, 74). I now offer an example of Socratic self-disclosive storytelling.

WATCHING THE LAST BREATH

My mother, Andrea Cheek Frosolono, passed away not long ago. She had a major stroke in 2013, a few months after *Plato's Socrates as Narrator* was published. Her recovery was long and difficult. Eventually, my parents moved to an assisted living facility in Austin. After listening to them talk with each other during a lengthy hospital stay, it became clear to me that they did not consider their new place "home." Even though they were together, they did not feel at home. My sister and I decided to move my parents from Texas to Colorado to live with her and Kelly, my brother-in-law. Although I fully supported the decision, like Simmias, I did have some "private misgivings (*Phd.*, 107b). I feared that being such a long distance away that I might not be present when my mother passed away. I was not worried that I would be kept away by "illness" as Plato was from the death of Socrates. I was concerned about geographic distance. As it turns out, I was among those whom I can list as present as I recount the story of her death.

The Christian narrative pervaded the room. The Christian story is the story of my parents' life. Their relationship to the Christian faith, at least from my perspective, has always seemed rather uncomplicated. It worked for them. They went to Sunday school and church each week. Service to the church structured their lives together. Mom spent many years helping the nursery of Aldersgate United Methodist Church. She worked as a volunteer church secretary helping with the newsletter and collecting money in their church in Florida. Her life was filled with women's Bible study. She once told the story of coming to Bible study with her grandmother when she was a very small child. She sat quietly in the corner as the women read the Bible stories together. Their friends, regardless of the town we lived in, tended to be fellow members of the body of Christ. And who am I to judge the truth of that *muthos*? It, or something like it, captures what is true about the soul and its journey between life and death and life after death.

There was even Christian incantation in the hospital room. We talked with hospice workers who encouraged us to play music and speak with her as she passed. They informed us that hearing is the last sense organ to go, which has caused me to wonder all the more about the references to hearing at the beginning of the *Phaedo*. Did the Pythagoreans know this? Did Plato? So, my father brought a Bose speaker from the house. He selected the contemporary hymn "Jerusalem." This song was piped through the tour bus speakers as they arrived at the Old City of Jerusalem on their treasured trip to the Holy Land. Their local minister was also there. She prayed over us all during the passing. Her prayers and the words of "Jerusalem" served to "charm away our fears" (*Phd.*, 77e).

At the same time, various scientific *logoi* about death pervaded the room. Much like Anaxagoras, who was concerned with "bones and sinews" (*Phd.*, 98c), we knew her overall health was not good. She had little strength. She used a walker and needed help with a gait belt before she went to the hospital. The prognosis for recovery back to the limited mobility she had was not good. We, as a family, long ago had both a Do Not Resuscitate (DNR) order and a Do Not Intubate (DNI) order in place. We each had her medical power of attorney. We accepted the contemporary medical narrative regarding responsible death practices. We gave her a few days to turn around. At some point, there was nothing else to do that did not require doing what we had already decided not to do. We decided to turn off the oxygen. We watched the monitor. She took her last breath. The medical language of respiration and heartbeat existed alongside the Christian story. Both are "true" accounts.

There is also the experiential account I am recollecting. I felt enormously lucky to be in the room as she took her last breath. My awareness was focused on being present with her in that moment. My sister, Christina, was "the guide who had been appointed to lead her" (*Phd.*, 107e). She coached my mother through labored inhalations and exhalations. I remembered Jeffrey Gold's suggestion that "the end of the *Phaedo* provides a specific technique of meditation and pranayama technique that one can use to achieve liberation" (1996, 25).[18] Christina was vigilant about morphine timings to ease the passing. As I watched the last inhalation and exhalation, I felt gratitude for being the daughter of such "an exemplary mother," as my best friend, Lenore, described her in the first text I received from her after my mother had passed. Also, I was palpably aware that the draft of this chapter lay open on my computer that I had left on a chair in the waiting room as the time drew near. The Platonic and the Christian narratives both surrounded me in that liminal space around my mother's deathbed, that space where one receives some glimpse of what lies beyond our current incarnated existence. That glimpse struck me as not that different from the "great hope" (*Phd.*, 114c) that Socrates maintains as he "utters a prayer to the gods that the journey from here to yonder may be fortunate" (*Phd.*, 117c).

NOTES

1. Like most Platonic dialogues, the scholarship on the *Phaedo* is immense. There are many fine books, book chapters, and articles on the *Phaedo*. I have benefitted from the following works listed in alphabetical order: Altman (2016b), Ahrensdorf (1995), Brill (2013), Burger (1984), Dorter (1982), Eckstein (1981), Jansen (2013), Hartle (1986), Long (2014), Michael Morgan (1990), Northwood (2015), Romero (2016), Sherman (2013), Zoller (2018), and Zuckert (2009).

2. On Socratic autobiography in the *Phaedo*, see Gower (2008). In addition, see the response article by Hoinski (2008). Hoinski (2008, 350n6) refers to 63b–69a as a passage that one would need to account for if offering a full assessment of autobiography in the *Phaedo*.

3. On Xanthippe's important role in this dialogue, see Saxonhouse (2018).

4. For more on Socrates and Aesop, see Clayton (2008) and Northwood (2015).

5. On Socratic listening, see Naddaff (2019).

6. On the importance of this passage and its resonances with many other dialogues, see Altman (2016b, 366–67).

7. It is interesting to note that Socrates associates Homer with the harmony model (*Rep.*, 94d). Socrates seems intent on placing the Pythagoreans in the overall Greek pedagogical context rather than insisting that they offer a radically different way of life as he seems to suggest at *Rep.*, 600a.

8. The number imagery reinforces the Pythagorean dimensions of the conversation.

9. Socrates places Pythagoreans in the same philosophical family as the material monists. On a related issue, see Finkelberg (1986).

10. After reading Cicero's *Hortensius*, Augustine explains, "It altered my outlook on life. It changed my prayers to you, O Lord, and provided me with new hopes and aspirations. All my empty dreams suddenly lost their charm and my heart began to throb with a bewildering passion for the wisdom of eternal truth" (1984, 50).

11. On Plato's casting of Socrates as a new Homer, see Howland (2004), Gould (1990), Klonoski (1993), Madhu (1999), Rosenstock (1983), Segal (1978), Ferrari (1999), O'Connor (2007), and Brann (2004).

12. Socrates' inability fully to persuade his interlocutors occurs in almost every dialogue. The presentation of Socrates' pedagogical failure may be a rhetorical necessity to stimulate the

reader of the dialogue to think beyond the failures of the interlocutor. At the same time, that Plato so consistently portrays Socrates as failing, at least on some level, in his attempts to bring others to philosophical understanding suggests to me that Plato is, to a degree, critical of Socrates' pedagogical practices. I make some preliminary suggestions about the nature of this critique in "Looking beyond the Elenchus." See Bowery (1998).

13. Several recent books greatly enhance our understanding of Pythagoras, Pythagoreanism, and the communities that arose after the death of Pythagoras. See Cornelli (2013); Cornelli, McKirahan, and Macris (2013); Huffman (2014a); and Zhmud (2012).

14. There is significant debate about when this split actually occurred. Leonard Zhmud argues that the split is an invention of a later tradition in that the first written description of the two groups of Pythagoreans is not found until Clement of Alexandria. See Zhmud (2014, 93). For an alternative view, see Marciano (2014) in the same volume. Huffman notes that "Burkert and many others think that it occurred in the fifth century and is already found in the testimony of Aristotle" (2014b, 7). Elsewhere, I argue that the constant use of the *akouo* language in the *Phaedo* should be taken as evidence that the split had occurred during Socrates' and Plato's lifetimes. See Bowery (2002).

15. On the significance of Xanthippe and Phaedo's inclusion of her in the narrative, see Saxonhouse (2018) and Schultz and McLain (forthcoming).

16. On this dimension of Phaedo's background, see Nails (2002, 231).

17. On the importance of Socrates' bath, see Romero (2016).

18. On the *Phaedo* as being a coded set of breathing and meditative practices, see Gold (1996).

Chapter Six

Listening to Socratic Voices

SUMMARY OF SOCRATIC SELF-DISCLOSURE

Before exploring how three contemporary writers have functioned as Socratic figures in my own life, I will step back and summarize some key elements of the autobiographical narratives that Socrates tells.[1] Doing so will help guide the exploration of contemporary autobiography and also suggest some guidelines by which we might choose to share some of our own stories in the contemporary public sphere. Five aspects of these Socratic self-disclosing narratives seem important to emphasize here. First, the autobiographical passages in the *Theaetetus*, *Symposium*, *Apology*, and *Phaedo* all present Socrates in a largely sympathetic light. Throughout these moments of self-disclosure, Socrates consistently reveals his emotional states, his internal thought processes, and his experiences of aporia to his auditors. Socrates seems quite willing to present himself in an emotionally complex and, at times, even vulnerable light. This well-rounded portrait of himself draws people closer to him specifically and, hopefully, to the practice of philosophy more broadly. Second, Socrates tells stories about an educational process. By sharing how he learned from Diotima, the oracle, the daimon, and Anaxagoras, Socrates paints a portrait of his philosophical development, which illustrates the transformational power of education. Third, the autobiographies that he tells are aimed at getting people to recognize uncomfortable truths about themselves and about the society in which they live. We see this attempt most clearly in his presentation of Diotima's speech aimed at getting the symposiasts to see beyond their culturally limited conceptions of love and in his self-disclosing narratives in the *Apology*, which are aimed at getting the jurors to see that what is truly good and truly good for them transcend their particular political circumstances. Simply put, Socrates' self-disclosing narratives are aimed at helping his interlocutors recognize the shadows on the wall of the cave of Athenian society and how they are influenced by those shadows. Fourth, as we see, particularly in the *Phaedo* and to a degree in the *Apology*, Socrates' autobiographical discourse is aimed at creating communities of care which can help change community structures so that individual flourishing, philosophical and otherwise, can manifest. Holly Moore nicely articulates this potential for Socratic self-disclosure. She describes Socratic self-disclosure as "auto-narration." Auto-narration "produces an image of the political subject as open to difference, both synchronically (with others) and diachronically (with oneself), not only exposes the role of imagination in political discourse but of discourse in imagining (and thereby producing) the conditions for the possibility of the just polis" (2018, 14). Finally, Socratic self-disclosure promotes philosophical autonomy by presenting the importance of critical thinking and ongoing questioning of self and other with respect to matters of ultimate concern. Just as Phaedo learns to tell his own story, we also have to move beyond Socrates' stories and tell our own. Socrates' philosophical stories are good models to consider as we think about sharing our own stories and listening to the stories of others. I do not think an autobiography has to exhibit all these qualities to function in a Socratic manner. However, seeing these qualities in Socratic self-disclosing narrative will hopefully help us recognize a broad range of voices as Socratic interlocutors. With this idea of Socratic self-disclosing discourse in mind, we expand our worldview by getting out of conversational silos and engaging with many voices across social and political divides. One of the major challenges facing contemporary America today is polarization. The seemingly insurmountable divides between "red/blue," conservative/liberal, urban/rural appear to become even more insurmountable with each passing news cycle as the 2020 election draws near. In the wake of the mass shootings in Parkland, California, El Paso, Dayton, and Midland-Odessa, our governmental leaders still cannot come together to work for meaningful gun reform. We have approximately thirty-three years to do anything meaningful to redress the effects of global warming, and, still, political parties remain entrenched and unwilling to legislate massive environmental change. Certainly, there are abundant calls to work across the divide. Consider Martha Nussbaum's new book, *Monarchy of Fear*, written just after the 2016 elections.[2] She offers many concrete suggestions about how to become a more engaged, thoughtful, reflective citizen. But is it really possible? Are there ways that we can meaningfully talk to, and listen to, each other across these divides? Furthermore, am I, like Nussbaum herself, a little too optimistic to expect that sharing stories about ourselves inside and outside of the classroom could make a difference in this jagged landscape of increasingly dangerous political posturing? By way of response, let me say two things. First, as I mentioned in the preface, there is a significant body of literature that supports the transformative power of story sharing. Indeed, the popularity of numerous memoirs attest to the popular appeal of reading about the lives of others. Consider Michelle Obama's *Becoming*, Tara Westover's *Educated*, J. D. Vance's *Hillbilly Elegy*, and Lori Gottlieb's *Maybe You Should Talk to Someone: A Therapist, Her Therapist, and Our Lives Revealed*.[3] Alongside these popular works, many contemporary philosophers have engaged in autobiographical reflection in their scholarly work.[4]

Second, I am certainly not alone in seeing the contemporary value of Socratic philosophical practice. For instance, Cornel West uses Socrates as a powerful model for engaged democratic citizenship.[5] In 2004, Cornel West wrote *Democracy Matters* as a sequel to his now classic *Race Matters*, published in 1994. West describes the decline in civic engagement in the public square aimed at the common good. Thirteen years and three tumultuous election cycles later, his words seem startlingly prophetic. If it is possible to regain anything like civil public space in the wake of the 2016 election and its ongoing aftermath, we would do well to return to his advice with renewed zeal. West maintains, "A narrow rant against the new imperialism or emerging plutocracy is not enough. Instead we must dip deep into often-untapped wells of our democratic tradition to fight the imperialist strain and plutocratic impulse in American life" (2005, 3). West isolates three main threats to our democratic lives: "the dogma of free market fundamentalism, aggressive militarism, and escalating authoritarianism" (2005, 3–5). Throughout this book, West vividly describes the dark underbelly of violence that pervades America's cultural history. He argues that we must find resources to expose our collective denial about the harm that our unreflective commitment to these three modes of engagement cost us on both the individual and the collective level. West locates three aspects of our democratic tradition that we must revive for our democracy to serve all of its citizens. These democratic underpinnings are Socratic questioning, the prophetic commitment to social justice, and tragicomic hope.

West describes the power of Socratic questioning and truth telling throughout the text of *Democracy Matters*. He writes, "Socratic questioning yields intellectual integrity, philosophic humility, and personal sincerity—all essential elements of our democratic armor for the fight against corrupt elite power" (2005, 208–209). West eloquently laments, "We desperately need the deep energy of this Socratic questioning in these times of rampant sophistry on the part of our political elites and their media pundits" (2005, 17). West acknowledges that practicing this Socratic art of plain speaking will not be universally welcome in our society any more than it was welcome by the Athenian demos. He insists that, "To engage in this Socratic questioning of America is not to trash our country, but rather to tease out those traditions in our history that enable us to wrestle with difficult realities we often deny" (West 2005, 41). West implores us to explore the dark side of our history, the stories we listen to just as reverently and unreflectively as Athenians listened to their Homer, the educator of Hellas. In *Democracy Matters*, Socrates emerges as a heroic figure for his time and ours: "In the great story of Athenian democracy, Socrates is the towering figure precisely because it was his central mission to combat the corruptions of elite power by questioning the narrow ideological and prejudicial thinking of his day" (2005, 208). I hope that this exploration of Socratic self-disclosure has added another element to our understanding of how Socrates practiced philosophy in his time and that we will embrace this aspect of his practice as another means of practicing Socratic philosophy in our time.

The Socratic practice of self-disclosure may offer a path forward through our tumultuous social/political arena where it seems so overwhelming to find common ground amid difference. The Socratic work we do in the classroom to encourage students to live the examined life perhaps offers hope that transformation is possible. bell hooks' observation applies to the way we engage with each other on the social and political domain as well. She writes, "In regards to pedagogical practices we must intervene to alter the existing pedagogical structure and to teach students *how to listen, how to hear one another*" (hooks 1994, 150). The same is true as we strive to do our work outside the classroom. In *Teaching Community*, hooks writes, "To successfully do the work of unlearning domination, a democratic educator has to cultivate a spirit of hopefulness about the capacity of individuals to change" (2003, 73). We must maintain a hopeful stance about the possibility for change. We must learn to listen to and learn from each other. But again the question remains. Is such genuine listening and learning from another with radically different views still possible? I think so. Here is one hopeful example. A 2016 American Enterprise Institute dialogue between Princeton University professors Robert George and Cornel West models how we might speak across divergent points of view.[6] Wilson Shirley, the event reporter, summarizes their main points of agreement about the purpose of liberal education. He writes, "Although Dr. George and Dr. West come from different political and personal backgrounds, they agreed on the answer about the purpose of liberal education. By making accessible the ideas posed by great thinkers throughout history, liberal arts education empowers students to live examined lives" (Shirley 2016). Their spirited debate illustrates how Tara Westover describes the transformative value of education. In an interview with Catherine Brown in *Forbes*, Westover asserts, "I think it's very unlikely that anyone who engages with a wide variety of different perspectives will come away with the same world view. That's true whether you've grown up very conservative or very liberal. I think education means access to different perspectives and understanding of different people and experiences and history. If all of that doesn't change your mind a bit, you're probably doing it wrong" (Brown 2017). My hope is that by practicing the art of Socratic self-disclosure, we will create new possibilities for liberal arts education that help cultivate the possibility of listening to and learning from a range of voices. More broadly, I hope our educational practices will shape a foundation for transforming the political landscape into communities that are oriented toward care for self and other.

THREE CONTEMPORARY SOCRATICS

One way we can overcome our philosophical and political hubris is by sharing and by listening to stories that populate the public sphere. To do this, we have to find our own voice and cultivate the capacity to listen to the voices of others. As a means of beginning the work of listening to a broad range of voices, I briefly engage with three thinkers who practice sharing stories of their own lives in their public intellectual work. I have chosen these particular writers because each one has functioned as a Socratic gadfly to me. Their writings have challenged me to recognize my complacency and privilege in three overlapping domains of my life: as a white feminist academic, as a liberal faculty member at a Christian university that is also a historically predominantly white institution, and as a white American citizen.

bell hooks: Her Teaching Trilogy

As I mentioned in the preface, reading bell hooks' *Teaching to Transgress* when I was just starting my teaching career radically altered the way I understood my role in the classroom.[7] Over the years, her work has consistently functioned in a Socratic manner for me individually. Her work causes me to think and rethink how I live the examined life as a white feminist educator at a conservative religious university. As a white female philosopher who has worked hard most of her life to succeed in an academic world largely defined by the work of white males, it is very easy to remain fixed in the gender binary of "male and female" because that is the most explicit power dynamic at work for me in the largely white culture in which I do my work. Unfortunately, it is often so difficult to work as a white female philosopher that I fail to see the "male and female" gender dynamic as also racially exclusionary— the number of nonwhite practitioners of philosophy is minuscule—because race has not been the battleground on which the white feminist philosophers have been fighting until rather recently. Reading bell hooks' work, I was forced to recognize that, as I taught from a feminist perspective, I was leaving unexamined the ways that I did not interrogate my racial or class privilege. I recognized myself in many of hooks' descriptions of white feminists: "Since well-educated white women with class privilege were uniquely situated to enter the academy via affirmative action policies in far greater numbers than black people, they were in turn able to make affirmative action boost their numbers. As the most immediate beneficiaries of affirmative action, their inclusion served to enhance 'white power and privilege' whether they were anti-racist or not" (hooks 2003, 3). I have taken hooks' observations about the early gains afforded by the feminist movement to heart and have embarked on a long self-reeducation process.[8] In *White Fragility*, Robin DiAngelo emphasizes that the process of interrogating white privilege is a lifelong undertaking. She writes,

> I believe that *white progressives cause the most daily damage to people of color*. I define a white progressive as any white person who thinks he or she is not racist, or is less racist, or in the "choir," or already "gets it." White progressives can be the most difficult for people of color because, to the degree that we think we have arrived, we will put our energy into making sure that others see us as having arrived. None of our energy will go into what we need to be doing for the rest of our lives: engaging in ongoing self-awareness, continuing education, relationship building, and actual antiracist practice. White progressives do indeed uphold and perpetrate racism, but our defensiveness and certitude make it virtually impossible to explain to us how we do so. (2018, 5)

This sustained questioning about the blindness of my white privilege pervades nearly every aspect of my existence. I now consider the numerous ways in which I uphold racial and class privilege simply by occupying the space that I do as a white American in general but, more specifically, as a faculty member at a conservative Christian university.[9] How can I, in this complicated context, truly learn to "teach from a standpoint aimed at liberating the minds of our students rather than indoctrinating them" (hooks 2003, 1)? hooks' descriptions of using autobiographical self-disclosure in the classroom motivated me to embrace that practice in my classrooms as a means of illustrating the liberating potential of philosophy to my students.

As I have spent the past few years examining Socratic autobiographical practices, I find that her own instances of self-disclosure have Socratic qualities. For instance, hooks, like Socrates, tells stories about her educational process. In the introduction to *Teaching to Transgress*, she outlines various stages of her educational journey. Starting with a positive experience in the segregated schools of her youth as a "location where I experienced learning as revolution" (hooks 1994, 2), she writes further, "Attending school then was sheer joy. I loved being a student. I loved learning" (hooks 1994, 3). From this sublime beginning, hooks was bussed for integration to a largely white school. Her experience of her educational process changed dramatically. She writes, "Knowledge was suddenly about information only." She explains that "We soon learned that obedience, and not a zealous will to learn, was what was expected of us" (hooks 1994, 3). hooks lost the "love of school," though she did manage to emerge from high school "believing that education was enabling, that it enhanced our capacity to be free" (1994, 4).

College reinforced the importance of "obedience to authority" rather than the "practice of freedom" (hooks 1994, 4). In graduate school, her sense of the possibility of transformative education devolved further. She writes, "The university and the classroom began to feel more like a prison, a place of punishment and confinement rather than a place of promise and possibility" (hooks 1994, 4).

Autobiographical reflections like these permeate the essays in *Teaching to Transgress* and much of hooks' extensive corpus.[10] hooks cautions educators about the necessity of overcoming their own vulnerability as the work to make the classroom a space that relates the subject matter to real-life concerns. We must share our own stories about how content relates to our lives if we want students to make this same sort of connection. She writes, "professors who expect students to share confessional narratives but who are themselves unwilling to share are exercising power in a manner that could be coercive" (hooks 1994, 21). Many teachers are uncomfortable with this process because "when professors bring narratives of their experiences into classroom discussions it eliminates the possibility that we can function as all-knowing, silent interrogators" (hooks 1994, 21). We should cultivate the practice of sharing our stories as a part of cultivating liberatory educational possibilities for our students. hooks exhorts us, "Professors who embrace the challenge of self-actualization will be better able to create pedagogical practices that engage students, providing them with ways of knowing that enhance their capacity to life fully and deeply" (1994, 22). In her dialogue with Ron Scapp, titled "Building a Teaching Community," hooks articulates the importance of developing voice. She explains, "one of the most misunderstood aspects of my writing on pedagogy is the emphasis on *voice*. Coming to voice is not just the act of telling one's experience. It is using that telling strategically—to come to voice so that you can also speak freely about other subjects" (hooks 1994, 148). In her 2018 autobiography, *Becoming*, Michelle Obama affirms the importance of voice that hooks eloquently articulates. Obama writes, "If there's one thing I've learned in life, it's the power of using your voice. I've tried my best to speak the truth and shed light on the stories of people who are often brushed aside" (2018, 241).

hooks has continued to write autobiographical self-reflections about the importance of teaching as the practice of freedom throughout her prolific career. In 2004, she published *Teaching Community*, and she recently completed *Teaching Critical Thinking*. Each of these books is filled with opportunities for self-study and reflection. Her reflections on her unique teaching career, both inside and outside the academy, exhorts the reader to find ways to make education truly be about the practice of freedom. She writes about the impact of this work, "In the last twenty years, educators who have dared to study and learn new ways of thinking and teaching so that the work we do does not reinforce systems of domination, of imperialism, racism, sexism or class elitism have created a pedagogy of hope" (hooks 2003, xiv). As I have been writing this book, I reread *Teaching to Transgress* after a twenty-five-year teaching career. I am struck by its startlingly prophetic quality. She writes, "As backlash swells, as budgets are cut, as jobs become even more scarce, many of the few progressive interventions that were made to change the academy, to create an open climate for cultural diversity are in danger of being undermined or eliminated. These threats should not be ignored" (hooks 2003, 33). Unfortunately, we have done just that. In many institutions of higher education, there is backlash against attempts to become more welcoming and diverse. hooks writes, "Conservative dominator culture responded to these chases by attacking public policies like affirmative action that had provided the means by which institutions of higher learning could include disenfranchised groups" (2009, 15). She observes, "Significantly the assault on progressive educators, and on new ways of knowing, was viciously launched not by educators but by policy makers and their conservative cohorts who control mass media" (hooks 2003, 8). Like Socrates exhorted his fellow citizens to question their received views about political reality, hooks consistently exhorts us to examine the shadows on our own cave walls. As part of our pedagogical practices both inside and outside the classroom, philosophers and other academics should not be afraid to come to voice, to share strategically in ways that will benefit both self and other by creating the possibility of social and political change. hooks exhorts us: "We need mass-based political movements calling citizens of this nation to uphold democracy and the rights of everyone to be educated, and to work on behalf of ending domination in all its forms—to work for justice, changing or educational system so that schooling is the site where students are indoctrinated to support imperialist capitalist patriarchy or any ideology, but rather where they learn to open their minds, to engage in rigorous study and to think critically" (2003, xiii). She emphasizes that this is a communal endeavor: "Progressive education, education as the practice of freedom, enables us to confront feelings of loss and restore our sense of connection. It teaches us how to create community" (2003, xv). I hope philosophers will follow her Socratic call to become more engaged wide variety of public settings.

Kathy Khang: *Raise Your Voice*

I have chosen for several reasons to include the work of Kathy Khang as an example of someone who practices Socratic self-disclosure. First, Khang gives numerous helpful guidelines for online engagement and in real-life engagement as means of learning to raise your voice in productive manners (2018, 112–132). Second, she regularly discloses facts about her personal life story in her writing. In doing so, she practices what I describe as Socratic self-disclosure. Third, I am trying to engage with voices from across a spectrum of social, political, and theological perspectives. Even though it seems pointless and impossible at times, I want to practice listening and learning from voices who occupy different spaces than I inhabit as an academic philosopher. Fourth, her work illustrates the fact that precisely how one can function as a Socratic voice will depend on the context in which one operates. Practicing Socratic public self-disclosure is a multivalent art. Each practitioner must figure out the best ways to tell their own stories.

Khang herself is a Christian motivational speaker, writer, and blogger.[11] Khang explains that the title of her recent work, *Raise Your Voice*, "tells as much about the content as it does about me. It connects the hope of 'more' to that of a stereotypical image of both 'Asian' as represented by the West—submissive servant—and 'women' as represented by the West, the East, and by some interpretations of Biblical womanhood" (2018, 3). Within the white Christian evangelical world, she challenges many social and political norms. Khang uses her voice to push the evangelical Christian community to recognize the limits of the experience of Christianity as filtered by white patriarchal heteronormativity. She maintains that "we need to address voice and identity through the intersections of race, ethnicity, gender, and class, as well as in personal and public spheres of communication" (Khang 2018, 23). She makes clear that her positionality as a person of color, of Korean descent, gives her the ability to see things that others in her evangelical Christian community fail to acknowledge; "As a Korean American immigrant woman who is married and the mother of three, I can't help but speak out against racism, sexism, xenophobia, and a host of other issues of injustice" (Khang 2018, 40). Her honesty has motivated me to affirm that Christianity itself is not the main cause of these challenges. Her ability to see Christianity as a practice that offers the possibility of individual and communal transformation helps me hold onto the good in my faith tradition. Often, I get discouraged when I encounter the sexism and racism that some strands of Christianity uphold as central to the Christian story. Her work made me recognize that what I am actually discouraged by is a mode of Christian culture that aligns with heteronormative, politically conservative values while asserting that those values are inherent, universal Christian values. This recognition gave me the courage to continue abiding in the difficult pedagogical and political contexts that arise when working for more liberal and inclusive understandings of Christian praxis.

Throughout *Raise Your Voice*, Khang offers concrete examples of her intersectional way of reading stories from the Judeo-Christian narrative. Here is one example:

> I can't teach the story of Queen Esther the same way a white man would because our minds and hearts encounter the story from such different starting points. I often have heard male pastors gloss over the selection of a new queen

> or portray it as an ancient version of the Miss Universe competition. Women are more likely to be aware of the sexual exploitation and power dynamics implicit in the story because we live in those same dynamics today. And as an immigrant woman of color, I have always been drawn to Esther's dual identity. I find that to be the core of the story, whereas someone from the majority culture may not dwell on that because they are the baseline for what is considered to be "normal." (Khang 2018, 40)

I find her work heartening because the Christian community I live and work within is often not progressive on issues of social justice.[12] Often, I find myself in a confrontational state of mind with respect to how I try to promote change in my campus community. Sometimes, it is difficult not to focus on Christianity as part of the problem. Khang's writing has motivated me to see my voice as an agent for change as redemptive rather than confrontational. She writes, "Learning to use your voice is about understanding how we each are created in God's image. It's about the space in which gender, faith, ethnicity, and race converge, adding to the power and beauty of individual voices effectively" (Khang 2018, 11). Later, she notes that "voice is not limited to what comes out of my mouth but out of my being" (Khang 2018, 21).

Khang also directly acknowledges the difficulties of speaking into this truth: "Raising my voice comes at some cost. Outspoken women are often called aggressive, arrogant, or abrasive" (2018, 3). She emphasizes further, "Women of color sit precariously and boldly in the intersection of race and gender, where raising our voices is a subversive, countercultural act that can earn us the labels of defiant or threatening: the angry Latina or black woman, the dragon lady, or even Pocahontas" (Khang 2018, 3). Despite these challenges, Khang proceeds in a Socratic fashion. She challenges the white heteronormative Christian community on white privilege and the exclusion of members of the LGBTQA community. She describes the pushback she received after speaking out about inappropriate representations of Asians in a prominent Bible study curriculum. She reports that many were "saying I was being too sensitive, prioritizing my ethnic identity over my Christian identity or that I was a reverse racist. (That's not a thing.)" (Khang 2018, 60). Differently put, Khang is accused of playing "the race card." On this point, hooks notes, "Of course the irony is that we are not actually allowed to play at the game of race, we are merely pawns in the hands of those who invent the games and determine the rules" (2003, 35).

Khang consistently acknowledges that:

> there is a chance that your community will experience tension and confusion as you experiment with raising your voice. Both Asian American and white friends, some of whom encouraged me to write and speak publicly, have told me that I've become too outspoken on matters of injustice and that my speak-

ing out only increases division. Speaking up doesn't increase division. It brings injustice and sin to the forefront. Speaking up can be an avenue of truth and healing, which can be painful for you and your friends. (2018, 66)

She asks Socratic questions of herself as well, "Can I love my neighbors, the white sisters and brothers I sit with in the pews, even as I wrestle through my confusion and frustration with the church's relative silence and delay in addressing systemic racism and injustice?" (2018, 65). The power of her Socratic provocation came to a head recently at my own university when she mentioned the recent case of an eleven-year-old student who was arrested for refusing to stand for the pledge of allegiance.[13] A white male student stood and interrupted her to object to her characterization of the event. Khang reports that "a university administrator asked me to consider rephrasing my description of the news story despite the fact that multiple news outlets connect the arrest to the child's refusal to stand for the pledge."[14] In the aftermath that ensued, it became clear that her remarks unsettled many faculty, students, and administrators of the largely conservative university community.[15] However, her honesty and courage in the face of this difficulty led me to regard her in deeply Socratic terms. Like Socrates, she stands up for her highest values even in the face of significant public resistance.

Ta-Nehisi Coates: *Between the World and Me*

I regard Coates as a contemporary American Socratic that the academic philosophical community in particular and American society more broadly should embrace as a valuable interlocutor. His work helps us think through and critically engage with a variety of social and political issues such as police brutality, race, and reparations.[16] Coates is an enormously successful writer. He is a regular contributor to *Atlantic Monthly* and won the MacArthur Fellowship for his interpretation of "complex and challenging issues around race and racism through the lens of personal experience and nuanced historical analysis."[17] Coates' work is beginning to receive sustained philosophical attention as well.[18] To my knowledge, Coates does not evoke Socrates as a model for his own work. In fact, in *Between the World and Me*, he outlines his journey from an early childhood belief that somehow the aim of education was "to create a carbon copy of white claims to civilization" (2015, 50). Coates minimizes mention of the traditional white intellectual canon. Instead, the text contains numerous references to African American thinkers, particularly those emerging out of Howard, which he calls the "crossroads of the black diaspora" (2015, 40). He mentions Charles Drew, Amiri Baraka, Thurgood Marshall, Ossie Davis, Doug Wilder, David Dinkins, Lucille Clifton, Toni Morrison, and Kwame Ture (Coates 2015, 40). Beyond specific thinkers and texts, Coates also emphasizes how "Mecca," the black intellectual community surrounding Howard, shaped his thinking. Coates describes it in these terms: "a machine, crafted to capture and concentrate the dark energy of all African peoples and inject it directly into the student body" (2015, 40). Much like Socrates was shaped by his city of Athens, Coates was shaped by his experiences at Howard.

Given Coates' refusal to connect himself with the white intellectual canon, I do have some hesitation about the comparison between Coates and Socrates. However, consider Michelle Alexander's description of him in her *New York Times* review of *Between the World and Me*: Coates is one "who now speaks unpopular, unconventional and sometimes even radical truths in his own voice, unfiltered. He is invariably humble, yet subtly defiant. And people listen" (Alexander 2015). If that does not describe a Socratic figure, I do not know what does. Coates has certainly functioned in a Socratic manner for me, causing me to interrogate my own "belief that I am white." I am not alone in seeing him in this way. Stephanie McCarter, an English professor at University of the South, compares him to both Antigone and Socrates in the *Apology*. She regards Socrates as agnostic, which makes a comparison with Coates' rejection of anything beyond the material easier (McCarter 2017). To be sure, frank speaking demands that we ask tough questions, and questioning yields an intellectual freedom to which Coates shows an irresistible attraction. Coates himself writes, "The greatest reward of this constant interrogation, of confrontation with the brutality of my country, is that it has freed me from ghosts and girded me against the sheer terror of disembodiment" (2015, 12). However, I see the Socratic aspects of Coates' writing in slightly different terms.

Coates's *parrhesia* has three primary aims. First, he seeks to undermine our unexamined commitment to American exceptionalism. Differently put, Coates "propose[s] to take our countrymen's claims of American exceptionalism seriously, . . . subjecting our country to an exceptional moral standard" (2015, 8). Second, Coates makes clear that the aim of unmasking the dream of American greatness is to aim at living in truth. Although Coates himself does not make this connection, I believe living in this awful truth is much like the Socratic practice of living in the truth of the fact that he knows that he knows nothing. Finally, Coates describes horrors of slavery and its legacy of ongoing racism, which becomes increasingly horrifying with every unfolding news cycle. He argues that our mythological belief in American greatness depends on the continued exploitation of its black citizens. And, if we are to become a country truly devoted to liberty, white Americans must come to terms with their complicity in this exploitation of black citizens, their bodies, and their souls.

With respect to waking from the dream of American exceptionalism, Coates writes, "America believes itself to be exceptional, the greatest and noblest nation ever to exist, a lone champion standing between the white city of democracy and the terrorists, despots, barbarians, and other enemies of civilization" (2015, 8). Observations like this one pervade *Between the World and Me*. They are evocative of Socrates' sense of Athens as a sleeping horse that needs to be awakened and reminded of the ways it has lost its greatness, a greatness that Pericles emphasizes in the Funeral Oration.[19] Coates is aware that this process of educating himself and educating America leads to living in the discomfort of truth. He writes, "It began to strike me that the point of my education was a kind of discomfort, was the process that would not award me my own special Dream but would break all the dreams" (Coates 2015, 52). Coates's writing is beginning to wake up the sleeping horse of white America.

Simply put, Coates, like Socrates, aims at making people see difficult truths about themselves and the world. Early in the book, he tells a story about talking with a reporter, stating, "I realized then why I was sad. When the journalist asked me about my body, it was like she was asking me to awaken her from the most gorgeous dream" (Coates 2015, 10–11). Coates continues, "But this has never been an option because the Dream rests on our backs, the bedding made from our bodies" (2015, 11). That gorgeous dream masks the horror that undergirds its possibility. Coates makes it impossible for his son to participate in this dream. He tells his son "that racism is a visceral experience, that it dislodges brains, blocks airways, rips muscle, extracts organs, cracks bones, breaks teeth. You must never look away from this" (Coates 2015, 10). Moreover, Coates' insistence on seeing and speaking the truth of America to his son is rhetorically aimed at the whole community. I am reminded of Socrates' exhortation to the Athenians to care for his children and hold them accountable to truth. He ends his defense exhorting the jurors to hold fast to the truth that he has spent his life trying to reveal: "When my sons grow up avenge yourselves by causing them the same kind of grief that I caused you, if you think they care for money or anything else more than they care for virtue or if they think they are somebody when they are nobody. Reproach them as I reproach you" (*Ap.*, 41e). In the spirit of Socrates, we must take up Coates' implicit exhortation and reproach ourselves as American citizens.

Coates steadfastly refuses a turn to religious or spiritual solace, which is a marked contrast with the Socratic practice of truth telling that is grounded in his spiritual commitment to understanding the meaning of the Delphic oracle. Nonetheless, Coates frequently appears on the public talk show and interview circuit, logically explaining his arguments with respect to the moral limitations of a vision of America that remains shaped by whiteness. Coates offers us, perhaps despite himself, a hopeful vision for the future.[20] On this point, James Haile writes, "He does not tell this to his son because he is pessimistic, but because he is optimistic: optimistic of the possibilities of his son for a meaningful life, for participation in a meaningful world-experience, for happiness and for joy" (2016, 13). Simply put, his evocative letters to his son contain an embedded enthymeme about a form of physically and psychically engaged citizenship.[21] On an individual level, he wants his son to have ownership of the fate of his body, to be a fearless questioner, to be aware of the legacy of violence and past oppression but not be bound by their reality.[22] His message to his son is a message to us all: to the extent that we all can inhabit this vision of citizenship, America might strive to achieve "a more perfect union" and embody the highest ideals of democracy by ending the exploitation of citizens at the margins and instead furthering the common good.

Finally, I think it is possible to regard Coates not only as a Socratic figure but also as a contemporary Plato lurking in our midst. Coates is an eloquent writer. In many ways, his articles, essays, and books function as Platonic dialogues do. His writing leads readers through a process of engaged argument, aporetic reassessment, toward a refined understanding of the issues at hand. His work should motivate us to enter the increasingly fragmented agora; after all, ours is a world shaped by a democracy in crisis, a world that needs philosophical gadflies willing to speak truth in the public political sphere—much the same as Socrates did in the Athenian agora.

NOTES

1. Some of the Ta-Neishi Coates and Cornel West material in chapter 6 appears in *Southwest Philosophy Review* "Stirring up the America's Sleeping Horses: Cornel West, Ta-Nehisi Coates, and Socratic Parrhesia and Platonic Writing in the Public Sphere." In *Southwest Philosophical Review* 34 (2018):1–16.

2. Nussbaum (2018). The book starts off with her description of her emotional state of mind on the night of the 2016 elections.

3. Westover (2018), Obama (2018), Vance (2016), and Gottlieb (2019).

4. Here are some recent examples of philosophers using their own experience as the occasion for philosophical reflection: Kittay (2019), Moore (2019), Kaag (2016), and Wright (2018). See also McWhorter (1999) and Barnes (1997). For a good treatment of Hazel Barnes and philosophical autobiography more broadly, see Wright (2006).

5. As a liberal American, I have the tendency to regard Socrates as a figure aligned with my own political framework. For a comprehensive assessment of how Greek thinkers including the reception of Socrates has shaped conservative thought, see Bloxham (2018).

6. bell hooks frequently engages in critical dialogue in her writing. *Teaching to Transgress* and *Teaching Community* have interviews between herself and Ron Scapp; see hooks (1994) and hooks (2003). *Breaking Bread* is a collection of exchanges between herself and Cornel West. See hooks and West (1991). Her dialogue with Mary Childers in *Conflicts in Feminism* is another example. See hooks and Childers (1990). While there are often strong points of convergence in thinking in these dialogues, the dialogical mechanism also highlights difference and the sustained ability to disagree in dialogue.

7. The website for the bell hooks (2019) Institute describes her in this way: "bell hooks is an acclaimed intellectual, feminist theorist, cultural critic, artist, and writer. hooks has authored over three dozen books and has published works that span several genres, including cultural criticism, personal memoirs, poetry collections, and children's books. Her writings cover topics of gender, race, class, spirituality, teaching, and the significance of media in contemporary culture."

8. On pernicious pervasiveness of the concept of whiteness, see Stovall (2019).

9. *Feminist Theory from Margin to Center* and *Feminism is for Everyone* clearly articulate the ways that early feminist gains capitalized on the gains of the civil rights movement and in many ways achieved ground without continuing to advance the work of social justice outside of narrowly circumscribed feminist concerns. See hooks (1984, 2000).

10. She chose to use the pseudonym bell hooks in her writing partly as a tribute to her grandmother, Bell Blair Hooks, but also as a way of taking the focus away from her as "the" author and to the ideas themselves, which is certainly a risk for any author who practices public self-disclosure.

11. Kathy Khang, n.d., Kathy Khang (website), accessed July 11, 2019, http://www.kathykhang.com/ .

12. On the white evangelical support of Donald Trump, see Frose, Uecker, and Vaughan (2017, 8). See also Sciupac and Smith (2018) and Newport (2018).

For an excellent exploration of the appeal of Trump to the Christian right, see Perry (2019).

13. Khang references a Fox News account in her blog. See Casiano (2019).

There are numerous other outlets that reported on the event; see, for example, Phillips (2019).

14. See Khang (2019b).

15. See Khang (2019b).

16. See Coates (2014). Coates recently testified before Congress on Reparations. See Stuart (2019).

17. See MacArthur Foundation (2015).

18. Adriel Trott has curated an extremely helpful collection of reviews of his work. See Trott (2015). Most of the reviews are in the popular media, but Coates' work is receiving academic attention as well. Ferrari's (2016) "A Tale of Fear: Racialization and Temporal Oppression in Coates' 'Between the World and Me'" and Haile's (2016) "Ta-Nehisi Coates: Quanta Matter and the Phenomenology of the Body" appeared on the SPEP program in 2016. In 2014, University of the South assigned *Between the World and Me* as the campuswide book to read. https://eidolon.pub/between-the-ancient-world-and-me-2c0ceee8cbdf#.hcgyuxqhf. See also Gordon (2017).

19. See Thucydides (1998, 2.34–46).

20. This is a significant dissimilarity with Socrates. Although Socrates' religious beliefs were clearly part of what led to his trial, Socrates did profess a strong, abiding commitment to the divine. On this point, see Beaty and Bowery (2003).

21. I thank my colleague Sam Perry for this formulation of Coates' rhetorical aim.

22. My thanks to Paul Carron for pointing out this rhetorical similarity.

Postscript

Becoming a Public Philosopher

People ask me all the time why I became a philosopher. One answer I like to give: I have always been a philosopher. It just took me awhile to wake up and realize it. I even have proof for my early affinity for philosophy. As an infant, I loved my father's statue of Rodin's *Thinker*. An old black-and-white photograph shows me teething on its head. In another photo from the same series, my arms are wrapped around it in an exuberant embrace. Here's another piece of evidence. I remember driving to my friend Naomi's house to study for an Advanced Placement chemistry exam. It was turning dark and getting cold. I was fiddling with the defrost mechanism on our drafty old Volkswagen bus. I had a vision of my future self. All of a sudden, this peaceful sense of well-being came over me. I knew that I wasn't going to be a doctor or a scientist, so this exam did not matter much. I knew, really knew, what I was going to be instead. I was going to be a philosopher and live on a mountaintop in Tibet. Now, at this time in my life, I had not read a single word of philosophy other than *Atlas Shrugged* and had only the vaguest sense of where Tibet was. It turns out that I am a philosopher, but I live in Texas. I got the location wrong, but I'm taking my fourth trip to India this year. Perhaps Tibet is not so far off. Nietzsche is right. Become what you are.

    I was a Platonist from the start. I remember the moment I learned to read. I was sitting on the crumpled edge of my pink and orange bedspread. It was just before bedtime. I remember the evening breeze and our two beagles barking outside. I was reading out loud from a book about pirates. My mother patiently listened as I tried to figure out the difference between the word "this" and the word "that." Prior to the particular evening, I'd been doing a lot of guessing about letters and practicing how to sound out words. Suddenly, as I watched my sister climb into the matching twin bed across the room, my young mind recollected how it all fit together. I could read. My mother confirms my memory of the moment. She said, "I could just see you get it. Your eyes were on fire. It was really exciting!" From picture books to philosophy. All of a sudden. Just like that.

But that isn't the kind of answer most people—particularly young philosophy students with anxious goal-oriented parents who have paid enormous sums of tuition dollars and have taken on the lifelong burden of student debt—are looking for. They want to know what hooked me, what hooked me hard enough to make me tell my parents that I was going to be an academic philosopher instead of a corporate lawyer. Why did I get a PhD and not an MD? A doctorate and not a diamond? That's a more difficult question. Even if I answer them, my answer can't be theirs. Truthfully, I don't have a clear memory of the very first philosophy class I took. Despite my beatific vision in the Volkswagen, I didn't take philosophy until my sophomore year. Finally, a distribution requirement forced me into an ethics class. So much for free will! We read the *Euthyphro*. Plato didn't hook me immediately. Piety was not something I was all that interested in thinking critically about after eighteen years of attendance in Methodist church services, Sunday school classes, and Bible studies. All I really remember about the class was meeting a very cute guy, Brent. Plato had already hooked him. He told me that he had renamed his childhood teddy bear, Socrates.

It took two classes for philosophy to grab me. Larry Kimmel's existentialism class did the trick. It wasn't so much the existentialism that got me. It was something he said about it. He said he was not sure if existentialism was a livable project. I don't know why that phrase struck me, but it did. It has really stuck with me as well. Is philosophy a livable project? I got my answer the next semester when I read Plato's *Symposium* with Chuck Salman. I fell in love with a dialogue about love. That's why I am a philosopher today.

* * *

Just the other day, a student asked me if reading the *Symposium* changed my understanding of love. I found myself quite unprepared to answer. "Yes, of course," I stammered. Dogged in her pursuit of knowledge, she asked, "How?" Still swimming in memory, I mentioned something about seeing beyond the heteronormative framework of our society. However, I knew I had not gone about the matter of answering her correctly. She wanted to know if what was happening to her happened to me, and, of course, the answer is "yes." I have been in love with this dialogue for over thirty years. From the moment I read it, I was entranced. I fell in love, and I fell in love hard. To this day, the text represents the beautiful itself for me. I am fascinated by its form. Its nested narrative frame. The dynamic personalities and the love triangles. The jokes, the stories, the flute girls, and the mixing vessels of wine. The Dionysian. The Apollonian. The idea that philosophy must necessarily encompass both. They are inexorably intertwined; that is what the *Symposium* teaches. We cannot escape our bodies any more than we can escape our minds. My love for the offspring of Plato's insight into the beautiful itself led me to an undergraduate major in philosophy, carried me through rigors of graduate school, sustained me in the tenure process and through the Byzantine career path of academia. Now, I find myself more prepared to answer her. Once more from the beginning. Yes, Plato's *Symposium* changed my understanding of love. *The Symposium* showed me that there is something larger to love. That love is an activity of soul, not a longing for beautiful bodies. I found comfort in this thought when I felt that all those beautiful college boys wanted was my own beautiful body and that no one would ever love my soul. *The Symposium* showed me the beautiful itself. Yes, the *Symposium* changed my understanding of love. It made me see philosophy as a form of love. It made me see philosophy as a livable project. Plato gave me a world I wanted to live in. Reading Plato made me happy. Teaching Plato made me even happier. That's why I am love teaching philosophy today.

* * *

Not long after I started teaching, my parents came to visit me for Thanksgiving. My mother saw a sign in Lake Air Mall advertising yoga classes with Walter Reece. She wrote down the phone number. This was before we all had cell phones. She told me, "Anne, I think you would really like yoga." She was right. I called Walter for information and took my first class the Saturday after Thanksgiving. I loved being a student of something again. This was when I was reading bell hooks and struggling with becoming the kind of teacher I wanted to be. I had no desire to teach yoga. Eventually, I took over some classes that Walter didn't want. I started teaching outside the academic setting. I was genuinely surprised when people kept coming to classes. I was so accustomed to teaching and learning happening within the confines of the classroom that it was hard for me to recognize that I was creating new learning environments in the local YMCA and in the sanctuary of Lake Shore Baptist Church. That was my first movement toward becoming a public philosopher, though I did not realize it at the time.

At first, I was not particularly interested in the philosophical aspects of yoga. I even enjoyed the break from philosophy. But it turns out there is really no escape from philosophy. As I started studying to be a Certified Iyengar Yoga teacher, I began to read Patanjali's *Yoga Sutras* and *The Bhagavad Gita*. I saw so many similarities with ancient Greek philosophy.[1] Just like the nested narrative frames of the *Symposium* hooked my English major mind, these texts drew my philosophically trained mind more deeply into the practice of yoga. I got more and more interested. Over time, I also started teaching philosophy to other aspiring teachers. Teaching philosophy in this context made me see that all sorts of people craved philosophy. These other yoga teachers generally had other professions. There were lawyers and bankers, fashion designers and freelance writers. River conservation managers and social workers. Fire fighters and kindergarten teachers. Massage therapists and stay-at-home moms. Engineers and English teachers. Everyone seemed to appreciate learning about yoga philosophy. That was my second movement toward becoming a public philosopher.

I started a blog during my first trip to India in 2007.[2] I started writing about my life as a teacher of philosophy and yoga and as a student of yoga and philosophy. I realized that all sorts of people were reading. Having an audience outside the classroom for my philosophical thoughts inspired me to write more and more. Blogging became an important part of my daily routine of philosophical writing and reflection. That was my third movement toward becoming a public philosopher. I have continued to develop my philosophical work outside the classroom in other ways as well. For example, the Black Lives Matter movement and other recent political events led me and my sister to start "Yoginis for Social Justice," a reading group in Austin. We focused our initial efforts around reading Chris Crass' *Towards the "Other America": Anti-Racist Resources for White People Taking Action for Black Lives Matter.* Ten yoga teachers carved time out from their busy schedules and met monthly for two years. I started reading even more widely as part of my own Socratic self-interrogation of white privilege .

With Plato's Socrates as public philosopher on my mind, I started thinking about how to use my pedagogical and professional spheres of influence to begin conversations about social justice issues. I started another Social Justice reading group in Waco. We are starting our third year of regular monthly meetings. I also decided to work for social change on campus. To this end, I became involved with the work of the Interfaith Youth Core and serve as a member of the Advisory Board for the Better Together chapter on campus. As I have moved out of the classroom and into the agora, I have found self-disclosure to be an important mode of interpersonal exchange that binds us together in the work that we do. I will end by stressing that my journey as a public philosopher is only beginning. I look forward to what the future holds.

NOTES

1. I'm working on a book that explores Plato's *Phaedo*, *The Bhagavad Gita*, and being a student of Iyengar Yoga during the years when the community experienced the passing of B. K. S. and Geeta Iyengar.

2. Schultz, n.d., *Thoughts on Teaching Philosophy and Yoga* (blog), accessed September 17, 2018, http://www.teachingphilosophyandyoga.blogspot.com.

References

Adams, Don. 2017. *Socrates Mystagogos*. New York: Routledge.
Ahbel-Rappe, Sara. 2018. *Socratic Ignorance and Platonic Knowledge in the Dialogues of Plato*. Albany: State University of New York Press.
Ahbel-Rappe, Sara, and Rachana Kamtekar, eds. 2006. *A Companion to Socrates*. Oxford: Blackwell.
Ahrensdorf, Peter. 1995. *The Death of Socrates and the Life of Philosophy*. Albany: State University of New York Press.
Alexander, M. 2015. "Ta-Nehisi Coates's *Between the World and Me*." Review of *Between the World and Me*, by Ta-Nehisi Coates. *New York Times*, August 27, 2015. https://www.nytimes.com/2015/08/17/books/review/ta-nehisi-coates-between-the-world-and-me.html .
Altman, William. 2012. *Plato the Teacher: The Crisis of "The Republic."* Lanham, MD: Lexington Books.
Altman, William. 2016a. *The Guardians on Trial: The Reading Order of Plato's Dialogues from* Euthyphro *to* Phaedo. Lanham, MD: Lexington Press.
Altman, William. 2016b. *The Guardians in Action: Plato the Teacher and the Post Republic Dialogues from* Timaeus *to* Theaetetus. Lanham, MD: Lexington Books.
Altman, William. 2018a. *Ascent to the Good: The Reading Order of Plato's Dialogues from* Symposium *to* Republic. Lanham, MD: Lexington Books.
Altman, William. 2018b. "Open Letter to Ariel Helfer." Accessed October 2, 2019. https://www.academia.edu/37168659/An_Open_Letter_to_Ariel_Helfer .
Anderson, Daniel. 1993. *The Masks of Dionysos: A Commentary on Plato's* Symposium. Albany: State University of New York Press.
Augustine. 1984. *Confessions*. Translated by R. S. Pine. London: Penguin Books.
Ausland, Hayden. 2000. "Who Speaks for Whom in the *Timaeus-Critias*?" In *Who Speaks for Plato*, edited by Gerald Press, 183–200. Lanham, MD: Rowman & Littlefield.
Baracchi, Claudia. 2006. "The 'Inconceivable Happiness' of 'Men and Women': Visions of Another World in Plato's *Apology of Socrates*." *Comparative Literature Studies* 43 (3): 269–84.
Barnes, Hazel. 1997. *The Story I Tell Myself*. Chicago: University of Chicago Press.
Barrett, James. 2001. "Plato's 'Apology': Philosophy, Rhetoric, and the World of Myth." *The Classical World* 95 (1): 3–30.
Barrett, James, and Angela Hobbs. 2000. *Plato and the Hero: Courage, Manliness and the Impersonal Good*. Cambridge: Cambridge University Press.
Bastianini, G., and D. Sedley. 1995. *Edition of the Anonymous In Theaetetum in Corpus Dei Papyri Filosofici Greci E Latini, Commentari*, III, Firenze.

References

Baylor University. 2019. "Better Together BU." Baylor. Accessed October 1, 2019. https://www.baylor.edu/multicultural/index.php?id=929860.
Beaty, Michael, and A. M. Bowery. 2003. "Cultivating Christian Citizenship: Martha Nussbaum's Socrates, Augustine's *Confessions*, and the Modern University." *Christian Scholar's Review* 31 (1): 21–52.
Benardete, S. 1984. *The Being of the Beautiful*. Chicago: University of Chicago Press.
Benardete, S. 1986. "On Interpreting Plato's *Charmides*." *Graduate Faculty Philosophy Journal* 11 (2): 9–16.
Benardete, S. 1997. "Plato's 'Theaetetus': On the Way of the Logos." *The Review of Metaphysics* 51 (1): 25–53.
Benardete, S. 2000a. "On Plato's *Symposium*." In *The Argument of the Action: Essays on Greek Poetry and Philosophy*, 167–85. Chicago: University of Chicago Press.
Benardete, S. 2000b. *The Argument of the Action*. Edited by Ronna Burger and Michael Davis. Chicago: University of Chicago Press.
Berg, Steven. 2010. *Eros and the Intoxications of Enlightenment: On Plato's "Symposium."* Albany: State University of New York Press.
Bergen, Benjamin K. 2012. *Louder than Words: The New Science of How the Mind Makes Meaning*. New York: Basic Books.
Blondell, Ruby. 2002. *The Play of Character in Plato's Dialogues*. Cambridge: Cambridge University Press.
Blondell, Ruby. 2006. "Where Is Socrates on the 'Ladder of Love'?" In *Plato's "Symposium": Issues in Interpretation and Reception*, edited by J. H. Lesher, Debra Nails, and Frisbee C. C. Sheffield, 147–78. Cambridge, MA: Harvard University Press.
Bloxham, John. 2018. *Ancient Greece and American Conservatism: Classical Influence on the Modern Right*. London: I. B. Tauris.
Bortolussi, Marisa, and Peter Dixon. 2003. *Psychonarratology: Foundations for the Empirical Study of Literary Response*. Cambridge: Cambridge University Press.
Bostock, David. 1988. *Plato's* Theaetetus. Oxford: Oxford University Press.
Bowery, Anne-Marie. 1998. "Looking Beyond the Elenchus." *Southwest Philosophy Review* 14: 157–68.
Bowery, Anne-Marie. 2003. "Recovering and Recollecting the Soul." In *Plato's Forms: Varieties of Interpretation*, edited by William Welton, 111–36. Lanham, MD: Lexington Books.
Brann, Eva. 2004. *The Music of the "Republic."* Philadelphia: Paul Dry Books.
Brickhouse, Thomas C., and Nicholas D. Smith. 1983. "The Origin of Socrates' Mission." *Journal of the History of Ideas* 44 (4): 657–66.
Brickhouse, Thomas C., and Nicholas D. Smith, eds. 2002. *The Trial and Execution of Socrates: Sources and Controversies*. Oxford: Oxford University Press.
Brill, Sara. 2013. *Plato on the Limits of Human Life*. Bloomington: Indiana University Press.
Brisson, Luc. 2006. "Agathon, Pausanias, and Diotima in Plato's *Symposium*: Paiderastia and Philosophia." Translated by Michael Chase. In *Plato's* Symposium: *Issues in Interpretation and Reception*, edited by James Lesher, Debra Nails, and Frisbee Sheffield, 229–51. Cambridge, MA: Harvard University Press.
Brown, Catherine. 2018. "She Never Saw a Classroom until College. Now She Has a Ph.D. and a Lot of Thoughts about Education." *Forbes*, August 27, 2018. https://www.forbes.com/sites/catherinebrown/2018/08/27/she-never-saw-a-classroom-until-college-now-she-has-a-ph-d-and-a-lot-of-thoughts-about-education/#4098da892787.
BU Bears for All. 2019. "Who We Are." Accessed October 1, 2019. https://bubearsforall.org/who-we-are.
Burger, Ronna. 1984. Phaedo: *A Platonic Labyrinth*. New Haven, CT: Yale University Press.
Bussanich, John. 2006. "Socrates and Religious Experience." In *A Companion to Socrates*, edited by Sara Ahbel-Rappe and Rachana Kamtekar, 200–213. Malden, MA: Blackwell.
Carsetti, Arturo. 2010. *Causality, Meaningful Complexity and Embodied Cognition*. Dordrecht: Springer Science & Business Media.
Casiano, Louis. 2019. "Florida Boy, 11, Arrested after Refusing to Recite 'Racist' Pledge of Allegiance: Report." *Fox News*, February 17, 2018. https://www.foxnews.com/us/florida-boy-11-arrested-after-refusing-to-recite-racist-pledge-of-allegiance.

Chance, Thomas. 1992. *Plato's* Euthydemus. Berkeley: University of California Press.
Chappell, Timothy. 2005. *Reading Plato's "Theaetetus."* Indianapolis: Hackett.
Clayton, Edward. 2008. "The Death of Socrates and the Life of Aesop." *Ancient Philosophy* 28 (2): 311–28.
Coates, Ta-Nehisi. 2014. "The Case for Reparations." *Atlantic Monthly*, June 2014. http://argumentcenterededucation.com/wp-content/uploads/2018/04/The-Case-for-Reparations-by-Ta-Nehisi-Coates-The-Atlantic.pdf.
Coates, Ta-Nehisi. 2015. *Between the World and Me*. New York: Random House.
Colaiaco, John. 2013. *Socrates against Athens: Philosophy on Trial*. New York: Routledge.
Collins, James Henderson, II. 2015. *Exhortations to Philosophy: The Protreptics of Plato, Isocrates, and Aristotle*. Oxford: Oxford University Press.
Connelly, Joan Breton. 2007. *Portrait of a Priestess: Women and Ritual in Ancient Greece*. Princeton, NJ: Princeton University Press.
Corcoran, Clinton DeBevoise. 2016. *Topography and Deep Structure in Plato: The Construction of Place in the Dialogues*. Albany: State University of New York Press.
Corey, David. 2005. "Socratic Citizenship: Delphic Oracle and Divine Sign." *The Review of Politics* 67 (2): 201–28.
Corey, David. 2015. *The Sophists in Plato's Dialogues*. Albany: State University of New York Press.
Cornelli, Gabriele. 2013. *In Search of Pythagoreanism*. Berlin: De Gruyter.
Cornelli, Gabriele, Richard McKirahan, and Constantinos Macris, eds. 2013. *On Pythagoreanism*. Berlin: De Gruyter.
Corrigan, Kevin, and Elena Glazov-Corrigan. 2004. *Plato's Dialectic at Play Argument, Structure, and Myth in the* Symposium. University Park, PA: Penn State Press.
Cotter, Joseph. 1992. "The Joke on Apollodorus's Demotic." *Classical Philology* 87 (2): 131–34.
Crooks, James. 2000. "Writing Conversation: Notes on the Structure of the *Phaedo*." In *Retracing the Platonic Text*, edited by John Russon and John Sallis, 155–74. Evanston, IL: Northwestern University Press.
Cupchik, Gerald C. 1997. "Identification as a Basic Problem for Aesthetic Reception." In *The Systemic and Empirical Approach to Literature and Culture as Theory and Application*, edited by S. T. de Zepetnek and I. Sywenky, 11–22. Edmonton: Research Institute for Comparative Literature and Cross-Cultural Studies.
Destrée, Pierre, and Zina Giannopoulou, eds. 2017. *Plato's* Symposium*: A Critical Guide*. Cambridge Critical Guides. Cambridge: Cambridge University Press.
DiAngelo, Robin. 2018. *White Fragility*. Boston: Beacon Press.
Dorion, Louis-André. 2012. "The Delphic Oracle on Socrates' Wisdom: A Myth?" In *Plato and Myth: Studies on the Use and Status of Platonic Myths*, edited by Catherine Collobert, Pierre Destrée, and Francisco J. Gonzalez, 419–34. Leiden: Brill.
Dorion, Louis-André. 2018. "Comparative Exegesis and the Socratic Problem." In *Plato and Xenophon: Comparative Studies*, edited by Gabriel Danzig, David M. Johnson, and Donald R. Morrison, 55–70. Mnemosyne Supplements 417. Leiden: Brill.
Dorter, Kenneth. 1982. *Plato's* Phaedo*: An Interpretation*. Toronto: University of Toronto Press.
Dover, Kenneth. 1978. *Greek Homosexuality*. Cambridge, MA: Harvard University Press.
Eagan, Kevin. 2013. "Interview with Christopher Long of the *Public Philosophy Journal*." Critical Margins. August 21, 2013. https://criticalmargins.com/interview-with-christopher-long-of-the-public-philosophy-journal-b9d6ffcc6350.
Eckstein, Jerome. 1981. *The Deathday of Socrates*. New York: Columbia Publishing Company.
Edmonds, Radcliffe G. 2017. "Alcibiades the Profane: Images of the Mysteries." In *Plato's* Symposium*: A Critical Guide*, edited by Pierre Destrée and Zina Giannopoulou, 194–215. Cambridge: Cambridge University Press.
Electronic Agora. 2019. "About." Accessed October 1, 2019. https://theelectricagora.com/.
Ellis, Walter. 1989. *Alcibiades*. New York: Routledge.

Ferrari, A. 2016. "A Tale of Fear: Racialization and Temporal Oppression in Coates's' *Between the World and Me*." Speech presented at the Society for Phenomenology and Existential Philosophy, Salt Lake City, 2016.
Ferrari, G. R. F. 1999. *City and Soul in Plato's "Republic."* Chicago: University of Chicago Press.
Finkelberg, Aryeh. 1986. "On the Unity of Orphic and Milesian Thought." *Harvard Theological Review* 79 (4): 321–35.
Finkelberg, Margalit. 2018. *The Gatekeeper: Narrative Voice in Plato's Dialogues*. Leiden: Brill.
Frey, Jennifer. 2019. Podcast audio. Sacred and Profane Love. Episode Sixteen. "King Lear's Vision." September 20, 2019. https://thevirtueblog.com/2019/09/20/episode-16-king-lears-vision/.
Frose, Paul, Jeremy Uecker, and Kenneth Vaughan. 2017. "The Sacred Values of Trumpism." In *American Values, Mental Health, and Using Technology in the Age of Trump: Findings from the Baylor Religion Survey, Wave 5*, 7–28. Waco, TX: Institute for Study of Religion and Baylor Sociology.
Frosolono, Anne-Marie. 1993. "Narrating Plato's *Symposium*: A Critique of Socratic Discipleship." Dissertation, Pennsylvania State University.
Gagarin, M. 1969. "The Purpose of Plato's *Protagoras*." *Transactions and Proceedings of the American Philological Association* 100: 133–64.
George, Robert, and Cornel West. 2016. "The Examined Life: Robert George and Cornel West on the Purpose of Liberal Arts Education." Speech presented at the AEI State of the American Campus Event. Washington, D.C., November 30, 2016. Accessed October 2, 2019. http://www.aei.org/events/the-examined-life-robert-george-and-cornel-west-on-the-purpose-of-liberal-arts-education/.
Giannopoulou, Zina. 2017. "Narrative Temporalities and Models of Desire." In *Plato's Symposium: A Critical Guide*, edited by Pierre Destrée and Zina Giannopoulou, 9–27. Cambridge: Cambridge University Press.
Gill, Mary Louise. 2012. *"Philosophos": Plato's Missing Dialogue*. Oxford: Oxford University Press.
Glass, Emily. 2015. "A Therapeutic *Symposium*: Obstructive Shame in Plato's Dialogues." Dissertation, Baylor University.
Gold, Jeffrey. 1996. "Plato in the Light of Yoga." *Philosophy of East and West* 46 (1): 17–32.
Gordon, Jill. 1999. *Turning Toward Philosophy*. University Park: Pennsylvania State University Press.
Gordon, Jill. 2017. "Black Bodies Matter: A Reading of Ta-Nehisi Coates' *Between the World and Me*." *Graduate Faculty Philosophy Journal* 38 (1): 199–221.
Gottlieb, Lori. 2019. *Maybe You Should Talk to Someone: A Therapist, Her Therapist, and Our Lives Revealed*. Boston: Houghton Mifflin Harcourt.
Gould, T. 1990. *The Ancient Quarrel Between Poetry and Philosophy*. Princeton, NJ: Princeton University Press.
Gower, O. S. L. 2008. "Why Is There an Autobiography in the *Phaedo*?" *Ancient Philosophy* 28 (2): 329–46.
Gulley, Norman. 1962. *Plato's Theory of Knowledge*. London: Metheun.
Guthrie, W. K. C. 1965. *A History of Greek Philosophy*. Vol. 2. Cambridge: Cambridge University Press.
Hadot, Pierre. 1988. *Philosophy as a Way of Life*. Translated by Michael Chase. Oxford: Blackwell Press.
Hadot, Pierre. 2004. *What Is Ancient Philosophy?* Cambridge, MA: Belknap Press.
Haile, James. 2016. "Ta-Nehisi Coates: Quanta Matter and the Phenomenology of the Body." Speech presented at the Society for Phenomenology and Existential Philosophy, Salt Lake City, 2016.
Halperin, David. 1990a. *One Hundred Years of Homosexuality*. New York: Routledge.
Halperin, David. 1990b. "Why Is Diotima a Woman?" In *100 Years of Homosexuality and Other Essays on Greek Love*, 113–52. London: Routledge.

Halperin, David. 1992. "Plato and the Erotics of Narrativity." In *Oxford Studies in Ancient Philosophy: Methods of Interpreting Plato and His Dialogues*, edited by Julia Annas, J. C. Klagge, and Nicholas D. Smith, 93–129. Oxford: Clarendon Press.

Hartle, Ann. 1986. *Death and the Disinterested Spectator: An Inquiry into the Nature of Philosophy*. Albany: State University of New York Press.

Helfer, Ariel. 2017. *Socrates and Alcibiades: Plato's Drama of Political Ambition and Philosophy*. Philadelphia: University of Pennsylvania Press.

Hesiod. 1968. *Theogony*. Translated by Richard Lattimore. Ann Arbor: University of Michigan Press.

Hoinski, David F. 2008. "Context, Decision, and Autobiography in Plato's 'Phaedo.'" *Ancient Philosophy* 28 (2): 347–55.

hooks, bell. 1984. *Feminist Theory from Margin to Center*. New York: Routledge.

hooks, bell. 1994. *Teaching to Transgress*. New York: Routledge.

hooks, bell. 2000. *Feminism Is for Everyone*. Cambridge, MA: South End Press.

hooks, bell. 2003. *Teaching Community*. New York: Routledge.

hooks, bell. 2009. *Teaching Critical Thinking*. New York: Routledge.

hooks, bell. 2019. "About." Bell Hooks Institute. Accessed October 1, 2019. https://bellhooksinstitute.squarespace.com/#/about.

hooks, bell, and Mary Childers. 1990. "A Conversation about Race and Class." In *Conflicts in Feminism*, edited by Marianne Hirsch and Evelyn Fox Keller, 60–81. New York: Routledge.

hooks, bell, and Cornel West. 1991. *Breaking Bread: Insurgent Black Intellectual Life*. Boston: South End.

Hopkins, Burt. 2011. "The Unwritten Teachings in Plato's *Symposium*." *Epoche* 15 (2): 279–98.

Howland, Jacob. 1991. "Re-Reading Plato: The Problem of Platonic Chronology." *Phoenix* 45 (3): 189–214.

Howland, Jacob. 1993. *The Republic: The Odyssey of Philosophy*. Philadelphia: Paul Dry Books.

Howland, Jacob. 1998. *The Paradox of Political Philosophy: Socrates' Philosophic Trial*. Lanham, MD: Rowman & Littlefield.

Howland, Jacob. 2004. *The Republic: The Odyssey of Philosophy*. Philadelphia: Paul Dry Books.

Howland, Jacob. 2018. "Socrates' Daimonic Ethics: Myth and Heroism in Plato's *Apology*." In *Readings of Plato's* Apology of Socrates*: Defending the Philosophical Life*, edited by Vivil Valvik Haraldsen, Olof Pettersson, and Oda E. Wiese Tvedt, 89–100. Lanham, MD: Lexington Books.

Howland, Jacob. 2019. *Glaucon's Fate: History, Myth, and Character in Plato's Republic*. Philadelphia: Paul Dry Books.

Hubbard, Thomas. 2003. *Homosexuality in Greece and Rome: A Sourcebook of Basic Documents*. Berkeley: University of California Press.

Huffman, Carl A., ed. 2014a. *A History of Pythagoreanism*. Cambridge: Cambridge University Press.

Huffman, Carl A. 2014b. "Introduction." In *A History of Pythagoreanism*, edited by Carl A. Huffman, 1–23. Cambridge: Cambridge University Press.

Humanities Commons. 2019. "The Humanities Commons." Accessed October 1, 2019. https://hcommons.org/.

Hyland, Drew. 2015. "Strange Encounters: Theaetetus, Theodorus, Socrates and the Eleatic Stranger." In *Proceedings of the Boston Area Colloquium in Ancient Philosophy*, edited by Gary Gurtler and William Wians, XXX:102–17. Leiden: Brill.

Iacoboni, Marco. 2009a. "Imitation, Empathy, and Mirror Neurons." *Annual Review of Psychology* 60: 653–70.

Iacoboni, Marco. 2009b. *Mirroring People: The New Science of How We Connect with Others*. New York: Macmillan.

Interfaith Youth Core. 2019. "About." IFYC. Accessed October 1, 2019. https://www.ifyc.org/about.

Irigaray, Luce. 1988. "Sorcerer Love: A Reading of Plato's 'Symposium,' Diotima's Speech." Translated by Eleanor H. Kuykendall. *Hypatia* 3 (3): 32–44.
Jansen, Sarah. 2013. "Plato's 'Phaedo' as a Pedagogical Drama." *Ancient Philosophy* 33 (2): 333–52.
Jong, Irene J. F. de. 2006. "The Homeric Narrator and His Own Kleos." *Mnemosyne* 59 (2): 188–207.
Kaag, John. 2016. *American Philosophy: A Love Story*. New York: Farrar, Straus and Giroux.
Kahn, Charles. 2013. *Plato and the Post-Socratic Dialogue: The Return to the Philosophy of Nature*. Cambridge: Cambridge University Press.
Kasimis, Demetra. 2018. *The Perpetual Immigrant and the Limits of Athenian Democracy*. Classics after Antiquity. Cambridge: Cambridge University Press.
Keysers, Christian. 2011. *The Empathic Brain: How the Discovery of Mirror Neurons Changes Our Understanding of Human Nature*. Charleston, SC: CreateSpace.
Khang, Kathy. 2018. *Raise Your Voice*. Downers Grove, IL: IVP Books.
Khang, Kathy. 2019. "About." Kathy Khang (website). Accessed July 11, 2019. http://www.kathykhang.com/about/.
Khang, Kathy. 2019. "I'm Sorry. A Story." Kathy Khang (website). Accessed October 1, 2019. http://www.kathykhang.com/2019/04/23/im-sorry-a-story/.
Kingsley, Peter. 1995. *Ancient Philosophy, Mystery, and Magic: Empedocles and Pythagorean Tradition*. Oxford: Oxford University Press.
Kittay, Eva Feder. 2019. *Learning from My Daughter: The Value and Care of Disabled Minds*. Oxford: Oxford University Press.
Klonoski, Richard J. 1993. "The Preservation of Homeric Tradition: Heroic Re-Performance in the 'Republic' and the 'Odyssey.'" *Clio* 22 (3): 251–71.
Krentz, Peter. 1982. *The Thirty at Athens*. Ithaca, NY: Cornell University Press.
Lampert, Laurence. 2013. *How Philosophy Became Socratic*. Chicago: University of Chicago Press.
Lara, Emma Cohen de. 2007. "Socrates' Response to the Divine in Plato's 'Apology.'" *Polis* 24 (2): 193–202.
Lear, Gabriel. 2006. "Permanent Beauty and Becoming Happy in Plato's *Symposium*." In *Plato's Symposium: Issues in Interpretation and Reception*, edited by James Lesher, Debra Nails, and Frisbee Sheffield, 96–123. Hellenic Studies 22. Cambridge, MA: Harvard University Press.
Lee, Mi-Kyoung, and C. C. W. Taylor. 2016. "The Sophists." In *The Stanford Encyclopedia of Philosophy*, edited by Edward N. Zalta, Winter 2016 Edition. Accessed October 1, 2019. https://plato.stanford.edu/archives/win2016/entries/sophists/.
Leibowitz, D. 2010. *Ironic Defense of Socrates: Plato's* Apology. Cambridge: Cambridge University Press.
Lesher, James, Debra Nails, and Frisbee Sheffield, eds. 2006. *Plato's Symposium: Issues in Interpretation and Reception*. Hellenic Studies 22. Cambridge, MA: Harvard University Press.
Long, Christopher P. 2014. *Socratic and Platonic Political Philosophy: Practicing a Politics of Reading*. Cambridge: Cambridge University Press.
Long, Christopher P. 2018. "Practicing Public Scholarship." *Public Philosophy Journal* 1 (1): 1–8.
Lutz, Mark. 1998. *Socrates' Education to Virtue: Learning the Love of the Noble*. Albany: SUNY Press.
MacArthur Foundation. 2015. "Ta-Nehisi Coates." MacFound (website). September 28, 2015. https://www.macfound.org/fellows/931/.
Madhu, R. C. 1999. "Plato's Homer." *Ancient Philosophy* 19 (Special issue): 87–95.
Marciano, Gemelli. 2014. "The Pythagorean Way of Life and Pythagorean Ethics." In *A History of Pythagoreanism*, edited by Carl A. Huffman, 131–48. Cambridge: Cambridge University Press.
McCarter, Stephanie. 2017. "Between the Ancient World and Me: Modes of Defiance in Ta-Nehisi Coates, Sophocles, and Plato." *Eidolon*. February 23, 2017. https://eidolon.pub/between-the-ancient-world-and-me-2c0ceee8cbdf#.hcgyuxqhf.

McCoy, James. 1975. "The Identity of Leon." *The American Journal of Philology* 96 (2): 187–99.
McCoy, Marina. 2013. *Wounded Heroes*. Oxford: Oxford University Press.
McPherran, Mark. 2006. "Medicine, Magic, and Religion in Plato's *Symposium*." In *Plato's Symposium: Issues in Interpretation and Reception*, edited by James Lesher, Debra Nails, and Frisbee Sheffield, 71–95. Hellenic Studies 22. Cambridge, MA: Harvard University Press.
McWhorter, LaDelle. 1999. *Bodies and Pleasures: Foucault and the Politics of Sexual Normalization*. Indianapolis: Indiana University Press.
Metcalf, Robert. 2004. "The Philosophical Rhetoric of Socrates' Mission." *Philosophy and Rhetoric* 37 (2): 143–66.
Metcalf, Robert. 2009. "Socrates and Achilles." In *Re-Examining Socrates in the "Apology,"* edited by Patricia Fagan and John Russon, 62–84. Evanston, IL: Northwestern University Press.
Michelini, Ann N. 2003. *Plato as Author: The Rhetoric of Philosophy*. Leiden: Brill.
Miller, Mitchell. 2004. *The Philosopher in Plato's Statesman*. Las Vegas: Parmenides Publishing.
Miller, Mitchell. 2015. "'Making New Gods?': A Reflection on the Gift of the *Symposium*." In *Second Sailing: Alternative Perspectives on Plato*, edited by Debra Nails and Harold Tarrant, 285–306. Helsinki: Societas Scientiarum Fennica.
Moore, Holly. 2018. "Socrates as Narrator and the *Republic*'s Theory of Political Subjectivity." Speech presented at the Socrativa IV, Buenos Aires, Argentina, November 13–16, 2018.
Moore, Scott. 2019. *How to Burn a Goat*. Waco, TX: Baylor University Press.
Morgan, K. A. 2004. "Plato." In *Narrators, Narratees, and Narratives in Ancient Greek Literature*, edited by Irene J. F. de Jong, René Nünlist, and Angus Bowie. Vol. 1. Studies in Ancient Greek Narrative, 357–76. Leiden: Brill.
Morgan, Kathryn. 2003a. "Plato's Dream." In *The Ancient Novel and Beyond*, edited by Stelio Panayotakis, Maaike Zimmerman, and Wytse Keulen, 101–14. Leiden: Brill.
Morgan, Kathryn, ed. 2003b. *Popular Tyranny*. Austin: University of Texas Press.
Morgan, Kathryn A. 2000. *Myth and Philosophy: From the Presocratics to Plato*. Cambridge: Cambridge University Press.
Morgan, Michael. 1990. *Platonic Piety*. New Haven, CT: Yale University Press.
Mulhern, J. J. 2015. "Plato's Putative Mouthpiece and Ancient Authorial Practice: The Case of Homer." In *Second Sailing: Alternative Perspectives on Plato*, edited by Debra Nails and Harold Tarrant, 257–58. Helsinki: Societas Scientiarum Fennica.
Munn, Mark. 2003. *School of History*. Berkeley: University of California Press.
Naddaff, Ramona. 2019. "Hearing Voices: The Sounds in Socrates' Head." In *Antiquities Beyond Humanism*, edited by Emma Bianchi, Sara Brill, and Brooke Holmes, 5–20. Oxford: Oxford University Press.
Nails, Debra. 1993. "Problems with Vlastos' Developmentalism." *Ancient Philosophy* 13 (2): 273–91.
Nails, Debra. 1995. *Agora, Academy and the Conduct of Philosophy*. Dordrecht: Kluwer.
Nails, Debra. 2002. *The People of Plato: A Prosopography of Plato and Other Socratics*. Indianapolis: Hackett.
Nails, Debra. 2006a. "The Trial and Death of Socrates." In *A Companion to Socrates*, edited by Sara Ahbel-Rappe and Rachana Kamtekar, 5–20. Oxford: Blackwell.
Nails, Debra. 2006b. "Tragedy Off-Stage." In *Plato's "Symposium": Issues in Interpretation and Reception*, edited by J. H. Lesher, Debra Nails, and Frisbee C. C. Sheffield, 179–207. Cambridge, MA: Center for Hellenic Studies.
Nails, Debra. 2015. "Bad Luck to Take a Woman Abroad." In *Second Sailing: Alternative Perspectives on Plato*, edited by Debra Nails and Harold Tarrant, 73–90. Helsinki: Societas Scientiarum Fennica.
Newport, Frank. 2018. "5 Things to Know About Evangelicals in America." Polling Matters: Pew Research, May 31, 2018. https://news.gallup.com/opinion/polling-matters/235208/things-know-evangelicals-america.aspx.

Nguyen, C. Thi. 2019. "Manifesto for Public Philosophy." *Daily Nous*, July 1, 2019. http://dailynous.com/2019/07/01/manifesto-public-philosophy-guest-post-c-thi-nguyen/?fbclid=IwAR19yocxgvn-hZxm-np7mWH-jyvlnJPU8jOcTQVshEKWprspIUBtn5bZXVo.

Nichols, Mary P. 2007. "Philosophy and Empire: On Socrates and Alcibiades in Plato's 'Symposium.'" *Polity* 39 (4): 502–21.

Northwood, Heidi. 2015. "Making Music with Aesop's Fables in the 'Phaedo.'" In *Plato's Animals: Gadflies, Horses, Swans, and Other Philosophical Beasts*, edited by Jeremy Bell and Michael Naas, 13–26. Bloomington: Indiana University Press.

Nussbaum, Martha. 2018. *Monarchy of Fear*. New York: Simon & Schuster.

Nussbaum, Martha, and Juha Sihvola, eds. 2002. *The Sleep of Reason: Erotic Experience and Sexual Ethics in Ancient Greece and Rome*. Chicago: University of Chicago Press.

Nussbaum, Martha C. 1986. *Fragility of Goodness: Luck and Ethics in Greek Tragedy and Philosophy*. Cambridge: Cambridge University Press.

Nussbaum, Martha C. 1997. *Cultivating Humanity*. Cambridge, MA: Harvard University Press.

Nye, Andrea. 1989. "The Hidden Host: Irigaray and Diotima at Plato's *Symposium*." *Hypatia* 3 (3): 44–61.

Nye, Andrea. 2015. *Socrates and Diotima: Sexuality, Religion, and the Nature of Divinity*. New York: Palgrave Macmillian.

Obama, Michelle. 2018. *Becoming*. New York: Crown Publishing House Group.

O'Connor, D. 2007. "Rewriting the Poets in Plato's Characters." In *Cambridge Companion to Plato's "Republic,"* edited by G. R. F. Ferrari, 55–89. Cambridge: Cambridge University Press.

O'Connor, David K. 2015. *Plato's Bedroom: Ancient Wisdom and Modern Love*. South Bend, IN: St. Augustine's Press.

Perry, Sam. 2019. *Rhetorics of Race and Religion on the Christian Right: Barack Obama and the War on Terror*. Lanham, MD: Lexington Press.

Phillips, Kristine. 2019. "Florida Sixth-Grader Arrested after Dispute with Teacher over Pledge of Allegiance." *Washington Post*, February 17, 2019. https://www.washingtonpost.com/education/2019/02/17/florida-sixth-grader-charged-with-misdemeanor-after-refusing-recite-pledge-allegiance/.

Plato. 1997a. *Plato: Complete Works*. Edited by John M. Cooper. Indianapolis: Hackett.

Plato. 1997b. "Apology." In *Plato: Complete Works*, edited by John M. Cooper, translated by G. M. A. Grube, 17–36. Indianapolis: Hackett.

Plato. 1997c. "Charmides." In *Plato: Complete Works*, edited by John M. Cooper, translated by Rosamond Kent Sprague, 639–63. Indianapolis: Hackett.

Plato. 1997d. "Euthydemus." In *Plato: Complete Works*, edited by John M. Cooper, translated by Rosamond Kent Sprague, 708–45. Indianapolis: Hackett.

Plato. 1997e. "Parmenides." In *Plato: Collected Works*, edited by John M. Cooper, translated by Mary Louise Gill and Paul Ryan, 359–97. Indianapolis: Hackett.

Plato. 1997f. "Phaedo." In *Plato: Collected Works*, edited by John M. Cooper, G. M. A. Grube, 49–100. Indianapolis: Hackett.

Plato. 1997g. "Symposium." In *Plato: Complete Works*, edited by John M. Cooper, translated by Alexander Nehamas and Paul Woodruff, 457–505. Indianapolis: Hackett.

Plato. 1997h. "Theaetetus." In *Plato: Complete Works*, edited by John M. Cooper, translated by M. J. Levett, rev. Myles F. Burnyeat, 157–234. Indianapolis: Hackett.

Press, Gerald A. 2000. *Who Speaks for Plato?: Studies in Platonic Anonymity*. Lanham, MD: Rowman & Littlefield.

Press, Gerald A. 2018. "The State of the Question in the Study of Plato: A Twenty Year Update." *The Southern Journal of Philosophy* 56 (1): 9–35.

Raaflaub, Kurt. 2003. "Stick and Glue: The Function of Tyranny in Fifth-Century Athenian Democracy." In *Popular Tyranny*, edited by Kathryn Morgan, 59–84. Austin: University of Texas Press.

Ranasinghe, Nalin. 2012. *Socrates and the Gods*. South Bend, IN: St. Augustine's Press.

Reeve, C. D. C. 2006. "A Study in Violets: Alcibiades in the *Symposium*." In *Plato's Symposium: Issues in Interpretation and Reception*, edited by J. H. Lesher and Debra Nails, 124–46. Cambridge, MA: Harvard University Press.

Romero, M. Ross. 2016. *Without the Least Tremor: The Sacrifice of Socrates in Plato's "Phaedo."* Albany: State University of New York Press.
Roochnik, David. 2003. *Beautiful City.* Ithaca, NY: Cornell University Press.
Rosen, Stanley. 1987. *Plato's Symposium.* 2nd edition. New Haven, CT: Yale University Press.
Rosen, Stanley. 1999. *Plato's Sophist: The Drama of Original and Image.* South Bend, IN: St. Augustine's Press.
Rosen, Stanley. 2005. *Plato's Republic.* New Haven, CT: Yale University Press.
Rosenstock, Bruce. 1983. "Rereading the 'Republic.'" *Arethusa* 16 (1): 219–46.
Russon, John, and Patricia Fagan. 2009. *Reexamining Socrates in the "Apology."* Evanston, IL: Northwestern University Press.
Sallis, John. 2004. *Platonic Legacies.* Albany: State University of New York Press.
Sargeant, Winthrop, trans. 2009. *Bhagavad Gita.* Albany: State University of New York Press.
Saxonhouse, Arlene. 2006. *Free Speech and Democracy in Ancient Athens.* New York: Cambridge University Press.
Saxonhouse, Arlene. 2018. "Xanthippe: Shrew or Muse?" *Hypatia* 33 (4): 610–25.
Schultz, A. M., and Paul Carron. 2013. "Socratic Meditation and Emotional Self-Regulation: A Model for Human Dignity in the Technological Age." *Journal of Interdisciplinary Studies* 24: 1–29.
Schultz, Anne-Marie. 2013. *Plato's Socrates as Narrator: A Philosophical Muse.* Lanham, MD: Lexington Books.
Schultz, Anne-Marie. 2015a. "Listening to Socrates' Voice in the *Theaetetus*: Recovering a Lost Narrator." In *Second Sailing: Alternative Perspectives on Plato*, edited by Debra Nails and Harold Tarrant, 13:248–65. Societas Scientiarum Fennica. Helsinki.
Schultz, Anne-Marie. 2015b. "Socrates on Socrates: Looking Back to Bring Philosophy Forward." Edited by Gary M. Gurtler and William Wians. *Proceedings of the Boston Area Colloquium in Ancient Philosophy* 30: 123–41.
Schultz, Anne-Marie. 2017. "Socrates and the Psychology of the Examined Life." In *Identity, Freedom, and Responsibility*, edited by Fernando di Mieri, 13–33. Milano: Ripostes Edizioni.
Schultz, Anne-Marie. 2018. "Stirring up the America's Sleeping Horses: Cornel West, Ta-Nehisi Coates, and Socratic Parrhesia and Platonic Writing in the Public Sphere." *Southwest Philosophy Review* 34: 1–16.
Schultz, Anne-Marie. 2019. "Socrates as Public Philosopher: Using Plato's Apology and Protagoras as Models for Informed Public Engagement." In *The European Legacy: Toward New Paradigms*, July 25, 2019. Accessed October 2, 2019. DOI: 10.1080/10848770.2019.1641312.
Schultz, Anne-Marie, and Kris McLain. Forthcoming. "Wailing and Lamenting Like Women: Reconsidering the Place of Xanthippe in Plato's *Phaedo*." In *Auditory Metaphors in Ancient Greek and Roman Texts*, edited by Jill Gordon. Bloomington: Indiana University Press.
Sciupac, Elizabeth Podrebarac, and Gregory Smith. 2018. "How Religious Groups Voted in the Midterms." Pew Research: Fact Tank: News in the Numbers. November 7, 2018. https://www.pewresearch.org/fact-tank/2018/11/07/how-religious-groups-voted-in-the-midterm-elections/.
Scott, Dominic. 2000. "Socrates and Alcibiades in the *Symposium*." *Hermathena* 168 (Summer): 25–37.
Scott, Gary Alan. 2000. *Plato's Socrates as Educator.* Albany: State University of New York Press.
Scott, Gary Alan. 2004. *Does Socrates Have a Method?: Rethinking the Elenchus in Plato's Dialogues and Beyond.* Edited by Gary Alan Scott. University Park, PA: Penn State Press.
Sedley, David. 2004. *The Midwife of Platonism: Text and Subtext in Plato's* Theaetetus. Oxford: Oxford University Press.
Segal, C. 1978. "The Myth Was Saved." *Hermes* 106 (2): 315–37.
Sheffield, Frisbee. 2008. "Introduction." In *The Symposium*, edited by M. C. Howatson and Frisbee Sheffield, translated by M. C. Howatson, v–xxviii. Cambridge: Cambridge University Press.

Sherman, David. 2013. *Soul, World, and Idea: An Interpretation of Plato's "Republic" and "Phaedo."* Lanham, MD: Lexington Books.
Stovall, Natasha. 2019. "Whiteness on the Coach." *LongReads*, August 12, 2019. https://longreads.com/2019/08/12/whiteness-on-the-couch/?fbclid=IwAR136c_Cr1LoreZxdtoafo5JzV1euu1M6Ecpgl1_sBS9QQ4ai41D8S89aEk.
Strauss, Barry. 2013. "The Classical Greek 'Polis' and Its Government." In *A Companion to Ancient Greek Government*, edited by Hans Beck, 22–37. Blackwell Companions to the Ancient World. Malden, MA: Blackwell.
Strauss, Leo. 2001. *On Plato's Symposium*. Edited by Seth Benardete. Chicago: Chicago University Press.
Stuart, Tessa. 2019. "Ta-Nehisi Coates Dismantles Mitch McConnell's Remarks on Reparations." *Rolling Stone*, June 19, 2019. https://www.rollingstone.com/politics/politics-news/ta-nehisi-coates-dismantles-mitch-mcconnells-remarks-on-reparations-849976/?fbclid=IwAR0Kdtd0t6a3jNmz-IBKrlFoQx8CqmjxBY0XFgeqLssH4yMBkPIgSMaYmzE.
Szelzák, Thomas Alexander. 1999. *Reading Plato*. London: Routledge.
Tan, Ed S. 1995. *Emotion and the Structure of Narrative Film: Film as an Emotion Machine*. New York: Routledge.
Tarrant, Harold. 1996. "Orality and Plato's Narrative Dialogues." In *Voice into Text: Orality and Literacy in Ancient Greece*, edited by Ian Worthington, 129–47. Leiden: Brill.
Tarrant, Harold. 2010. "The 'Theaetetus' as a Narrative Dialogue." *Australian Society for Classical Studies Proceedings* 31 (14): 1–17.
Tejera, Victor. 1999. *Plato's Dialogues One by One*. Lanham, MD: University of America Press.
Thesleff, Holger. 1982. *Studies in Platonic Chronology*. Commentationes Humanarum Litterarum. Helsinki: Societas Scientiarum Fennica.
Thesleff, Holger. 1989. "Platonic Chronology." *Phronesis* 34 (1): 1–26.
Thesleff, Holger. 1993. "Looking for Clues: An Interpretation of Some Literary Aspects of Plato's 'Two-Level Model.'" In *Plato's Dialogues: New Studies and Interpretations*, edited by Gerald A. Press, 17–45. Lanham, MD: Rowman & Littlefield.
Thesleff, Holger. 2002. "Plato and His Public." In *Noctes Atticae*, edited by B. Amden, 289–301. Copenhagen: Museum Tusculanum Press.
Thesleff, Holger. 2015. "The Pedimental Structure of the Dialogues." In *The Bloomsbury Companion to Plato*, edited by Gerald Press, 121–23. London: Bloomsbury.
Thucydides. 1998. *The Peloponnesian War*. Translated by Steven Lattimore. Indianapolis: Hackett.
Trott, Adriel. 2015. "Collected Reviews of Ta-Nehisi Coates' *Between the World and Me*." *The Trott Line: Catching All Manner of Thought* (blog). September 26, 2015. https://adrieltrott.com/2015/09/26/collected-reviews-of-ta-nehisi-coates-between-the-world-and-me/.
Vance, J. D. 2016. *Hillbilly Elegy*. New York: HarperCollins.
Vlastos, Gregory. 1973. *Platonic Studies*. Princeton, NJ: Princeton University Press.
Vlastos, Gregory. 1981. "The Individual as the Object of Love in Plato." In *Platonic Studies*, 1–34. Princeton, NJ: Princeton University Press.
West, Cornel. 2005. *Democracy Matters: Winning the Fight Against Imperialism*. New York: Penguin Books.
Westover, Tara. 2018. *Educated*. New York: Random House.
Williams, Justin H. G., Andrew Whiten, Thomas Suddendorf, and David I. Perrett. 2001. "Imitation, Mirror Neurons and Autism." *Neuroscience & Biobehavioral Reviews* 25 (4): 287–95.
Winkler, John. 1990. *The Constraints of Desire: The Anthropology of Sex and Gender in Ancient Greece*. New York: Routledge.
Wright, J. Lenore. 2006. *The Philosopher's I: Autobiography and the Search for the Self*. Albany: State University of New York Press.
Wright, J. Lenore. 2018. "Relationality and Life: Phenomenological Reflections on Miscarriage." *International Journal of Feminist Approaches to Bioethics* 11 (2): 135–56.
Zhmud, L. 2012. *Pythagoras and the Early Pythagoreans*. Oxford: Oxford University Press.

Zhmud, Leonard. 2014. "Sixth-Fifth, and Fourth-Century Pythagoreans." In *A History of Pythagoreanism*, edited by Carl A. Huffman, 88–112. Cambridge: Cambridge University Press.

Zoller, C. 2018. *Plato and the Body*. Albany: State University of New York.

Zuckert, Catherine. 2009. *Plato's Philosophers: The Coherence of the Dialogues*. Chicago: University of Chicago Press. Kindle.

Index

academics, public and, 5
Achilles, Socrates and, 61
Aesop, 9, 73, 74, 75, 76, 79
affirmative action, 105
African-American thinkers, 111
Agathon, 7, 7–8, 25–27, 28–29; aporia and, 32–33; house of, 58; love and, 39; self-disclosure and, 30; Socrates and, 29–32, 34; speech of, 30
Alcibiades, 8, 41, 42, 43; Apollodorus and, 50; as drunk, 60n7; emotional state of, 47, 49; existential despair of, 48; hubris of, 49; narrative of, 48, 50; Plato and, 43, 59n5; politics of, 44; seduction plan of, 47; self-disclosure imitation by, 43–51; self-reflection of, 45; social reputation of, 49; Socrates and, 43, 44–51, 60n7; state of mind, 46–47, 49; in *Symposium*, 44; thought process of, 47
Allegory of the Cave, 42
Anaxagoras, 9, 74, 81, 82, 83, 85, 97
animals, intercourse of, 38
Anonymous Commentary on Theaetetus, 10n11
Antiochis, 67
Aphrodite, 34
Apollo, swans of, 73, 79, 89
Apollodorus, 7–8, 20, 26, 41, 52, 86; Alcibiades and, 50; Aristodemus and, 54, 55–57, 75; autobiography and, 26, 51, 56; Glaucon and, 53, 54–55, 57; narrative of, 56; negative view of self, 54–55; Phaedo and, 88; *Republic* and, 52; Socrates and, 53; in *Symposium*, 26, 42, 51

Apology (Plato), 1, 23, 112; autobiography in, 3, 8, 61–62, 70–71, 101; Delphic oracle in, 62–67; history in, 61; Socrates in, 61
aporia, 81, 101; Agathon and, 32–33; of Echecrates, 91; Phaedo and, 91; Socrates and, 65; Socratic method and, 33
Aristodemus, 8, 26, 27–28, 31, 41; Apollodorus and, 54, 55–57, 75; narrative of, 57; negative treatment of, 59; philosophical provocation and, 57; Socrates and, 57–58, 59; *Symposium* and, 92; voice of, 57
Aristophanes, 7, 29–32, 50, 62
arts, 74, 76
Athenian Council, 8, 62, 68
Athens, 35, 39, 113
authoritarianism, 103
autobiography, 3, 7, 10n5, 11; Apollodorus and, 26, 51, 56; in *Apology*, 3, 8, 61–62, 70–71, 101; Delphic oracle and, 63; elenchus and, 33; history and, 33; as parrhesia, 31–32; in *Phaedo*, 101; philosophical value of, 5, 37, 41; philosophy and, 5; politics and, 62;

preparation and, 51–52; *Republic* and, 53; in scholarship, 103; self and, 53; self-disclosure and, 5, 9; state of mind and, 32; storytelling and, 70; in *Symposium*, 25–27, 27, 101; in *Theaetetus*, 101. *See also* narrative; self-disclosure
auto-narration, self-disclosure as, 103

Battle of Munychia, 52
beauty, 39n11, 51, 93, 110; birth and, 35; Diotima on, 36; of Socrates, physical, 49
Becoming (Obama), 107
Benardete, Seth, 17, 22
Between the World and Me (Coates), 111–114, 115n18
Bible, 97, 110
birth, beauty and, 35
blogs, 4
body, soul and, 78, 79
Breaking Bread (hooks & West), 114n6

cause, mind and, 81
Cebes, 73, 75–80, 82–84, 85, 89, 91, 92, 93–95
Cephalus, 20, 52
Chaerephon, 64
Charmides, 50
Charmides (Plato), 13, 22, 64
Childers, Mary, 114n6
Christianity, 97, 109, 110
Cicero, 98n10
citizenship, 114
class privilege, 106
Clement of Alexandria, 99n14
Coates, Ta-Nehisi, 111–114, 115n18
communal responsibility, 6
community: LGBTQA, 110; Socrates and, 65–66, 71; structures, 103
Conflicts in Feminism (hooks & Childers), 114n6
Corybantes, 45
Crito, 54, 77, 86, 96
Crito (Plato), 63
Critobulus, 54
cultural diversity, 108
Cyrene, 17

daimon: love as, 35; self-disclosure on, 69–70; Socrates and, 62, 69–71, 101
death: definition of, 78; of Glaucon, 52, 69; last breath, 96–97; practice for, 77; of Pythagoras, 85, 99n13; of Socrates, 9, 73–74, 76, 77, 79, 86, 87, 88–89, 95–96, 97
deeds (*pragmata*), 16
Defense of Palamedes (Gorgias), 61
Delium, 50
Delos, 74
Delphic oracle, 8, 113; in *Apology*, 62–67; autobiography and, 63; Socrates and, 62–67, 67, 70
democracy, 114
Democracy Matters (West), 103–104
developmentalism, 23n1
dialogue, 2, 12–13, 13
DiAngelo, Robin, 106
Dionysodorus, 31, 70
Diotima, 8, 25–27; on beauty, 36; existence of, 33–34; lessons with, 27, 42; on love, 36; reproduction and, 38; self-presentation and, 34–39; as shaman, 38; Socrates as student of, 32–39, 82, 101; wisdom of, 35
divination, 33–34, 35
domination, 104, 108
dramatic action, narrative and, 5
dramatic structure: philosophical provocation and, 41–43; in *Symposium*, 41–43
dreams, of Socrates, 73, 74, 76

Echecrates, 86; aporia of, 91; emotional states of, 91; Phaedo and, 73, 87–88, 94, 96; thought process of, 91
education, 2, 24n10; philosophy and, 38; transformative value of, 104, 107. *See also* learning
elections, in U.S., 103
The Electronic Agora, 4
elenchus, autobiography and, 33
emotional states: of Echecrates, 91; narrative and, 5, 17; of Phaedo, 87–88; philosophy and, 91; self-disclosure and, 32, 57; Socrates and, 6, 66, 69, 75, 77, 81, 82, 83, 101
emulation, narrative and, 10n10

eros. *See* love
Eros, birth of, 34
Eryximachus, 7, 29, 30, 42, 58, 59n4
ethics: Socrates and, 82; of wisdom, 38
Euclides, 6–7, 11, 81; narrative and, 17; Socrates and, 15, 16, 20; Terpsion and, 12
eulogy, 31
Euthydemus, 31, 50, 70
Euthydemus (Plato), 6, 20, 24n18, 70, 71n7, 90
Euthyphro, Socrates and, 20
Evenus, 75, 76
examined life, 2
exceptionalism, 112–113
existentialism, of Alcibiades, 48

feminism, 105, 114n7
Feminist Theory from Margin to Center and Feminism is for Everyone (hooks), 115n9
Forbes, 104
freedom, 108
free market fundamentalism, 103
Frosolono, Andrea Cheek, 96

gender, 105
George, Robert, 104
Glaucon, 16, 51; Apollodorus and, 53, 54–55, 57; death of, 52, 69; self-disclosure of, 54; self-reflection of, 54; Socrates and, 55
God, 110; in narrative, 18; Socrates and, 67, 77, 78
Gordon, Jill, 80
Gorgias, 61
Gorgias (Plato), 13
Greek, in *Theatetus*, 7

happiness, 37
harmony model, 80
Hellenica (Xenophon), 69
Heracles, 61, 92
Hesiod, 4
Hillbilly Elegy (Vance), 2
Hippocrates, 21–22
history: in *Apology*, 61; autobiography and, 33

Homer, 28, 31, 73; poetry and, 84; Socrates and, 39n6, 57, 98n7
hooks, bell, 104, 105–108, 114n6–114n7, 115n9–115n10
Hortensius (Cicero), 98n10
Howard, 111–112
The Humanities Commons, 4
human nature, 36, 93

identity, self-disclosure and, 38
Iliad (Homer), 28
imagination, politics and, 103
immortality, 9, 85; reproduction and, 38; of soul, 85, 93, 94
incarnation, soul and, 80
intercourse, of animals, 38
interpretation, of narrative, 23

Khang, Kathy, 108–111
kleos, 84–86
knowledge, 19, 21, 106

learning: love of, 78; process, 82; of Socrates, 82; vulnerability and, 35
Leon from Salamis, 62, 68, 69
LGBTQA community, 110
liberalism, in U.S., 114n5
logoi, 37
love (eros), 7, 26, 29, 35; Agathon and, 39; art of, 30, 31, 36; as daimon, 35; definition of, 32–33; Diotima on, 36; interpersonal, 37; ladder of, 38, 59n4; between mortal and immortal, 34; nature of, 35; Plato on, 39n11; politics and, 38; relationships and, 37
Lysis, 13

maieutics, 12
marriage, 35
mass shootings, 103
meditation, 97
midwifery, 18–20
militarism, 103
mind, 81, 82
misanthropy, 79, 85, 92–93
misology, 79, 85, 92–93
Mnemosyne, 84
Monarchy of Fear (Nussbaum), 103
the Muses, 84

muthologia, 96
Myth of Er, 27

Nails, Debra, 33, 52
narrative, 1, 5–6, 10n12, 12, 13; affect on others, 18–20; of Alcibiades, 48, 50; of Apollodorus, 56; of Aristodemus, 57; autobiography in, 19, 23; Benardete on, 22; in *Charmides*, 22; dramatic action and, 5; emotional states and, 5, 17; emulation and, 10n10; Euclides and, 17; framing techniques, 3; God in, 18; interpretation of, 23; key elements of, 101; perception in, 22; in *Phaedo*, 3, 86–87; philosophical process and, 18; Plato and, 1–2, 11, 21–23, 24n4; self-disclosure and, 3, 23, 41, 51–59; state of mind in, 18; storytelling in, 18; style, 19, 22; in *Symposium*, 3, 41, 51, 73; *Theaetetus* and, 3, 13, 17–20, 21, 23; as tyranny, 22; word choice, 13
non-self, self and, 38
Nussbaum, Martha, 103
Nye, 33–34

Obama, Michelle, 107
obedience, 106–107
objectivity, truth and, 21
online forums, 4
On Plato's Symposium (Strauss), 53–54
opposites, interrelationship of, 74–75

pain, pleasure and, 74–75, 88
Parmenides, 11, 20
parrhesia: autobiography as, 31–32; of Coates, 112
The Partially Examined Life (podcast), 4
Pausanias, 7, 59n4
pedagogical practices: self-actualization and, 107; self-disclosure and, 27–32, 104; of Socrates, 83, 98n12
Peloponnesian War, 26
The People of Plato (Nails), 33
perception, 21; knowledge and, 19, 21; in Socratic narrative, 22
personal glory, 3
Phaedo, 86, 87; Apollodorus and, 88; aporia and, 91; death of Socrates and, 88–89, 95–96; Echecrates and, 73,
87–88, 94, 96; emotional states of, 87–88; sexual slavery of, 93; Socrates conversation with, 91–92, 92–93; thought process of, 87
Phaedo (Plato), 1, 7, 9, 11, 23, 59, 71; autobiography in, 101; beginning of, 97; end of, 97; imitation of self-disclosure and, 86–96; language in, 99n14; mediation and pranayama in, 97; narrative in, 3, 86–87; self-disclosure in, 71, 74; Socrates in, 73; *Symposium* and, 73
Phaedrus, 7, 29, 58
Phaedrus (Plato), 32
Philolaus, 91
philosophers, on Twitter, 4
philosophical kinship, 42
philosophical process: narrative and, 18; of Socrates, 83
philosophical provocation: Aristodemus and, 57; dramatic structure and, 41–43; in *Symposium*, 41–43
philosophy: autobiography and, 5, 41; as communal experience, 88; education and, 38; emotional states and, 91; politics and, 2, 3; self-disclosure and, 43, 74; Socrates and, 70
Phlians, 87
Phlius, 89, 91, 94
plain speaking, 103
Plato, 114; Alcibiades and, 43, 59n5; Allegory of the Cave, 42; death of Socrates and, 97; dialogue and, 12–13; literary production of, 13; on love, 39n11; narrative and, 1–2, 11, 21–23, 24n4; Socrates and, 98n12; tragedy and, 46. *See also specific works*
Plato's Philosophers (Zuckert), 70–71
Plato's Socrates as Narrator (Frosolono), 96
pleasure, pain and, 74–75, 88
pledge of allegiance, 111
poetry, 39; Homer and, 84; *kleos* and, 84; of Socrates, 75–76; Socrates on, 66
politics: of Alcibiades, 44; autobiography and, 62; imagination and, 103; love and, 38; philosophy and, 2, 3; self-disclosure and, 68; Socrates and, 63, 67, 69

Potidaea, 50, 64
pragmata (deeds), 16
pranayama, 97
preparation, autobiography and, 51–52
private, public and, 71
privilege, 105–106
professors, 107
prophets, 66
Protagoras, 31
Protagoras (Plato), 20, 21, 24n16, 71n7
Protagorean perspectivism, 21
Protagorean relativism, 21–23
protest, Socrates and, 69
public: academics and, 5; philosophy, 4–5, 70; private and, 71
purification, 78
Pythagoras, 85, 99n13
Pythagoreans, 85, 99n14

Race Matters (West), 103
racial privilege, 106
racism, 109, 110, 111, 112, 113
Raise Your Voice (Khang), 109–110
reality, fundamental nature of, 74
reasoning process, in self-disclosure, 57
relationships, love and, 37
relativism, 12, 21–23
reproduction: Diotima and, 38; immortality and, 38
Republic (Plato), 51; Apollodorus and, 52; autobiography and, 53; *Symposium* and, 52; *Theaetetus* and, 14

Sacred and Profane Love (podcast), 4
segregation, of sexes, 35
self: autobiography and, 53; non-self and, 38
self-actualization, 107
self-awareness, 106
self-care, 6
self-disclosure, 1, 2, 9, 10n5; Agathon and, 30; Alcibiades imitation of, 43–51; autobiography and, 5, 9; as auto-narration, 103; on Daimon, 69–70; emotional states in, 32, 57; feelings and, 32; of Glaucon, 54; identity and, 38; Khang and, 108–111; narrative and, 3, 23, 41, 51–59; pedagogical practices and, 27–32, 104; in *Phaedo*, 71, 74;
Phaedo and imitation of, 86–96; philosophy and, 43, 74; politics and, 68; reasoning process in, 57; state of mind and, 28; storytelling and, 96; summary of, 101–105; in *Symposium*, 71; in *Thaeatetus*, 71; as vulnerability, 28; wisdom and, 28–29
self-presentation, Diotima and, 34–39
self-reflection, 32; of Alcibiades, 45; of Glaucon, 54; of Socrates, 58
senses, 83
sexes, segregation of, 35
sexism, 109
Shirley, Wilson, 104
Silenus, Socrates and, 46
Simmias, 73, 76–80, 85, 89, 91, 92, 93–95
social context, Socrates and, 6
social justice, 103
Socrates, 11; Achilles and, 61; Agathon and, 29–32, 34; Alcibiades and, 43, 44–51, 60n7; alcohol and, 60n7; Apollodorus and, 53; in *Apology*, 61; aporia and, 65; Aristodemus and, 57–58, 59; Aristophanes and, 29–32, 62; Athenian Council and, 62, 68; Athens and, 113; auditors of, 6, 19, 22, 63; bath of, 95; burial of, 95; calmness of, 50; community and, 65–66, 71; conflict with city, 67–69; daimon of, 62, 69–71, 101; death of, 9, 73–74, 76, 77, 79, 86, 87, 88–89, 95–96, 97; Delphic oracle and, 62–67, 67, 70; development as philosopher, 10n3; dreams of, 73, 74, 76; emotional states and, 6, 66, 69, 75, 77, 81, 82, 83, 101; ethics and, 82; Euclides and, 15, 16, 20; Euthyphro and, 20; final prayer, 95; Glaucon and, 55; God and, 67, 77, 78; Heracles and, 61; as his own teacher, 83; Homer and, 39n6, 57, 98n7; hubris of, 49; identity of, 38; ignorance of, 81; imprisonment of, 6–7, 89; inner life of, 6, 32, 46, 69; learning of, 82; legacy of, 86; liberalism in U.S. and, 114n5; pedagogical practices of, 83, 98n12; in *Phaedo*, 73; Phaedo conversation with, 91–92, 92–93; philosophical process of, 83; philosophy and, 70; physical beauty of, 49; physical stature of, 57; Plato

and, 98n12; on poetry, 66; poetry of, 75–76; politics and, 63, 67, 69; prison activities of, 75; protest and, 69; as public philosopher, 3–4; reputation of, 62, 63, 65; second sailing, 80–84; self-reflection of, 58; Silenus and, 46; Simmias and, 77–78; social context and, 6; sophists and, 71n7; state of mind, 75, 77; as student of Diotima, 32–39, 82; students of, 85–86; *Symposium* and, 34; the Thirty and, 68–69; thought process of, 5, 81, 89, 101; trial, 39, 62–63, 64, 66, 68, 71, 73, 89; truth and, 80

Socrates and Diotima (Nye), 33–34

Socratic autobiography. *See* autobiography

Socratic method, 33

Socratic narrative. *See* narrative

Socratic self-disclosure. *See* self-disclosure

Sophist (Plato), 11

sophists, Socrates and, 71n7

soul, 83; body and, 78, 79; fate of, 80, 94; immortality of, 85, 93, 94; incarnation and, 80; journey of, 95

Sparta, Athens and, 68

state of mind: Alcibiades, 46–47, 49; autobiography and, 32; in narrative, 18; self-disclosure and, 28; Socrates, 77

Statesman (Plato), 11

storytelling, 7, 26; autobiography and, 70; in narrative, 18; self-disclosure and, 96

Strauss, Leo, 53–54

suicide, 76

Symposium (Plato), 1, 7, 11, 20, 23; Alcibiades in, 44; Apollodorus in, 26, 42, 51; Aristodemus and, 92; autobiography in, 25–27, 27, 101; dramatic structure of, 41–43; Glaucon, 16; narrative in, 3, 8, 41, 51, 73; *Phaedo* and, 73; philosophical provocation in, 41–43; publication date of, 39; *Republic and*, 52; secondary literature on, 39n1, 43; self-disclosure in, 71; Socrates and, 34

Tarrant, Harold, 7, 11–12, 13–14

teaching, outside conventional structures, 4

Teaching Community (hooks), 104, 107

Teaching Critical Thinking (hooks), 107

Teaching to Transgress (hooks), 105, 106, 107, 108, 114n6

Terpsion, 6–7, 12, 16, 81

thauma (wonder), 91

Theaetetus, 7, 12, 15, 18

Theaetetus (Plato), 1, 3, 6, 81; *Anonymous Commentary on*, 10n11; assumptions about, 11; autobiography in, 101; earlier version of, 10n11; Greek in, 7; narrative in, 3, 13, 17–20, 21, 23; prologue, 15; *Protagoras* and, 24n16; *Republic V* and, 14; self-disclosure in, 71; Tarrant on, 13–14; Thesleff on, 12–13

Theodorus, 7, 15, 18

Thesleff, Holger, 7, 11–12, 12–13

the Thirty, Socrates and, 68–69

thought process: of Echecrates, 91; of Phaedo, 87; of Socrates, 5, 81, 89, 101

tragedy, Plato and, 46

truth: objectivity and, 21; passion for, 98n11; Socrates and, 80; telling, 2, 113

Twitter, philosophers on, 4

tyranny, narrative as, 22

United States (U.S.): elections in, 103; exceptionalism in, 112–113; news in, 112; polarization in, 103

Vance, J. D., 2

virtues, 37, 78

voice, 107, 110

vulnerability: learning and, 35; self-disclosure as, 28

West, Cornel, 103–104, 114n6

Westover, Tara, 104

white intellectual canon, 111–112

white power, 106

white privilege, 105–106

wine, 48

wisdom: of Diotima, 35; ethics of, 38; human, 66; mirror of, 38; self-disclosure and, 28–29

women, divination and, 33–34

wonder (*thauma*), 91

Xanthippe, 74, 89

xenophobia, 109

Xenophon, 69

Zuckert, Catherine, 70–71

About the Author

Anne-Marie Schultz is professor of philosophy at Baylor University. She also serves as director of the Baylor Interdisciplinary Core. She is the author of *Plato's Socrates as Narrator: A Philosophical Muse* (2013). She has written numerous articles on Plato, Augustine, feminism, and issues in philosophical pedagogy. She is currently writing a third book on Plato's use of narrative, *Telling Tales of Socrates: Creating Philosophers of the Future*. She is an Intermediate Junior III Certified Iyengar Yoga teacher and is doing comparative work with Plato's *Phaedo* and *The Bhagavad Gita*.

www.ingramcontent.com/pod-product-compliance
Lightning Source LLC
Chambersburg PA
CBHW050909300426
44111CB00010B/1450